"Graham's cartoons are wonderfully inventive, and he share
ways. He can be wacky, clever and often poetic.
- Liza Donnelly, *New Yorker* cartoonist, *TED* speaker, *Forbes* writer.

"Graham Sale's cartoons
are crispy, pithy, surprising,
elegant, tasty, sophisticated,
stylish, clever, beautiful,
provocative, pertinent,
outrageous, timely,
perceptive, revolutionary,
and above all, absolutely
hilarious!"
- Randall Enos,
*Reknowned illustrator
and embellisher
of printed works.*

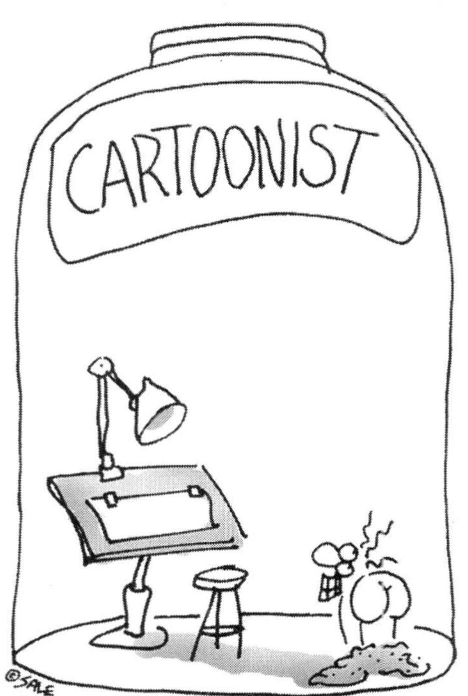

"Graham's cartoons and wit make
me grin, wince, groan and giggle.
I'm never sure what to expect from
his twisted, sardonic mind except
coffee-spitting entertainment.
Sure, he has light moments, but it's
his down and dirty satire that keeps
me coming back for more!"
- Sandee Beyerle,
Managing Editor,
Funny Times

W W W . G R A H A M S A L E . C O M

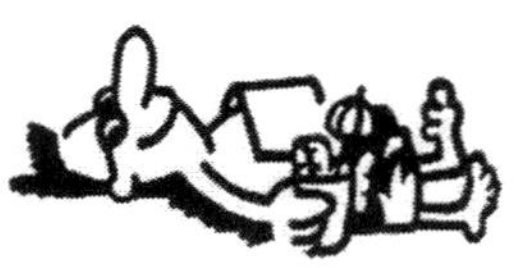

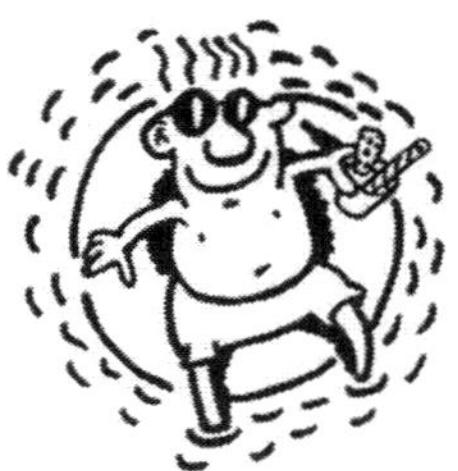

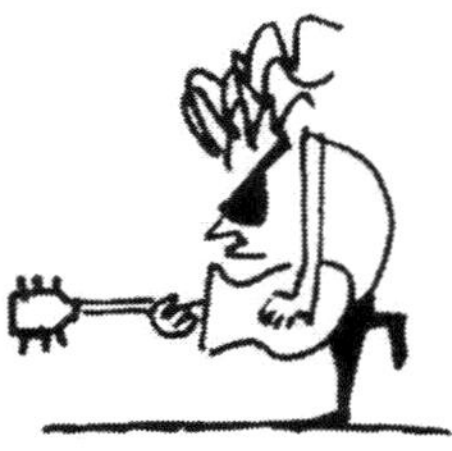

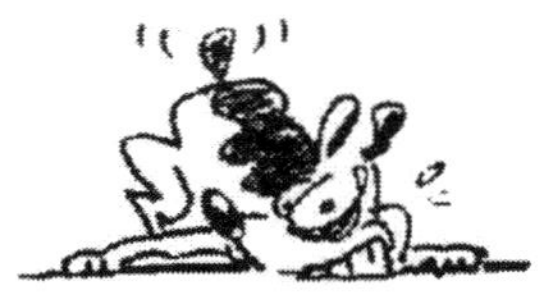

First Printing, 2014
ISBN 0-9672865-6-5
Little Black Book Press

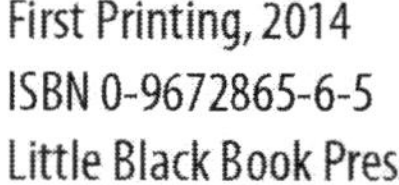

TO BUY THIS BOOK or CONTACT GRAHAM:

www.grahamsale.com
graham@grahamsale.com

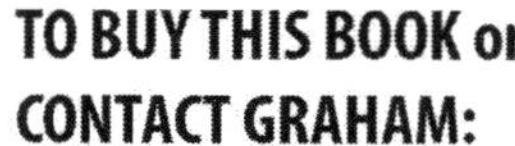

PURCHASE THESE CARTOONS

As prints, on greeting cards, mugs, t-shirts and more on the website!

Other collections by Graham.

Men in Hats, If Idiots Could Fly
Political Cartoons by Graham Sale

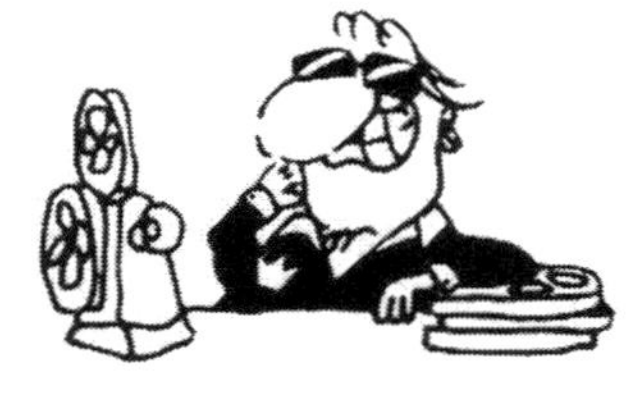

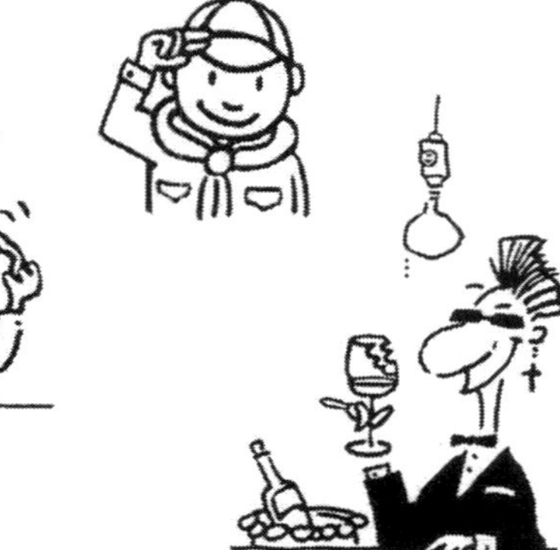

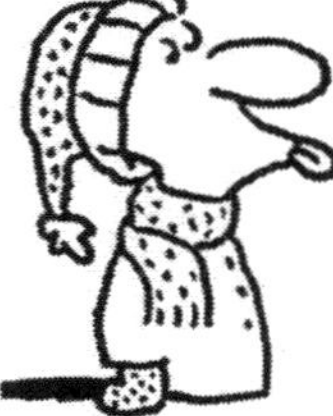

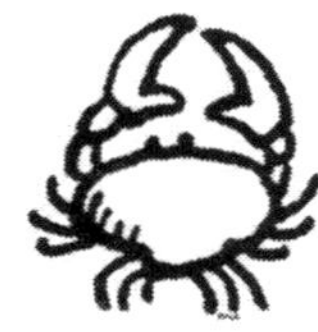

CARTOONS & ILLUSTRATIONS

By Graham Sale

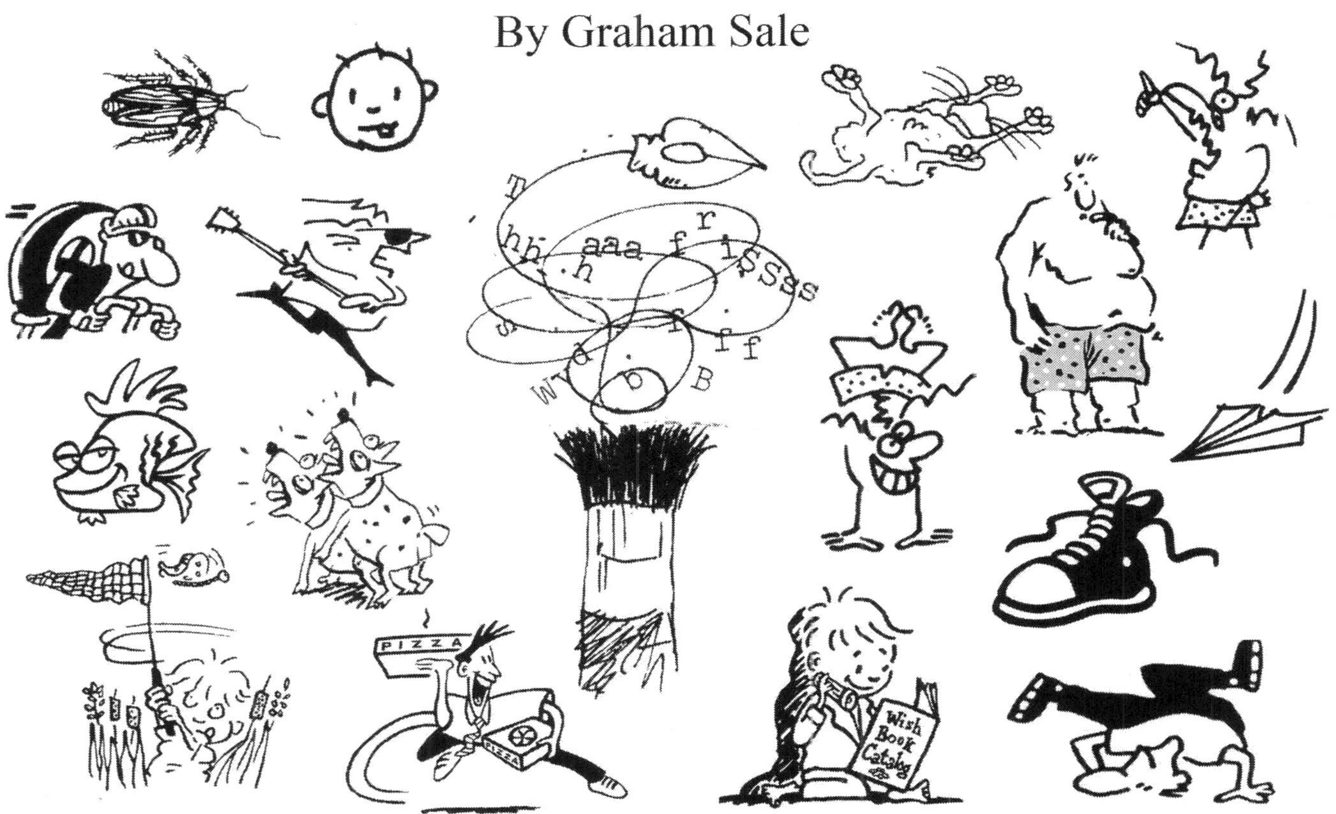

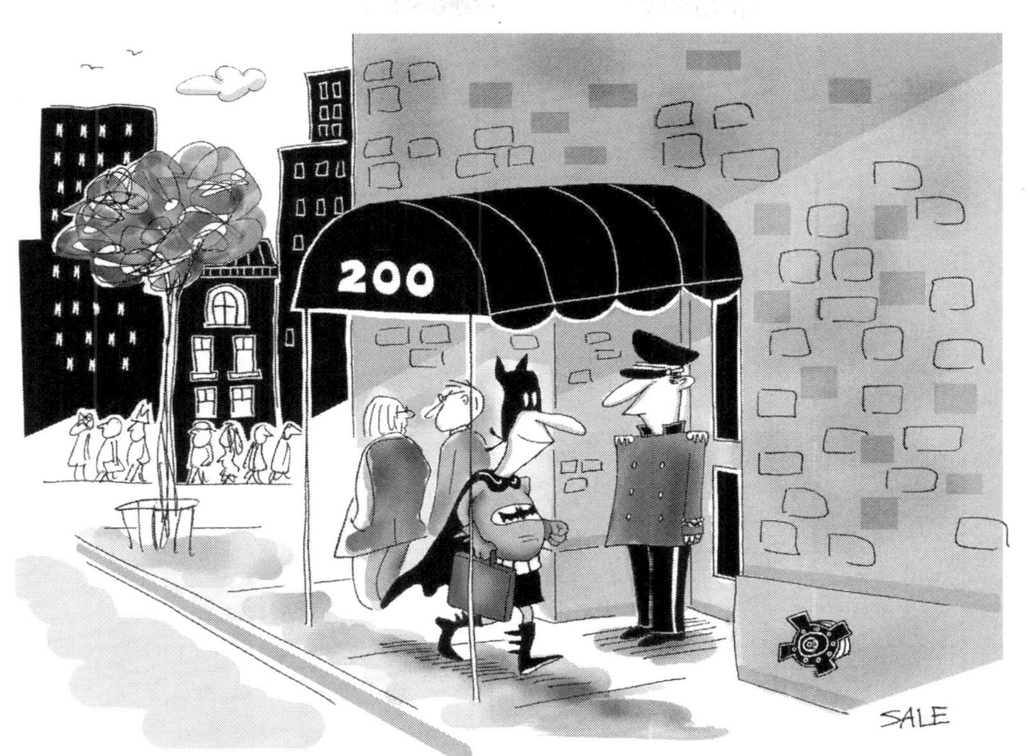

Miles was always looking for an edge in an uncertain world.

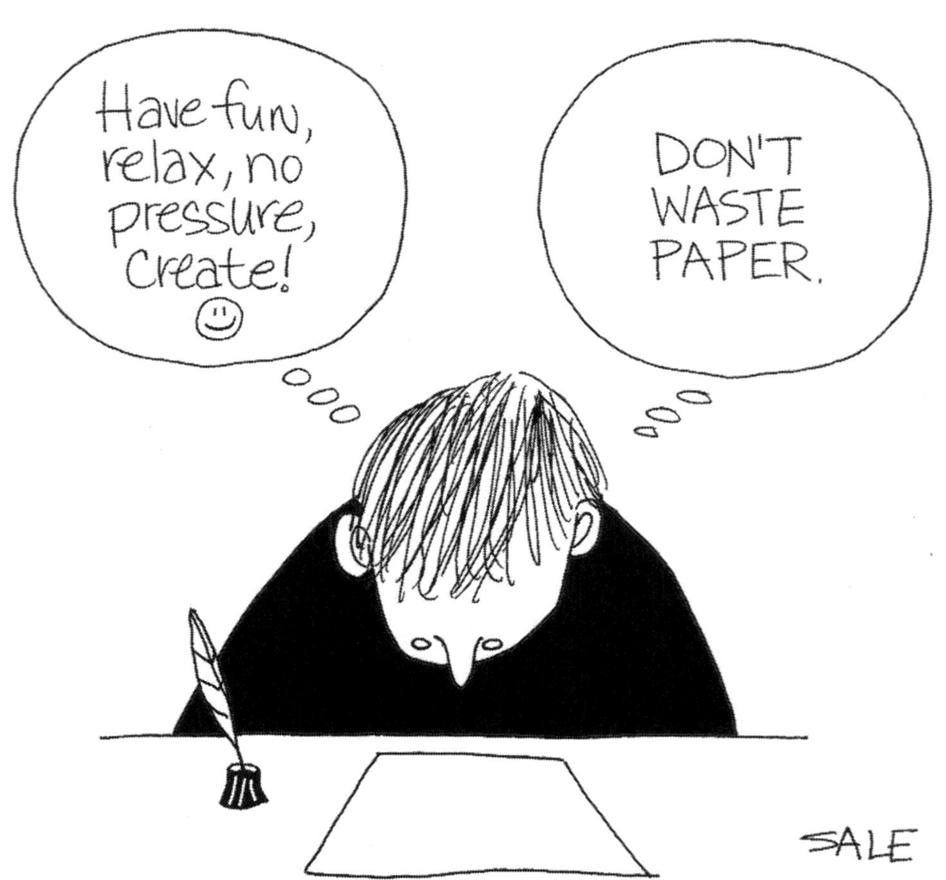

Have fun, relax, no pressure, create!
DON'T WASTE PAPER.
SALE

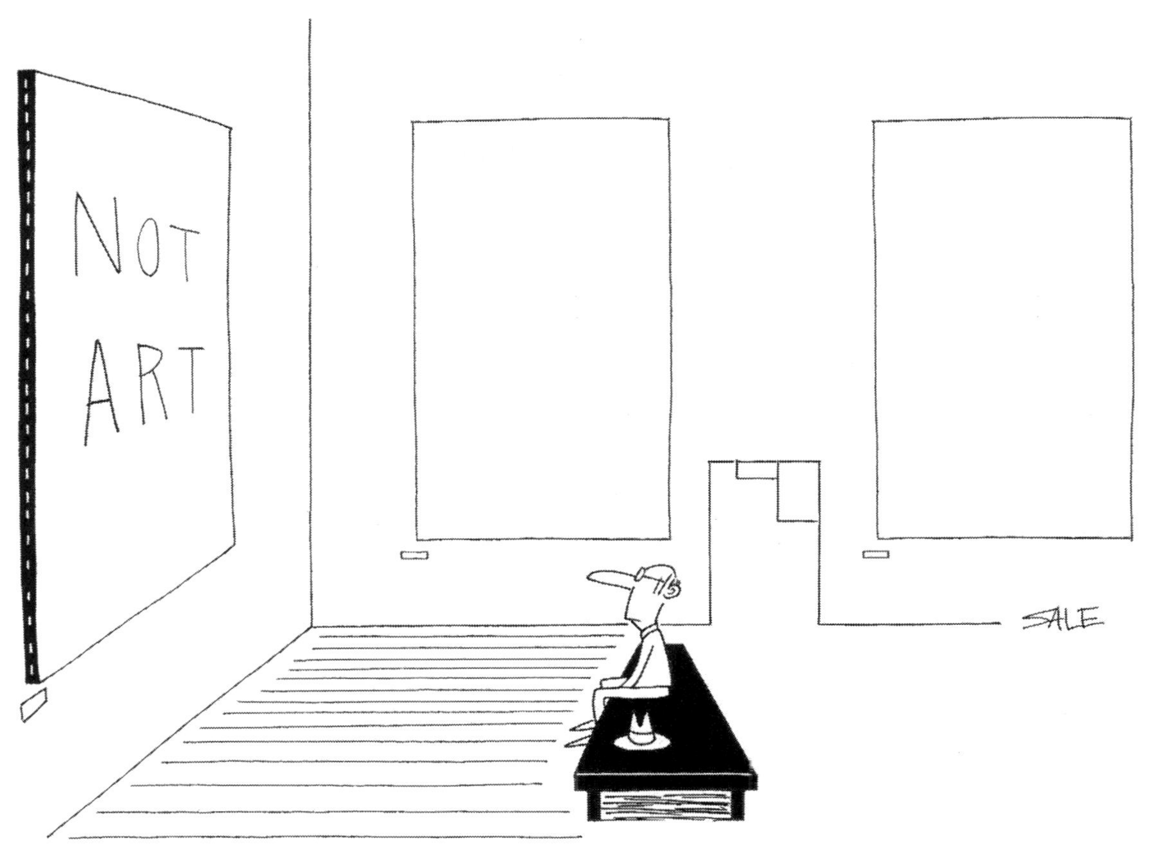

NOT
ART
SALE

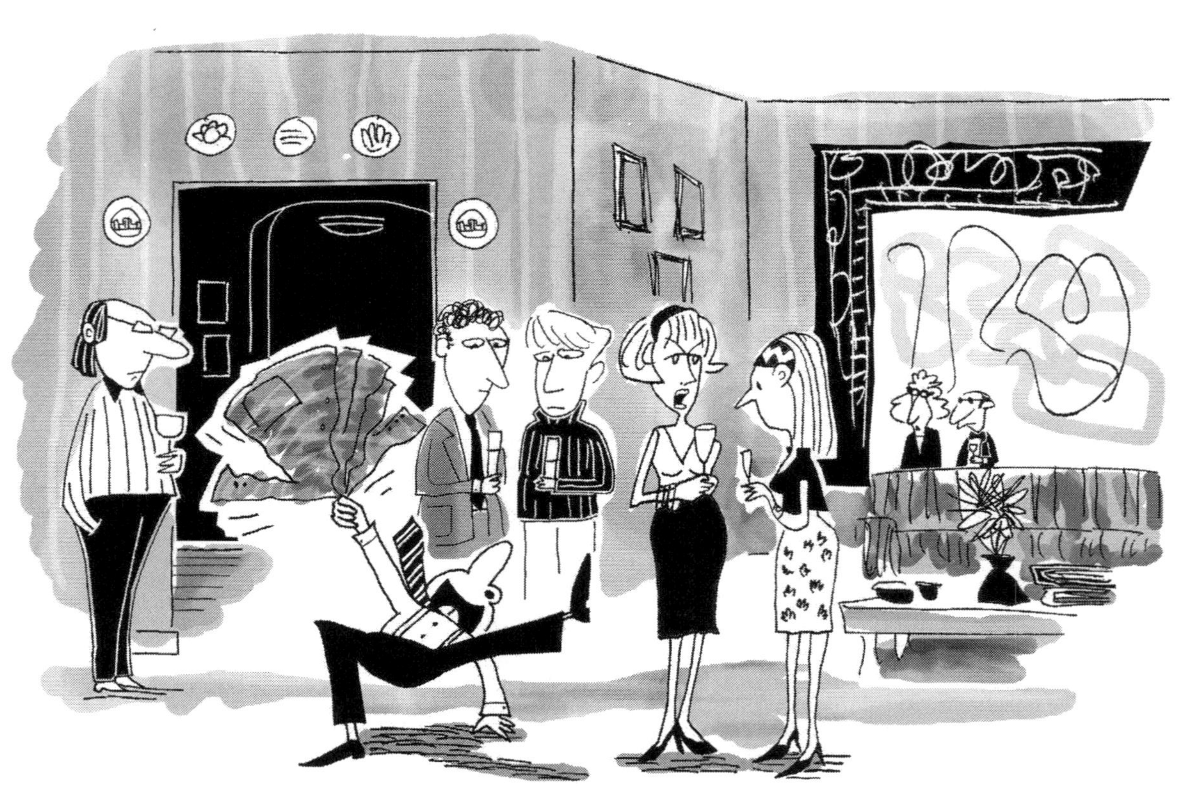

"That's Richard, his authentic self dances like nobody is watching."

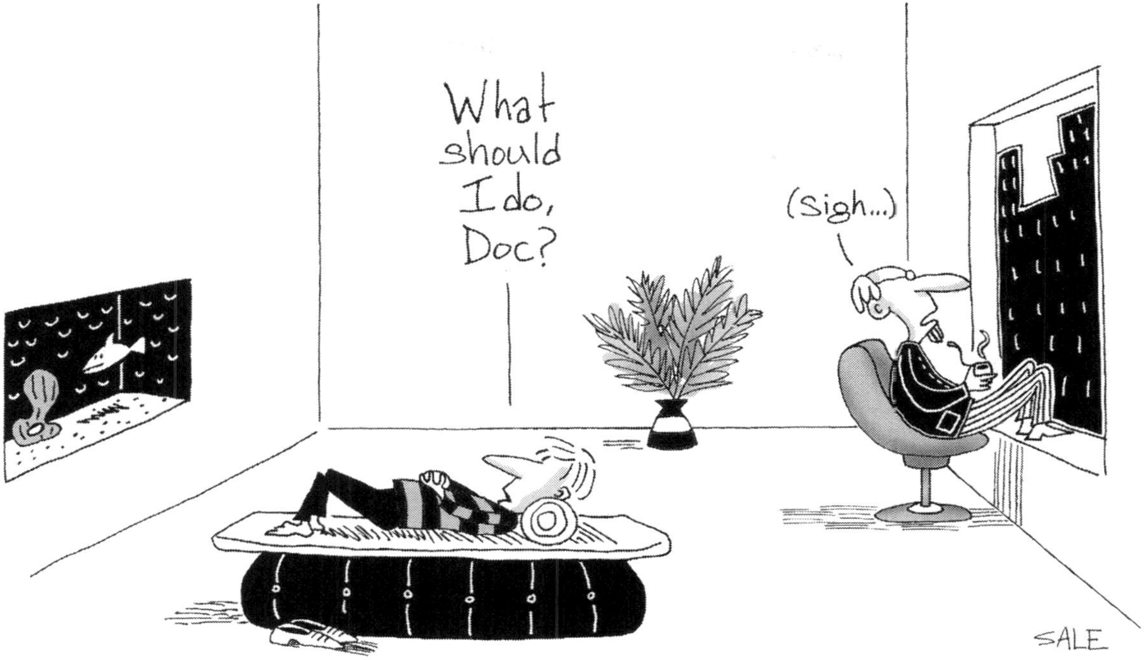

"Stop believing everything you think."

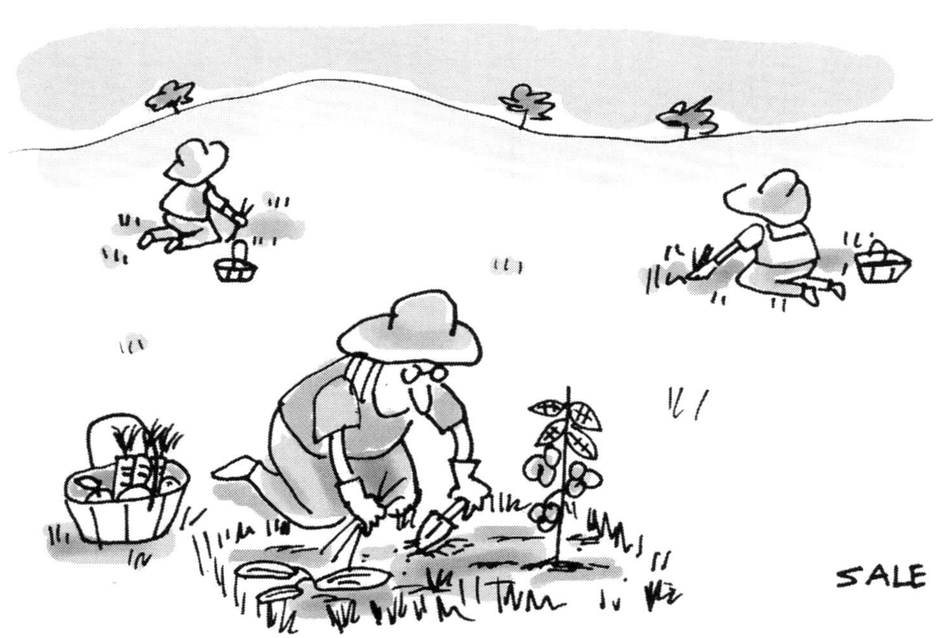

Free Range Gardners.

Want to Change the World?

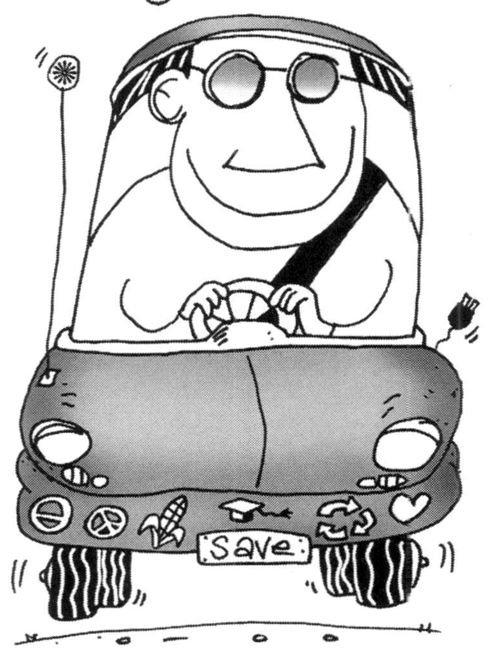

Start by using your turn signals.

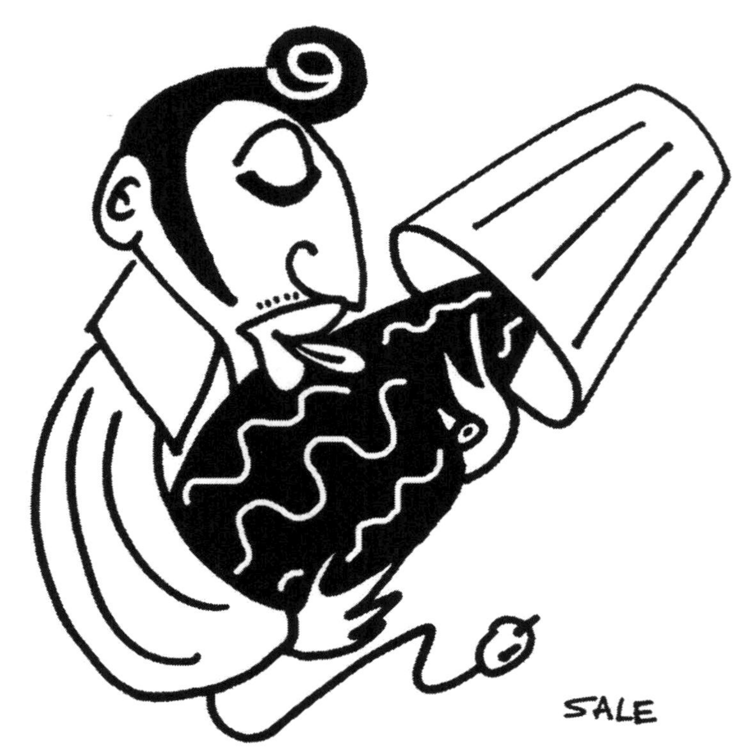

Carlos the Barracuda treated objects like women.

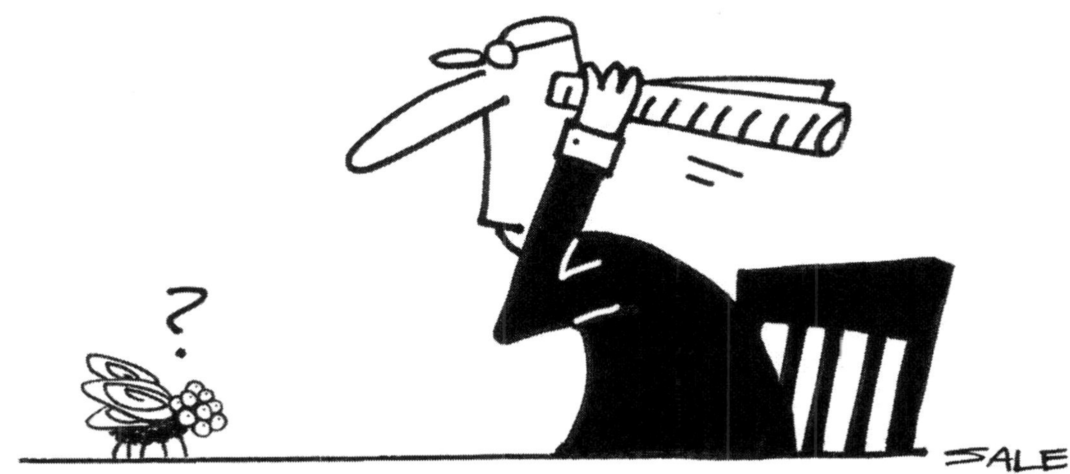

"Hmm...Now how in the world is he going to read that newspaper when it's all rolled up?"

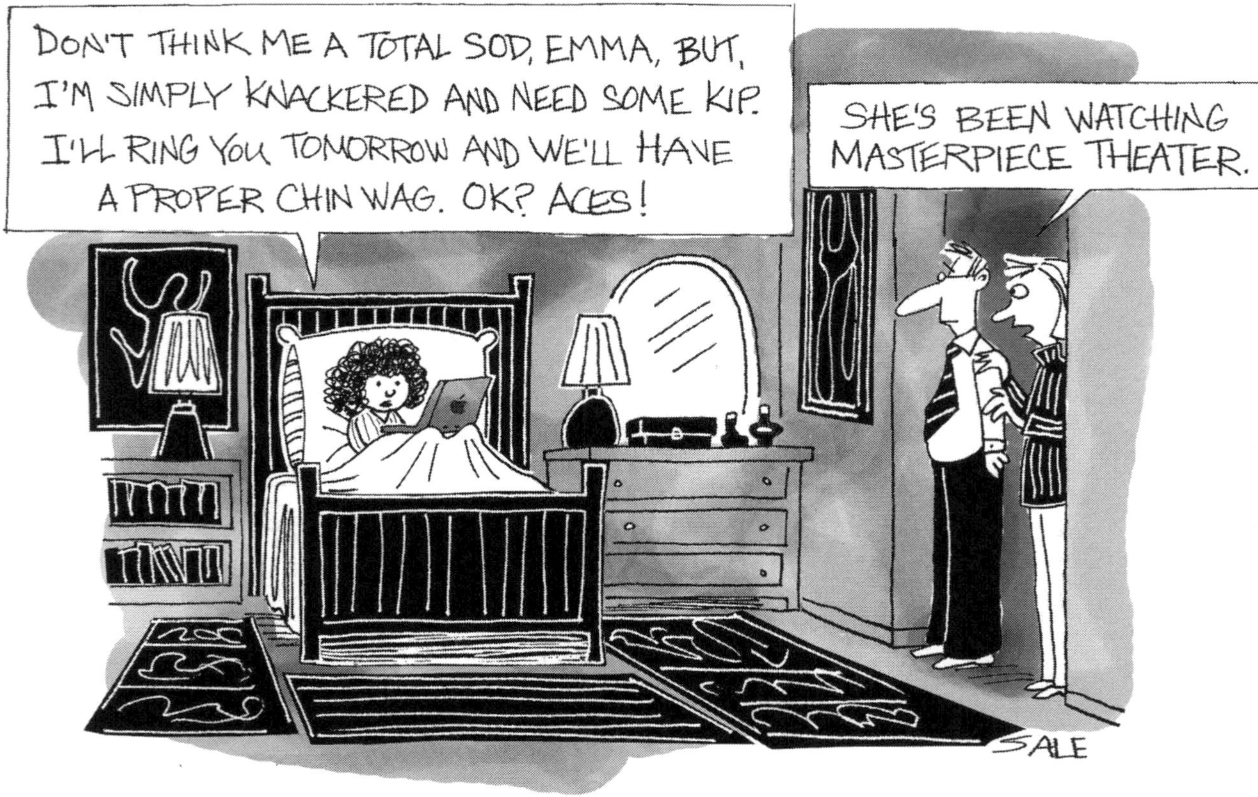

DON'T THINK ME A TOTAL SOD, EMMA, BUT, I'M SIMPLY KNACKERED AND NEED SOME KIP. I'LL RING YOU TOMORROW AND WE'LL HAVE A PROPER CHIN WAG. OK? ACES!
SHE'S BEEN WATCHING MASTERPIECE THEATER.
SALE

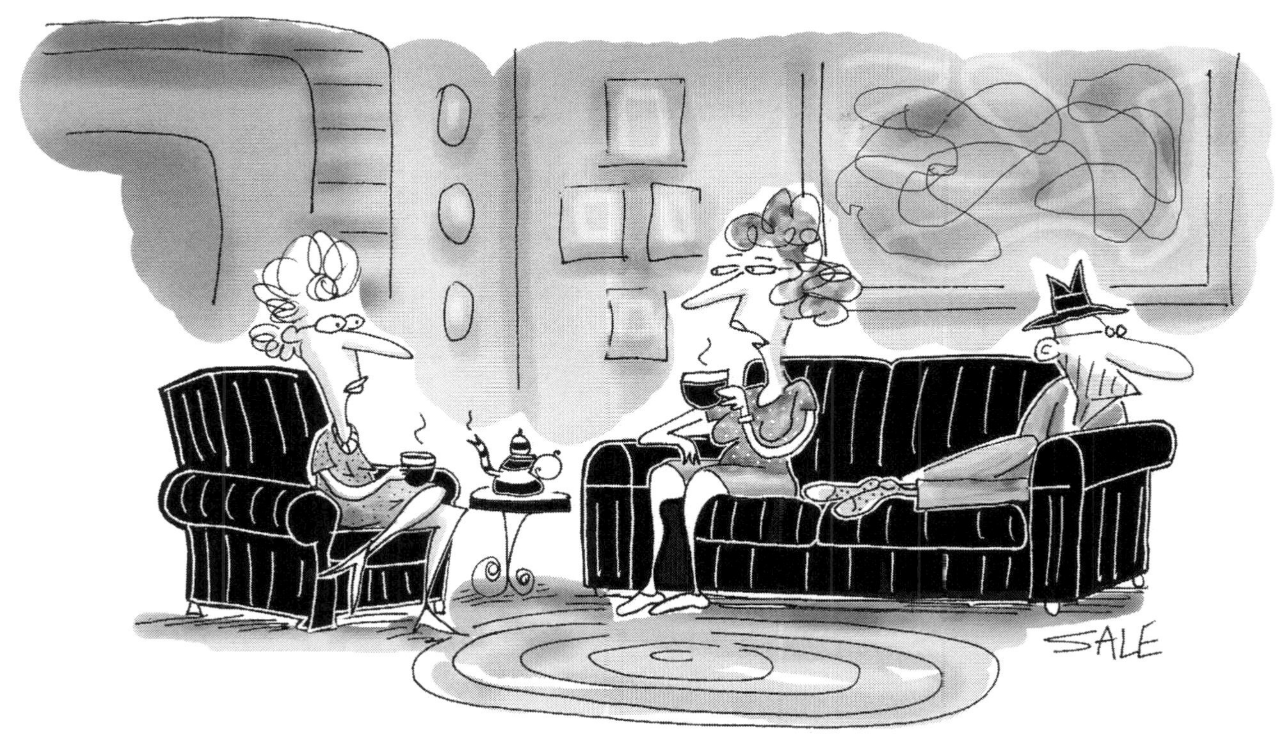

"*That's Jerome, he's a rescue.*"

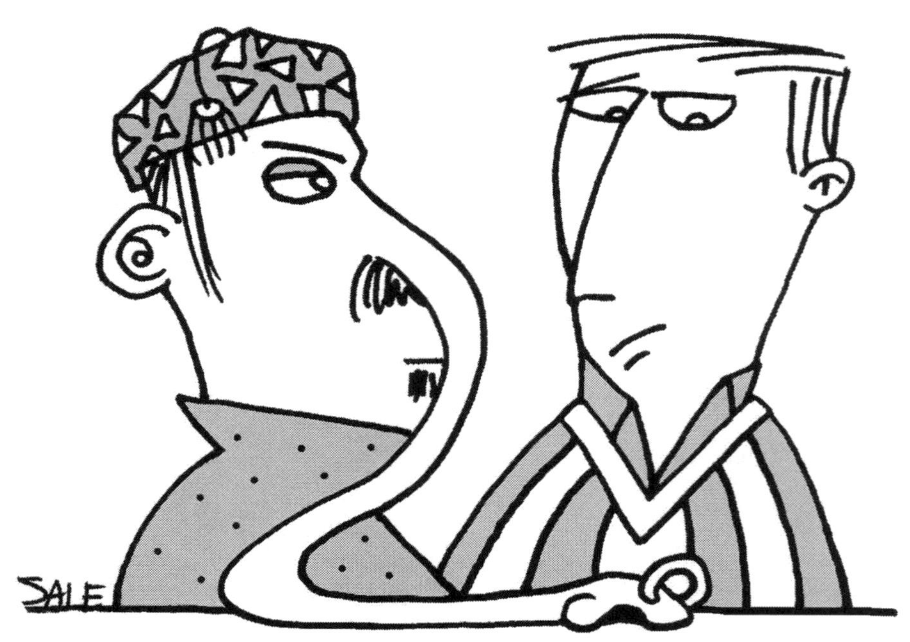

*Todd wanted to support his friend, but frankly,
Akbar's new nose ring kinda freaked him out.*

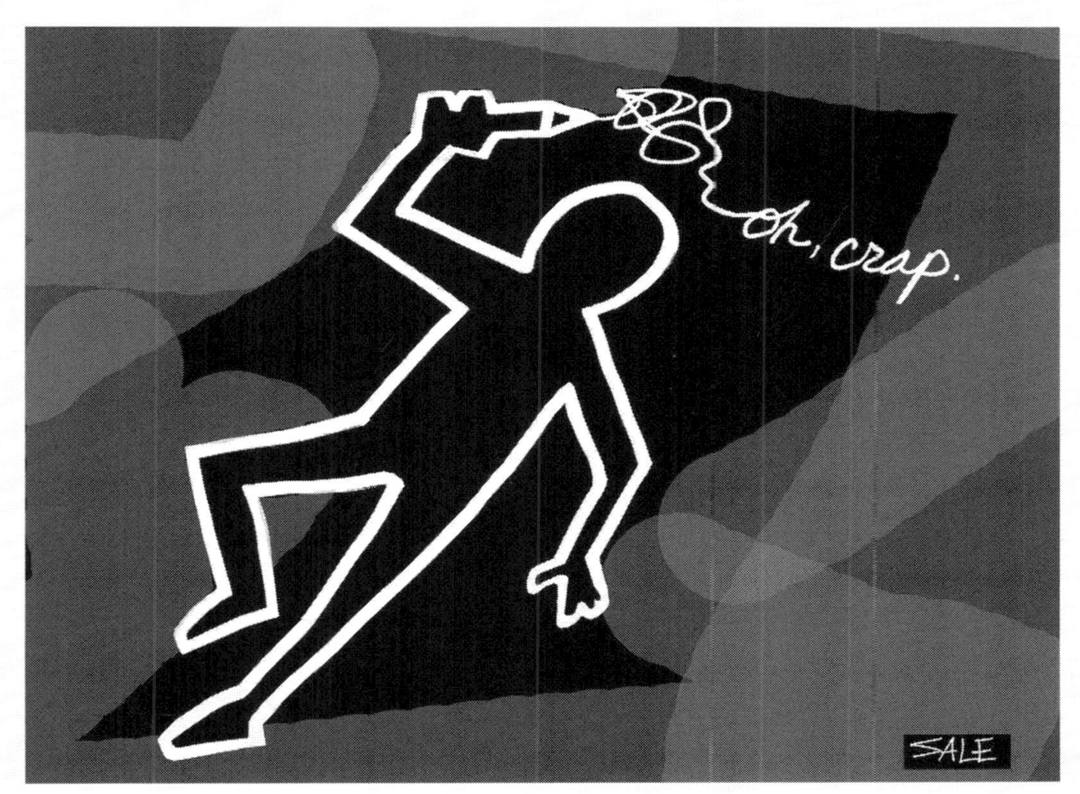

"Webster Riggs couldn't draw to save his life.
Eventually it caught up with him."

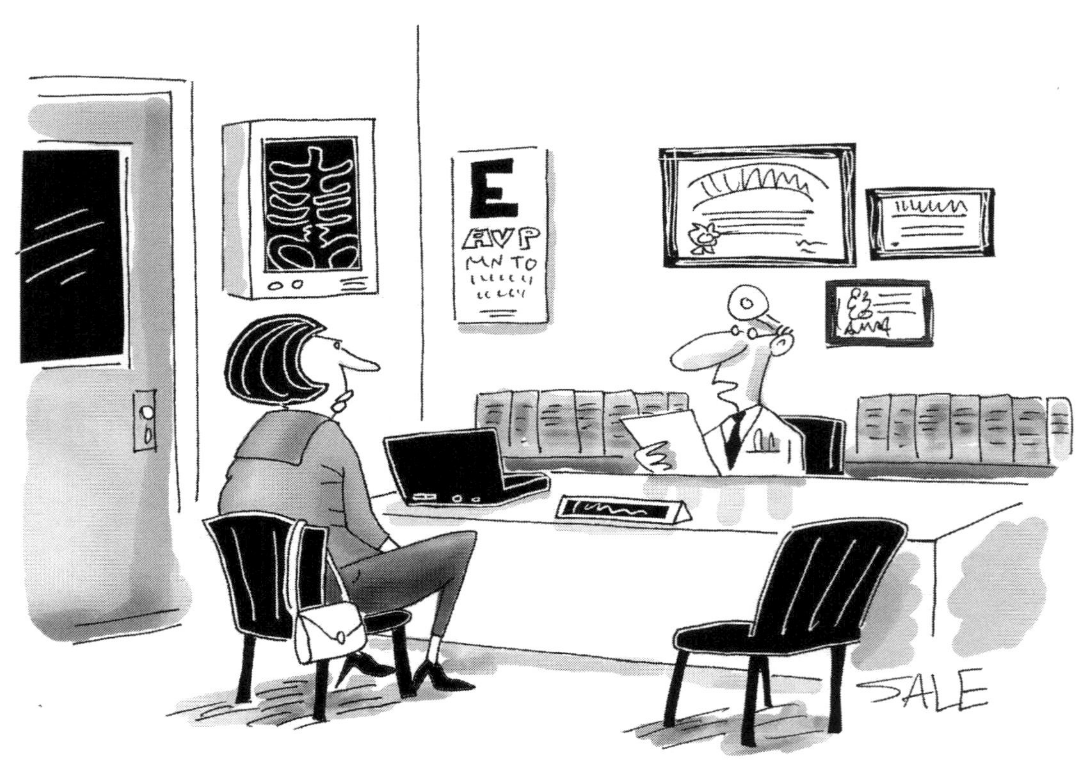

"*The test results confirm that, yes, your genes make you look fat. So, you can stop asking.*"

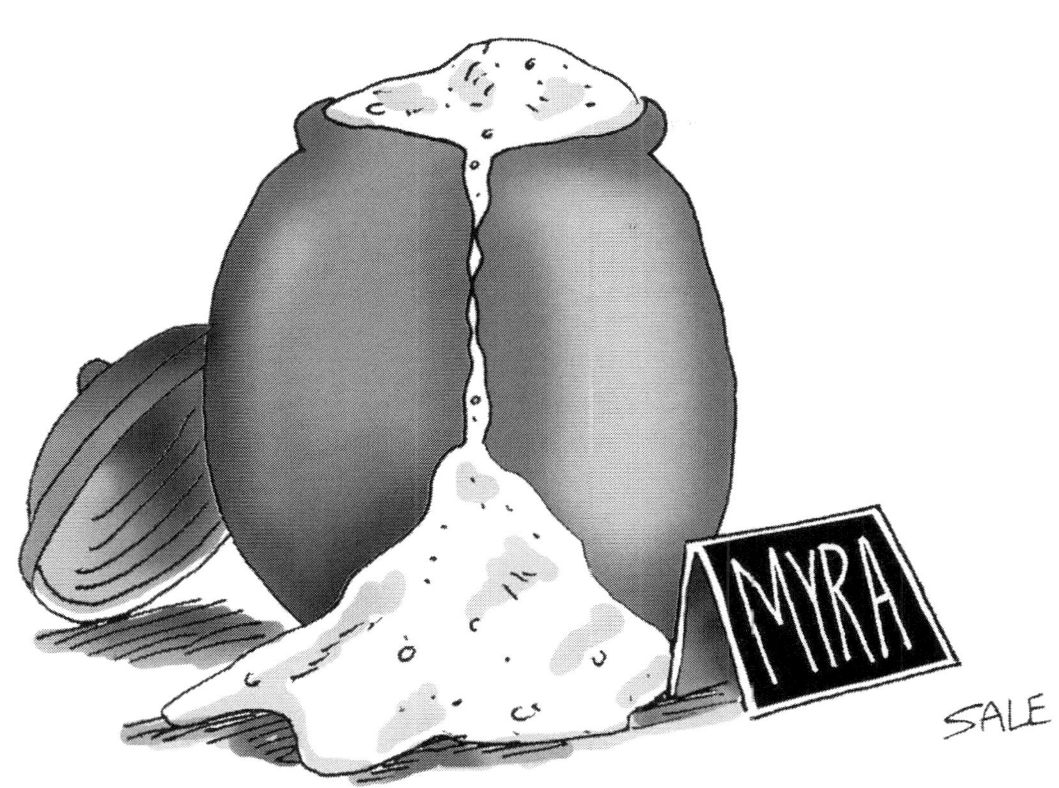

Even in death, Myra failed to attain her ideal weight.

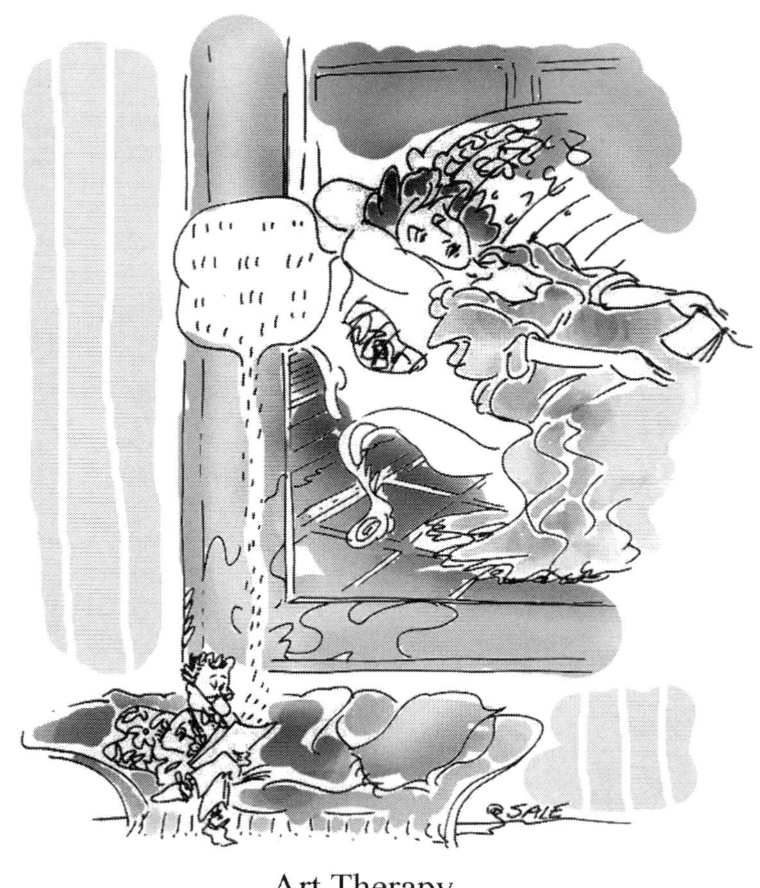

Art Therapy

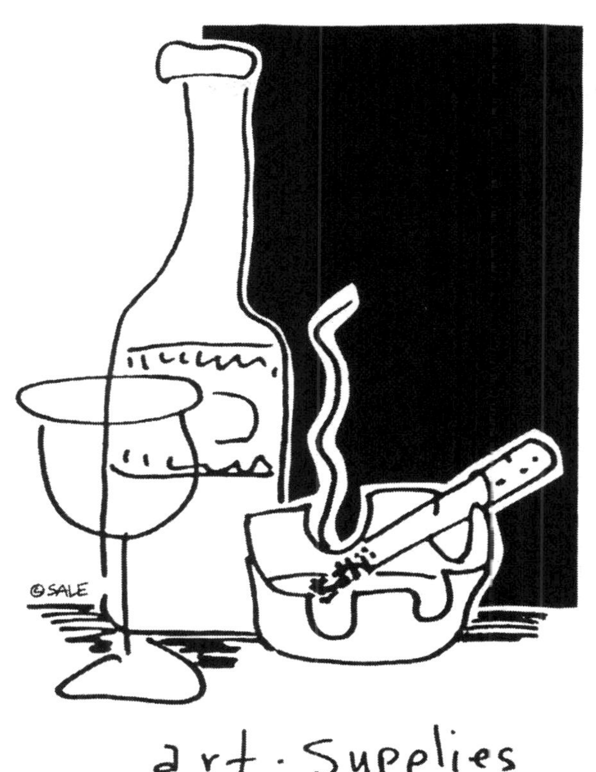

art . supplies

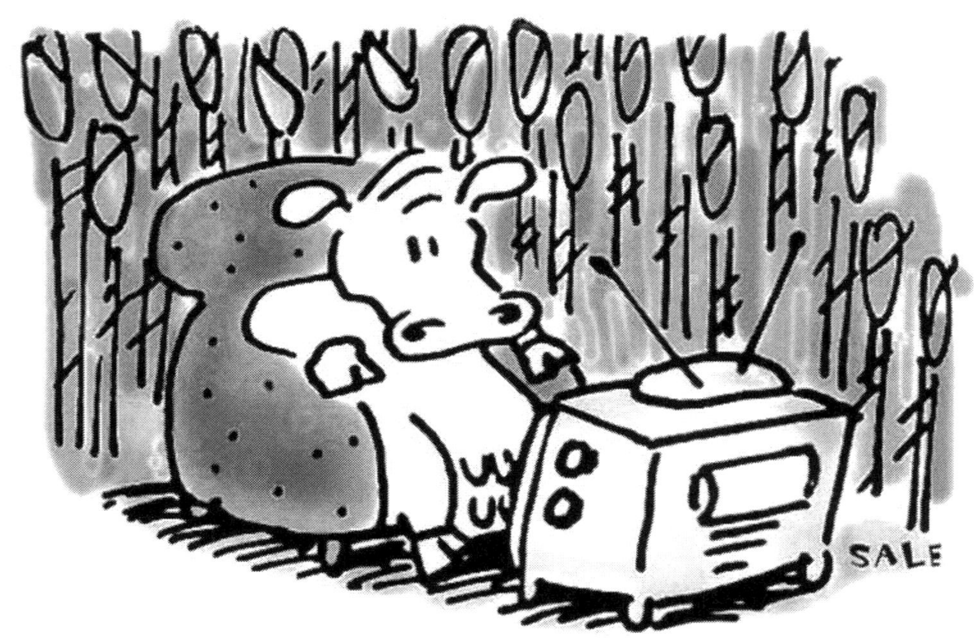

*A safer, more humane, drug-free way to
increase the size of livestock.*

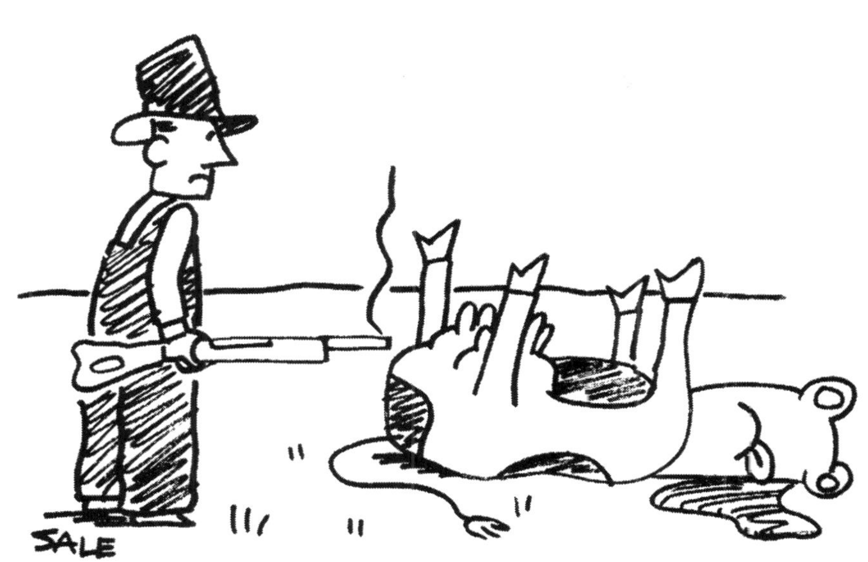

Lactose Intolerant.

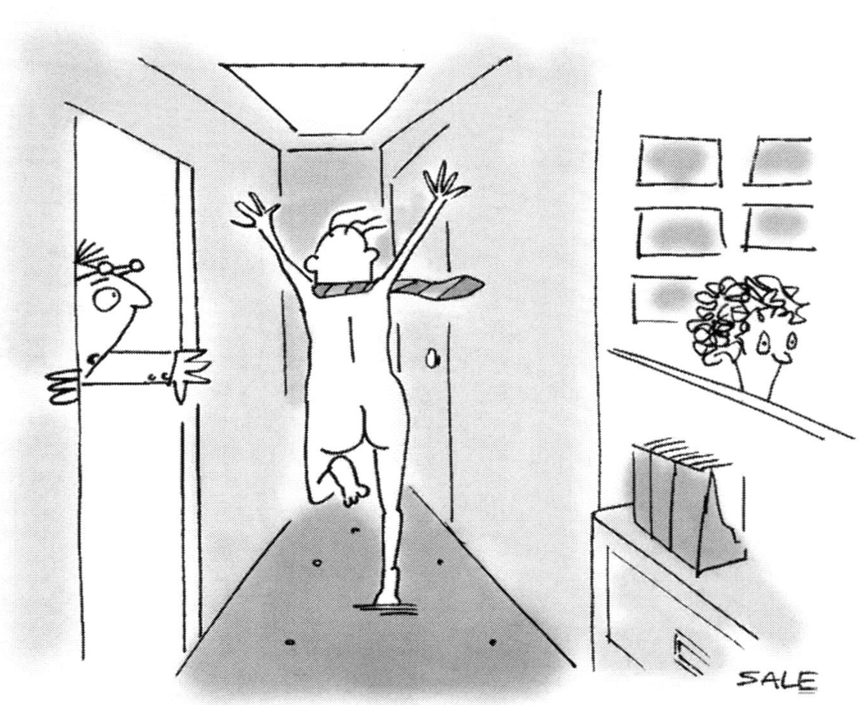

When told to give it the old college try, Stevenson smoked a bong, drank six jello shots, mooned the receptionist and streaked the office.

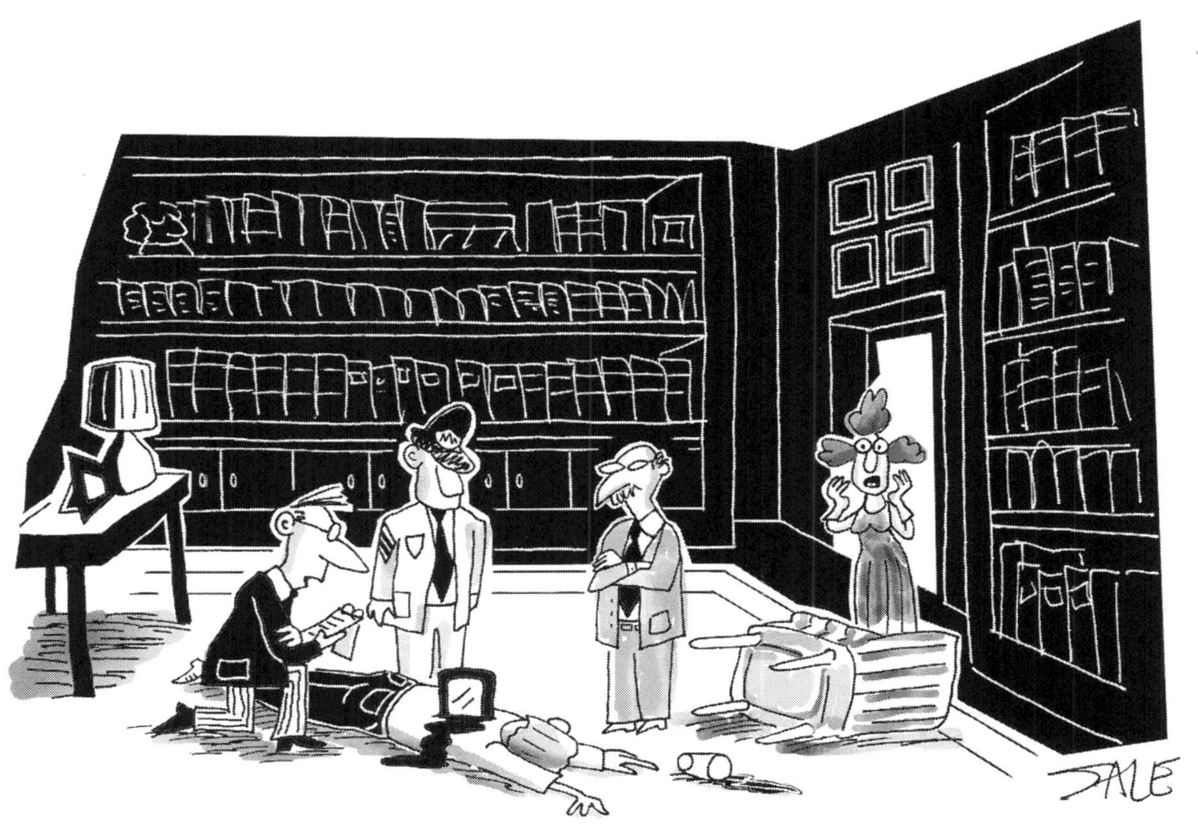

"*Boys, Colonel Mustard did this in the library with a Kindle.*"

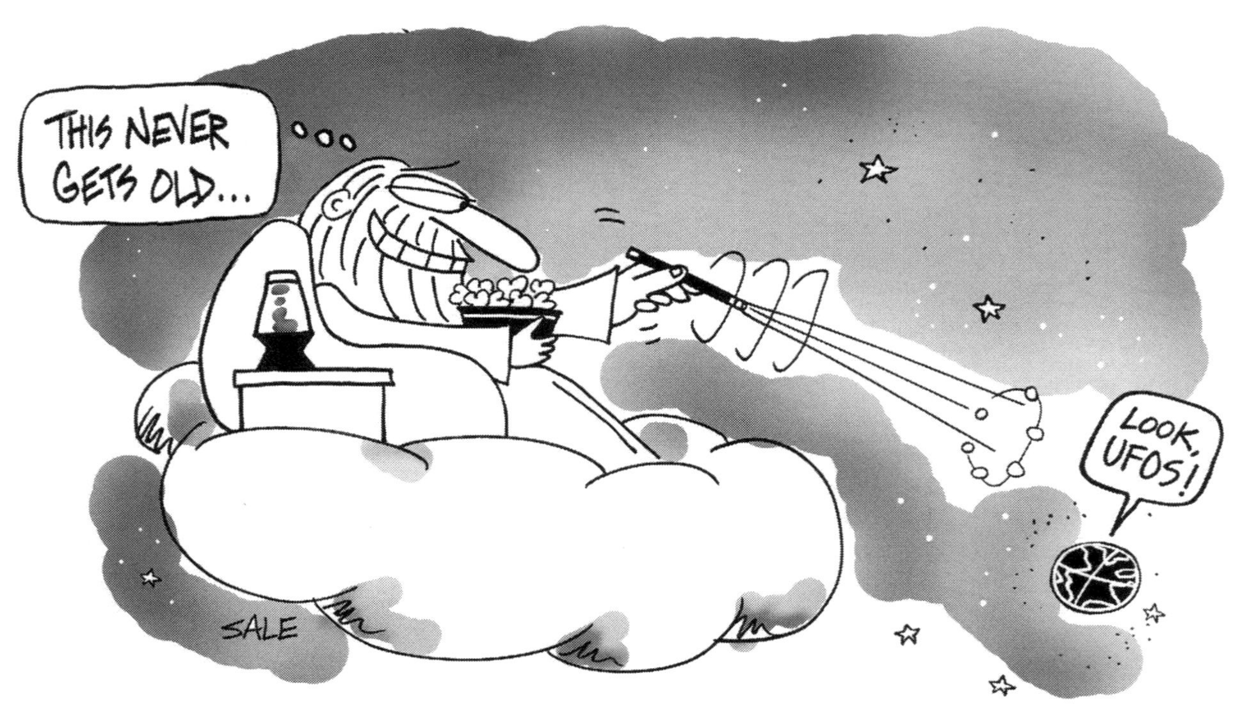

After a tough week, God loves to curl up with a bowl of popcorn and use his laser pointer to screw with people.

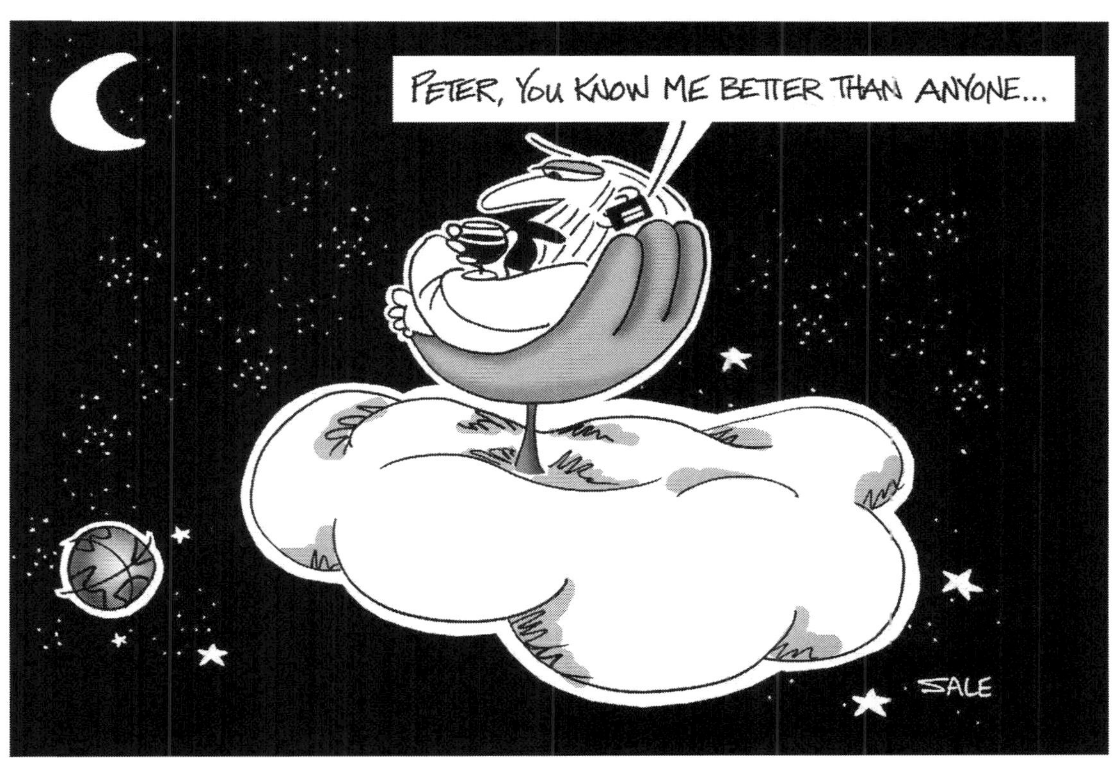

"Why do I attract so many crackpots?"

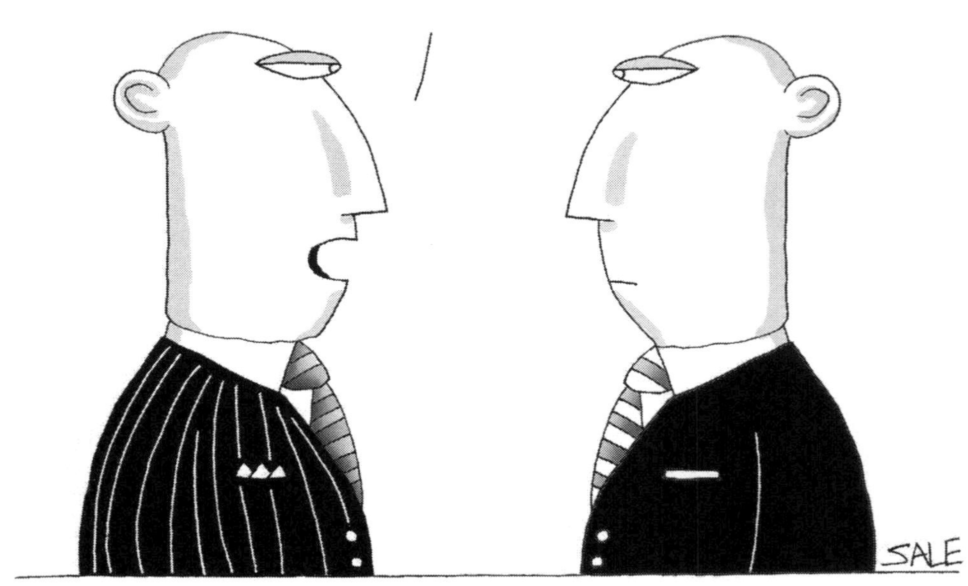

"It made me sick."

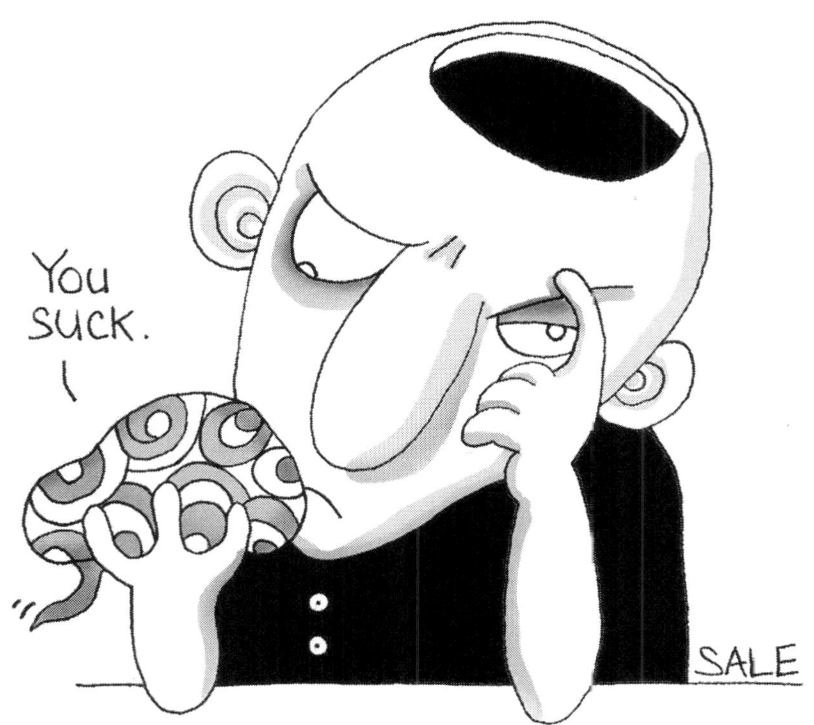

Guns don't kill people—introspection does.

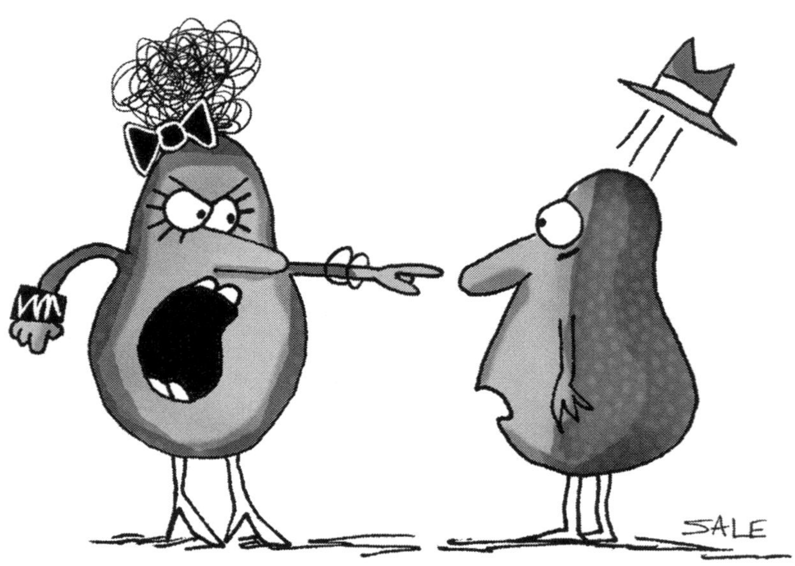

"*Stop saying I'm the good kind of fat!*"

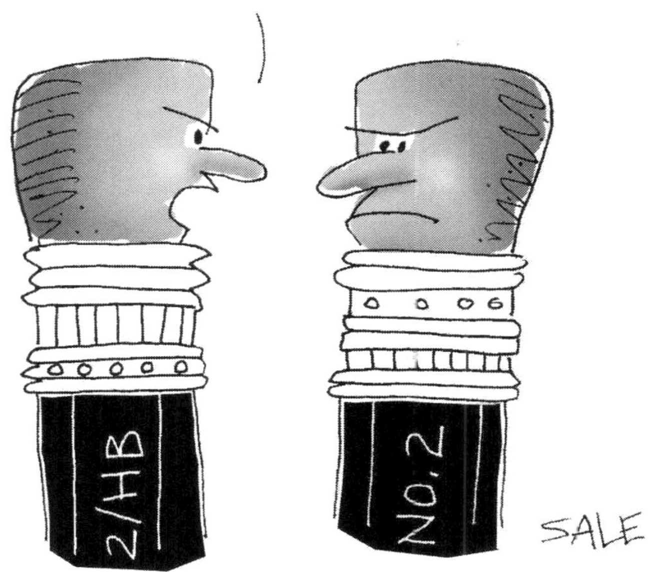

STOP CORRECTING ME!
2/HB
NO.2
SALE

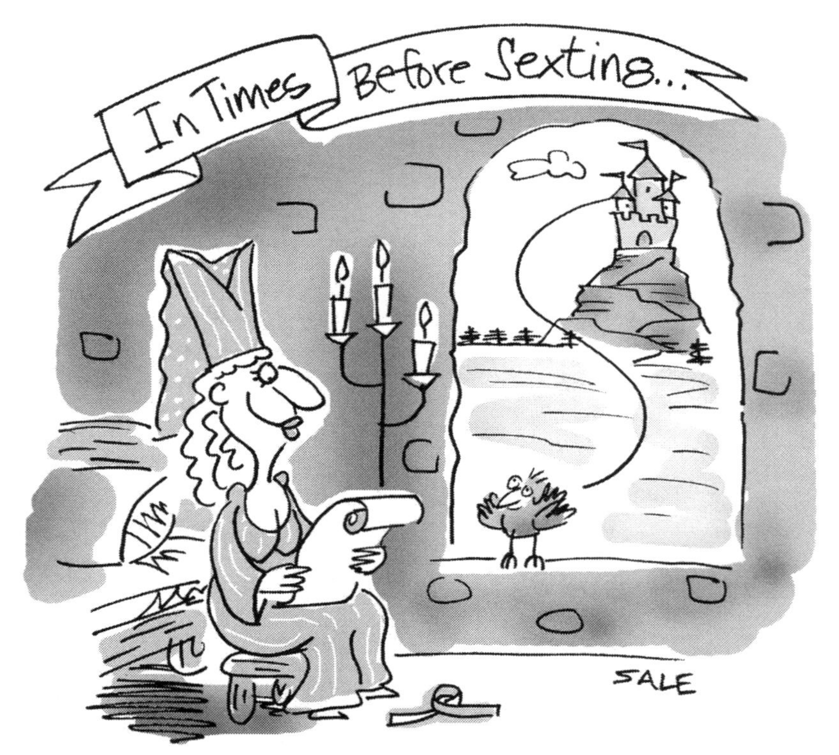

"What art thou wearing?"

Early American Tweeters...

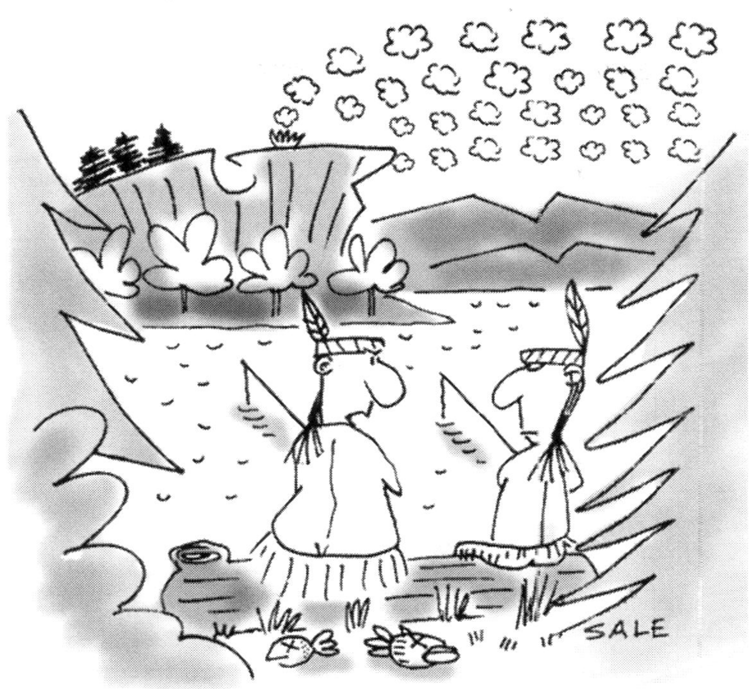

"Why does Bear Without Life think we care
about every little thing he think and do?"

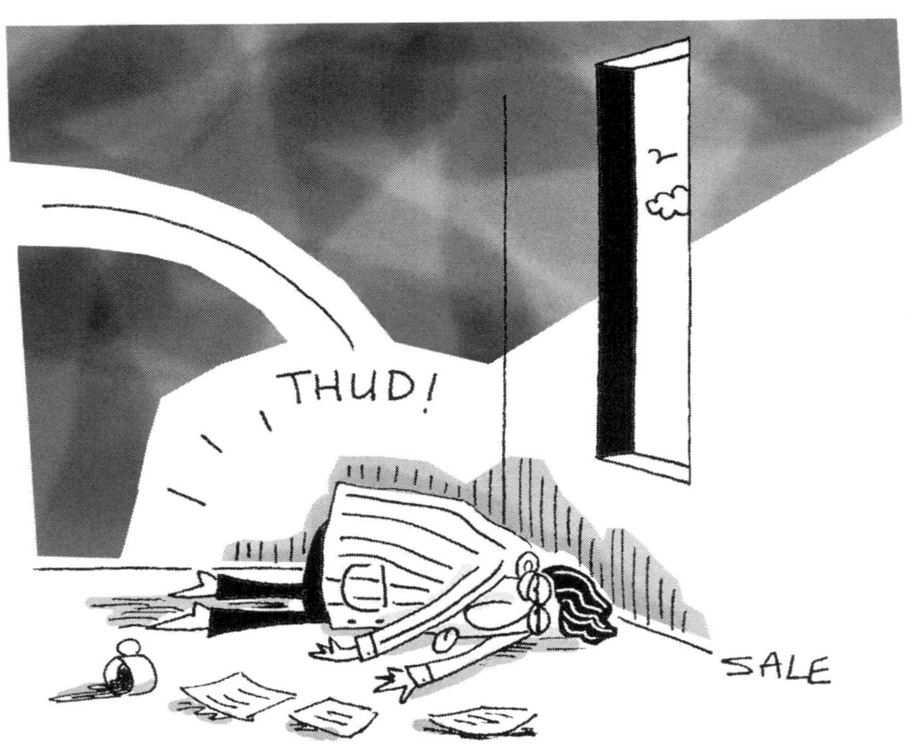

*Constant interaction with humanity finally caught up
with Rudy and dropped him in his tracks..*

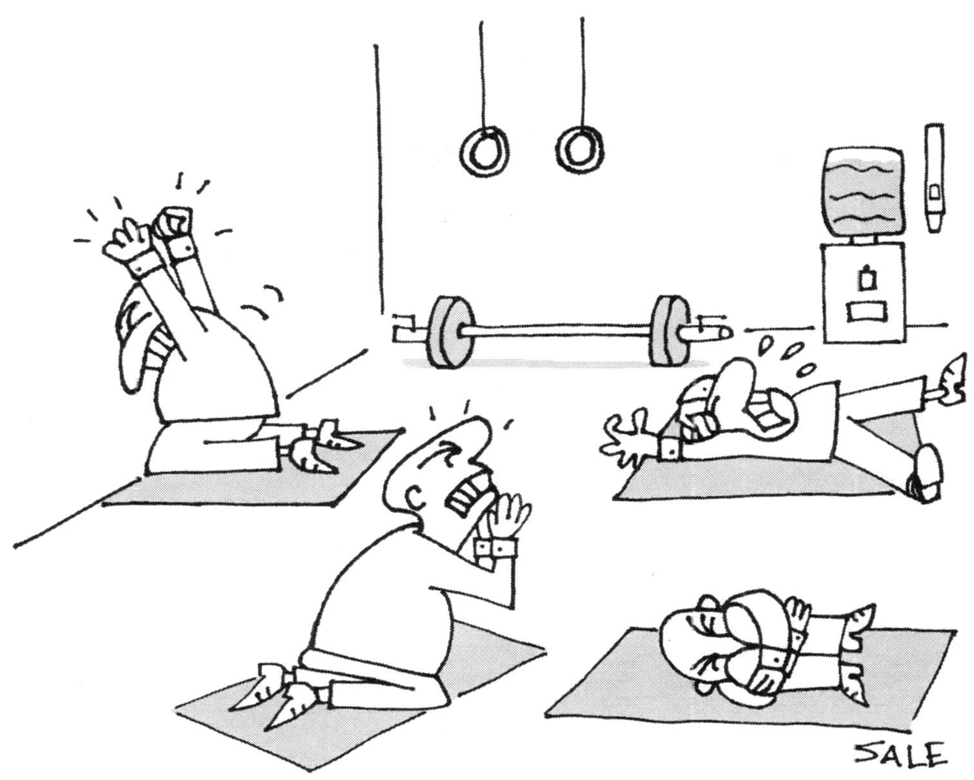

Inner Debate Team Practice.

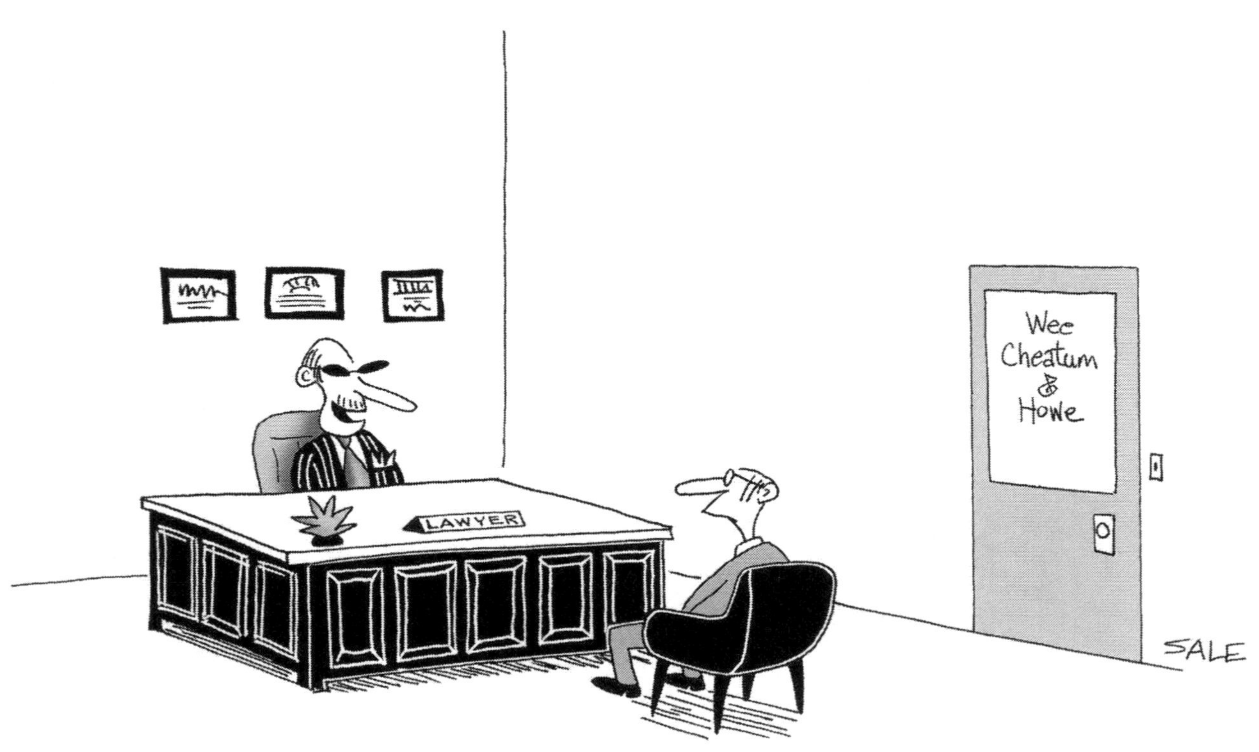

"Here, we consider you innocent until proven insolvent."

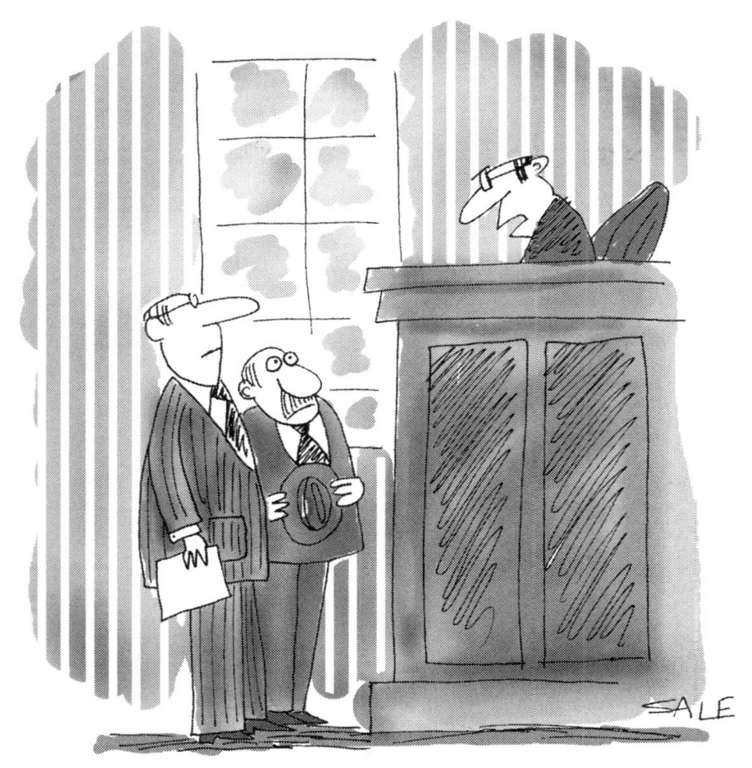

"*Counselor, instruct your client that hindsight is not a legal defense.*"

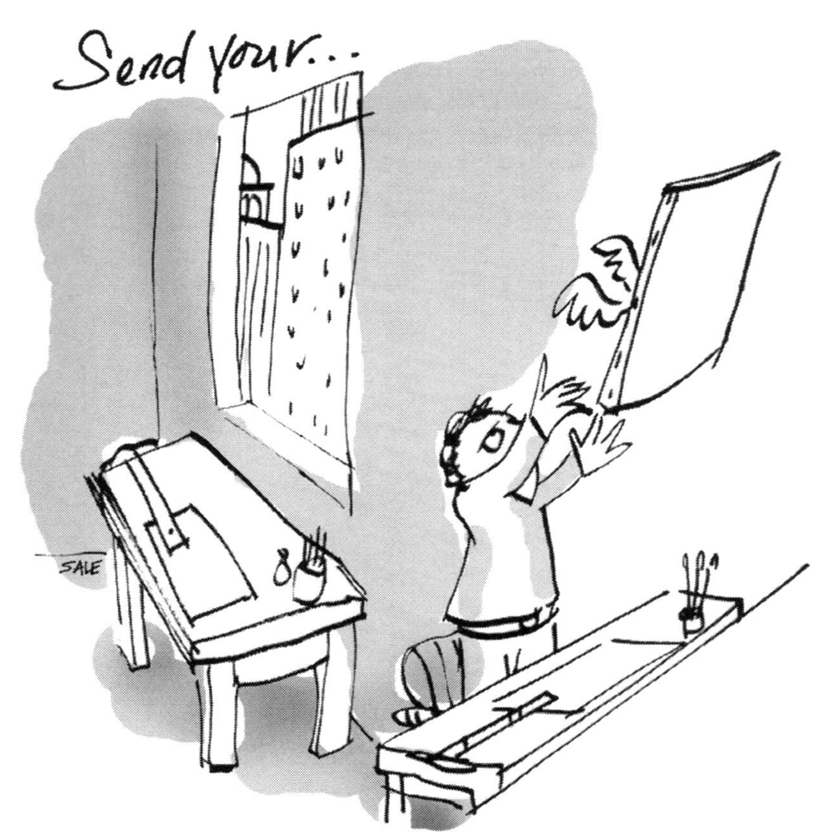

Send your...
Art into the world.

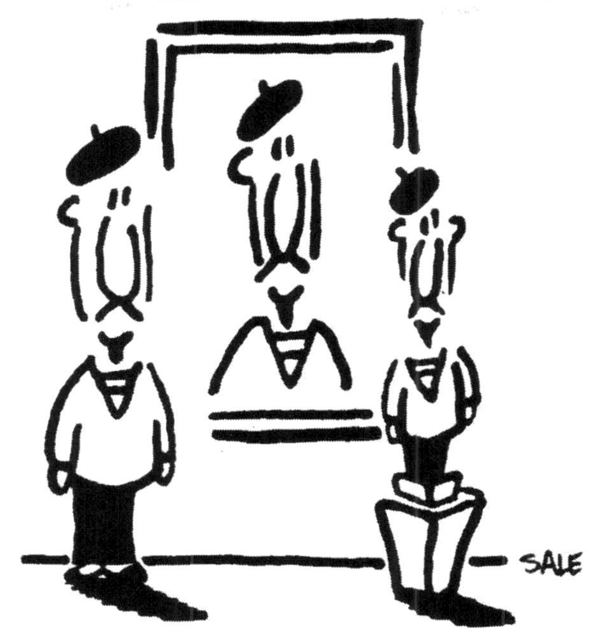

ME, MYSEF & MY EGO.

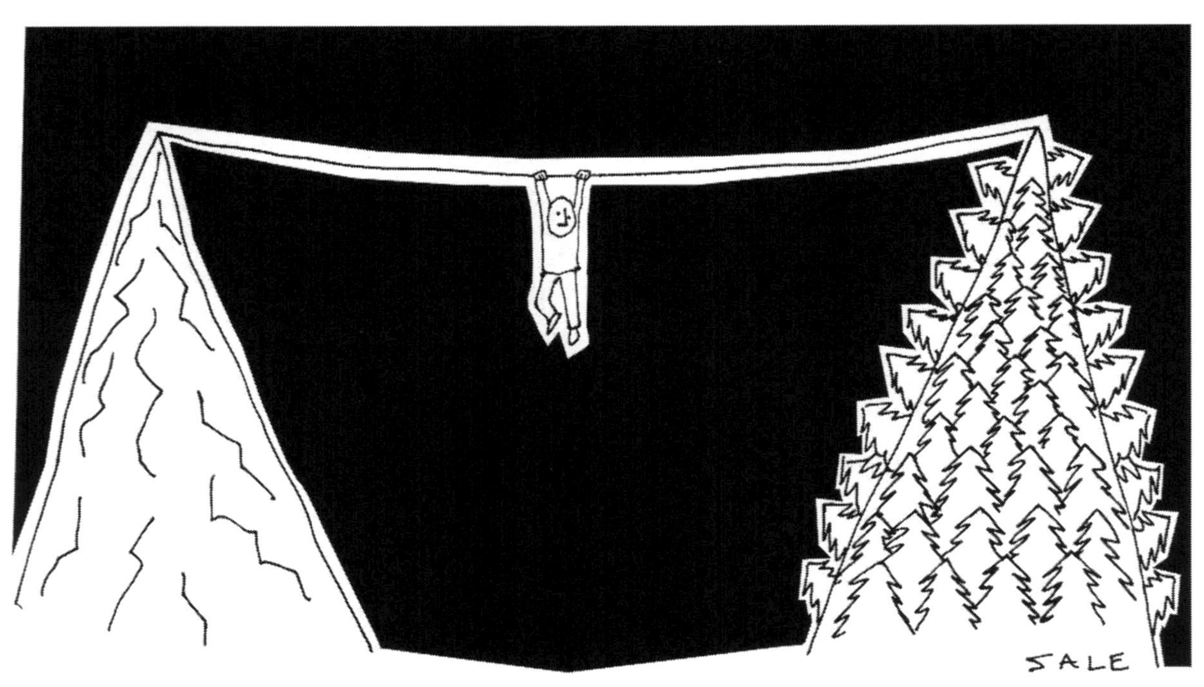

Change is good—it's the transition that'll kill you.

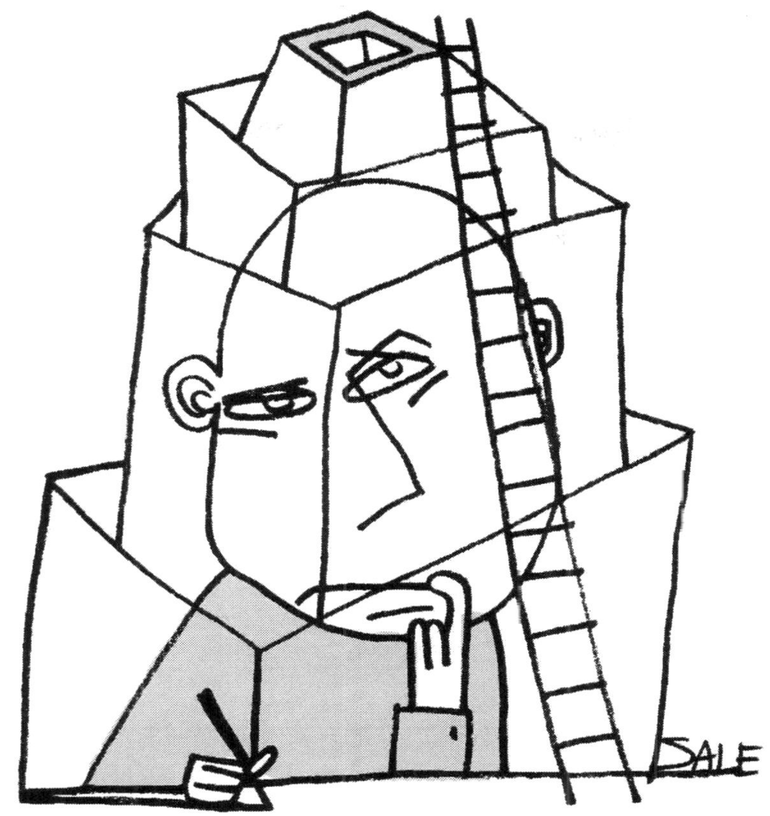

SALE

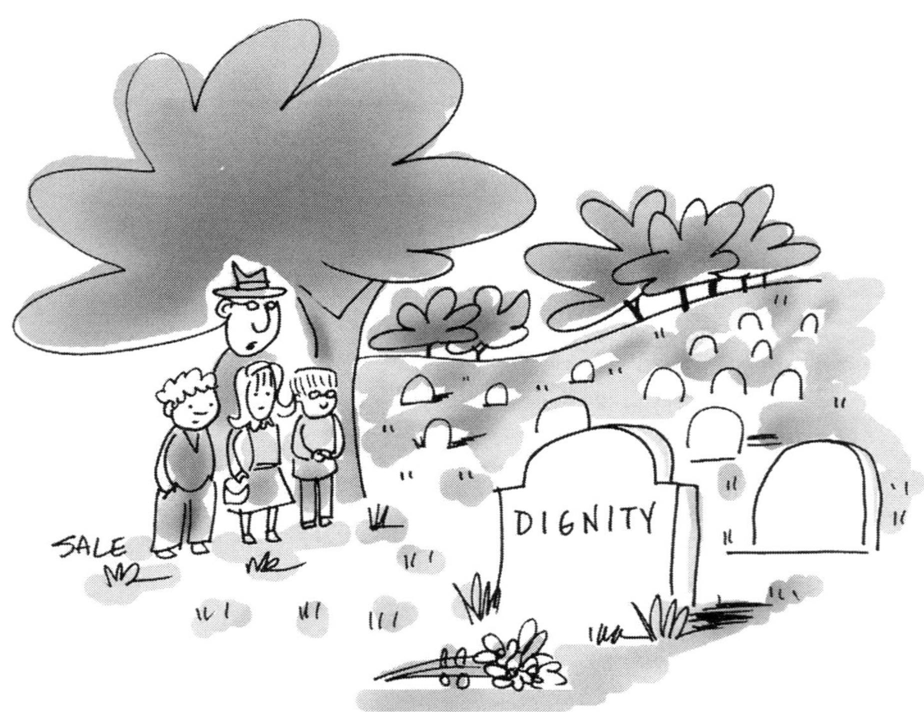

"*You see children, as the Internet grew, social networking, twitter and blogging fed peoples' compulsion to reveal every detail of their lives. Oh, look, there's modesty and self-respect.*"

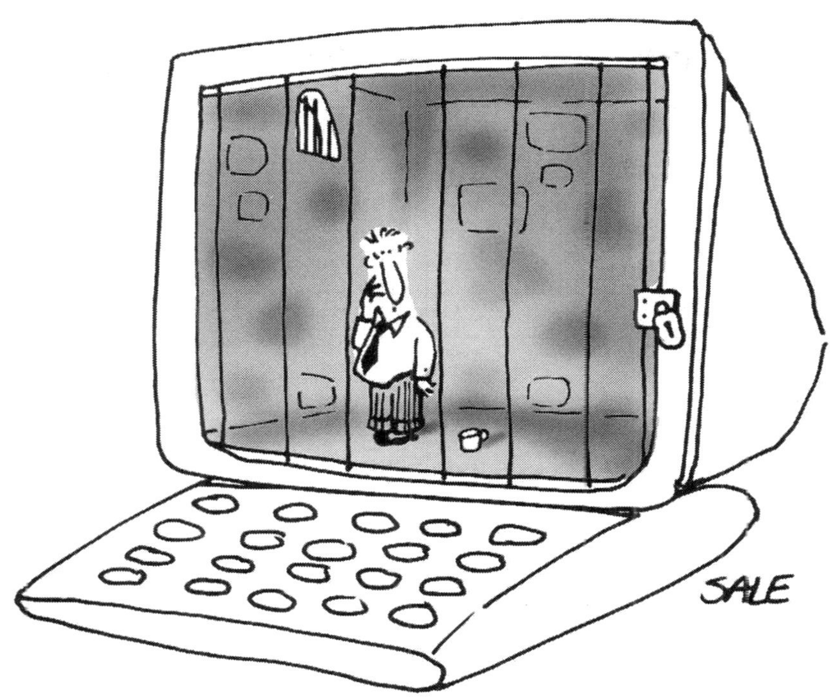
SALE

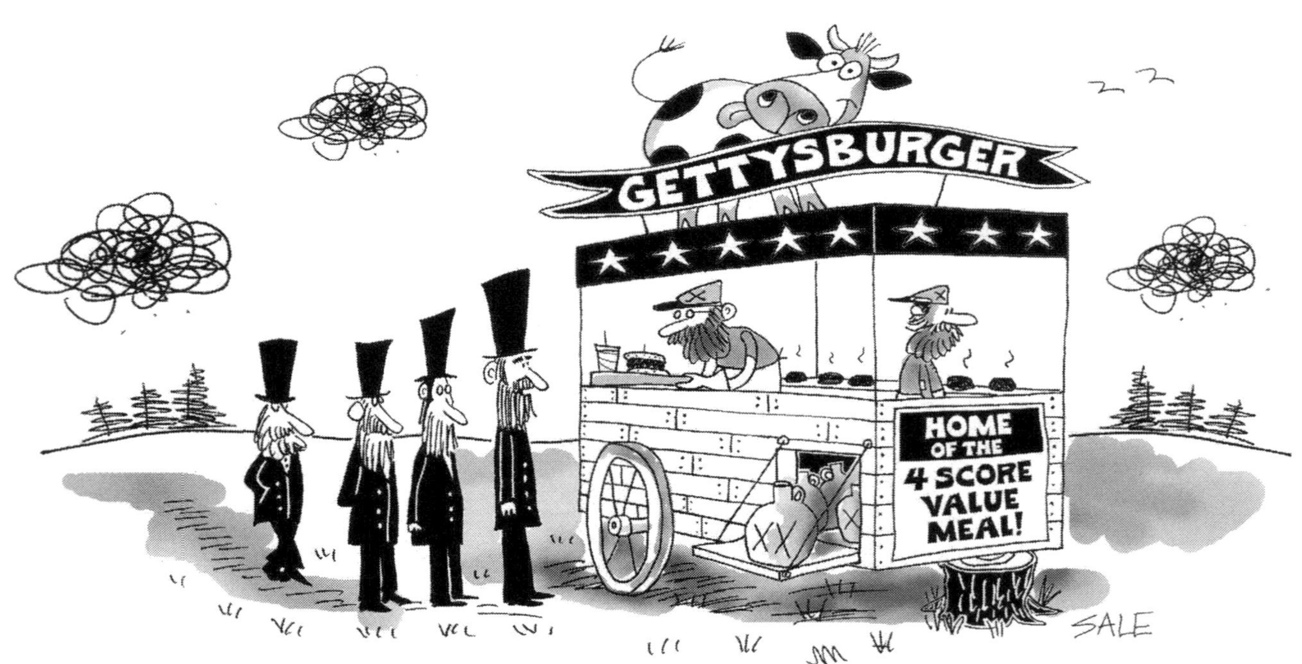

GETTYSBURGER
HOME OF THE
4 SCORE VALUE MEAL!
SALE

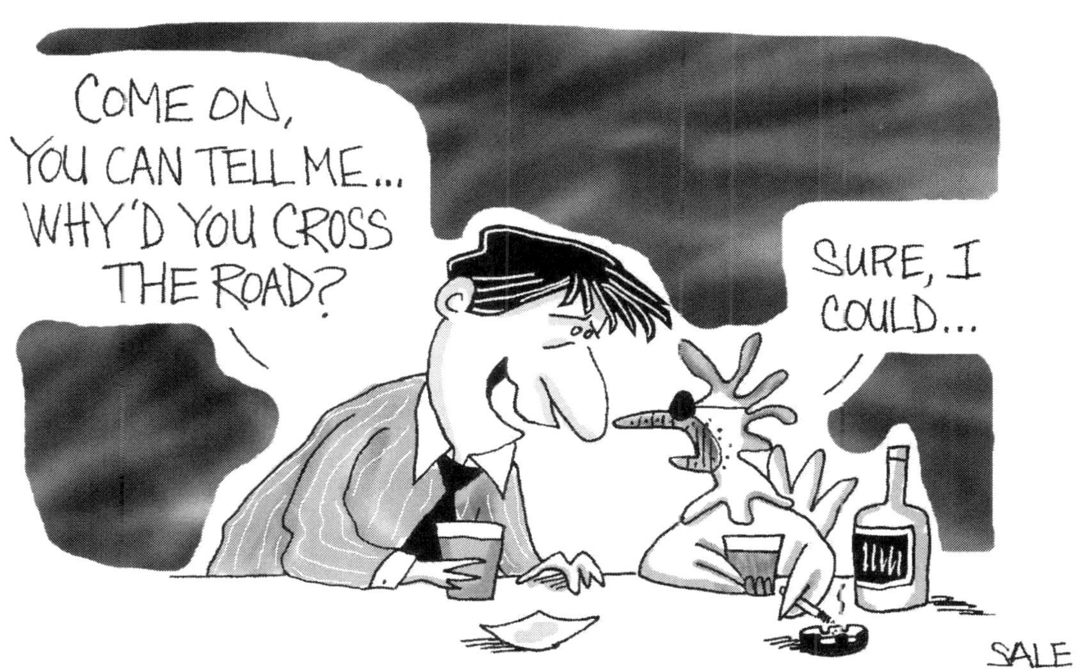

"...But then I'd have to kill you."

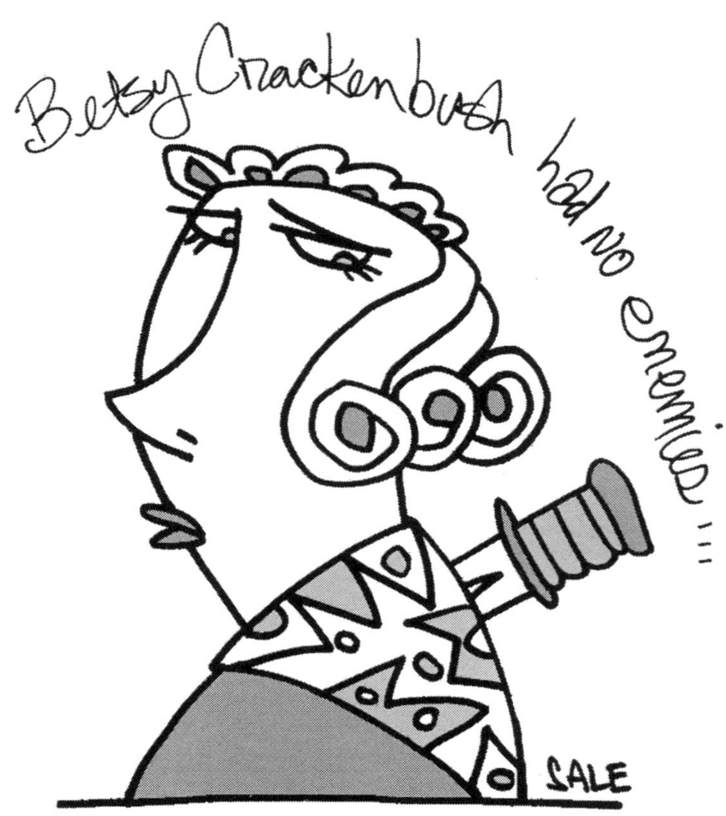

"But she did have some friends that
were not all that crazy about her."

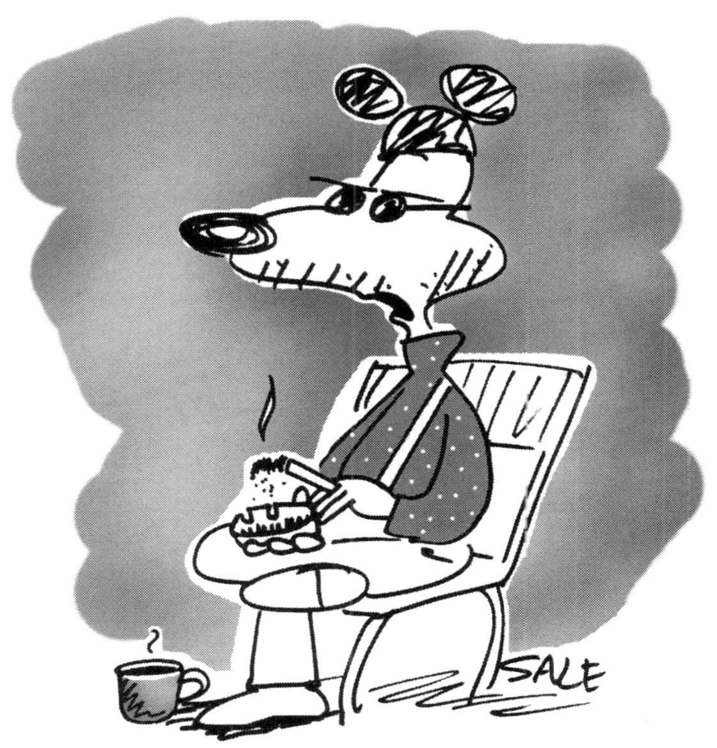

"Hello, my name is Mickey...and
I am powerless over cheese."

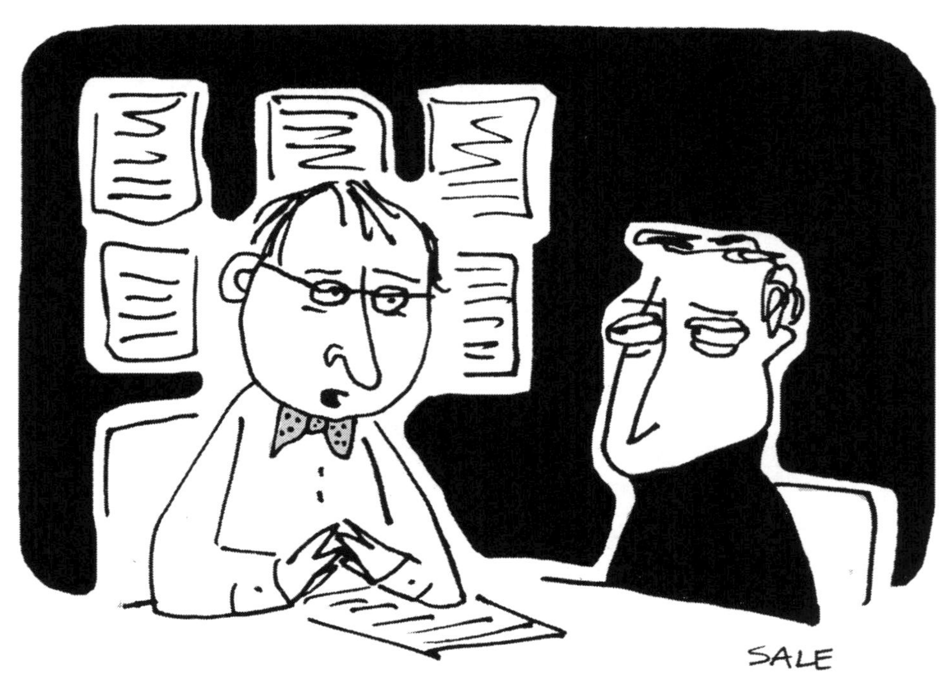

"*Medically speaking, you show signs of recovery;*
Existentially speaking, you are actively dying."

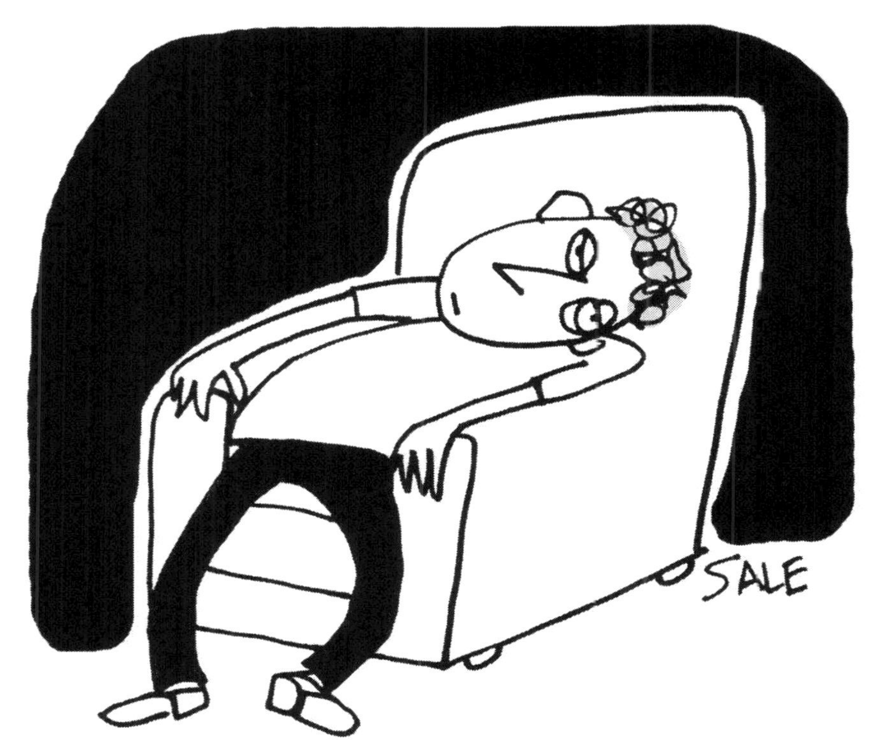

Premature stupidity made Jack a dull boy.

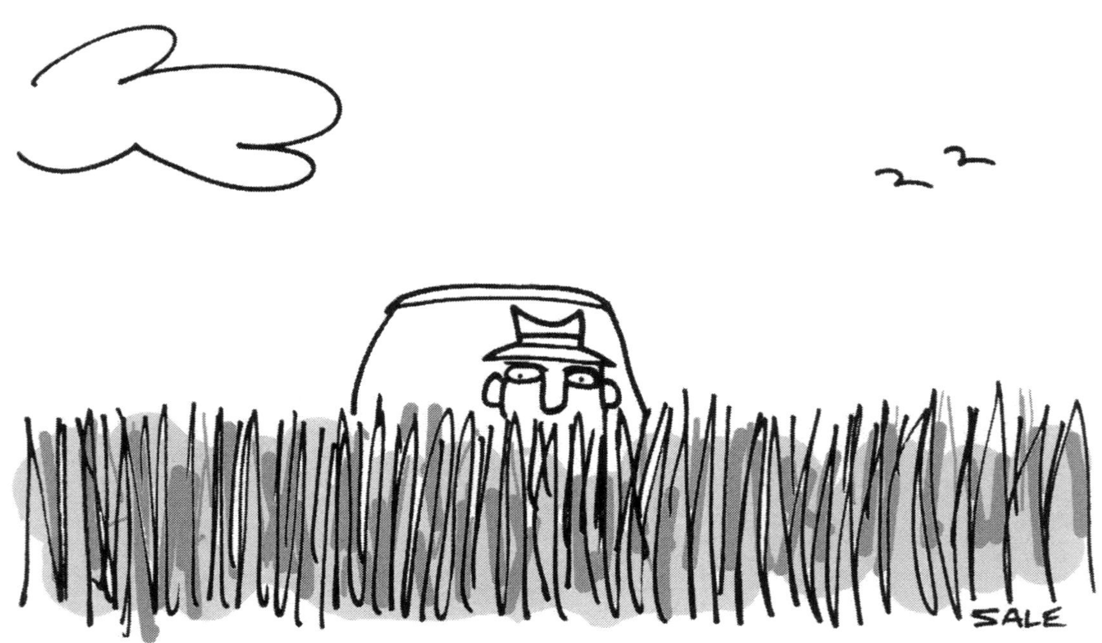

"*Mr. Frost, this is your OnStar Operator...*
It appears you've taken the road less traveled."

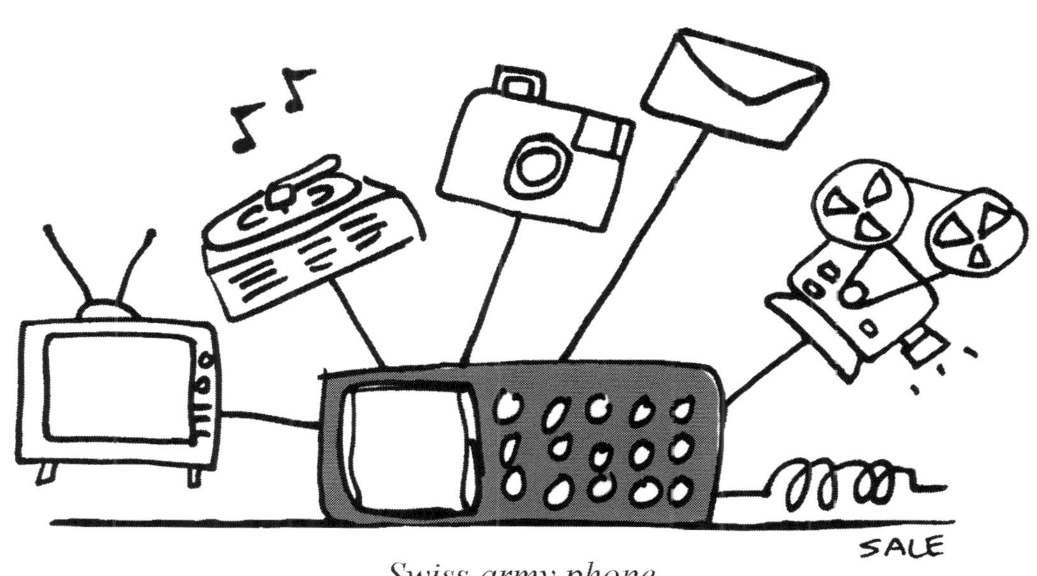

Swiss army phone.

Edwina Pokey.

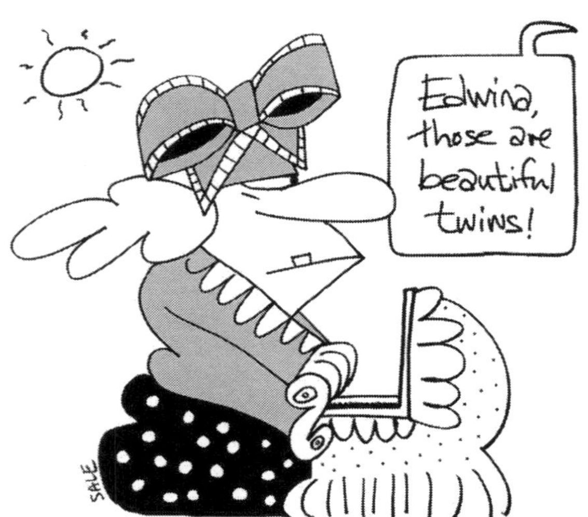

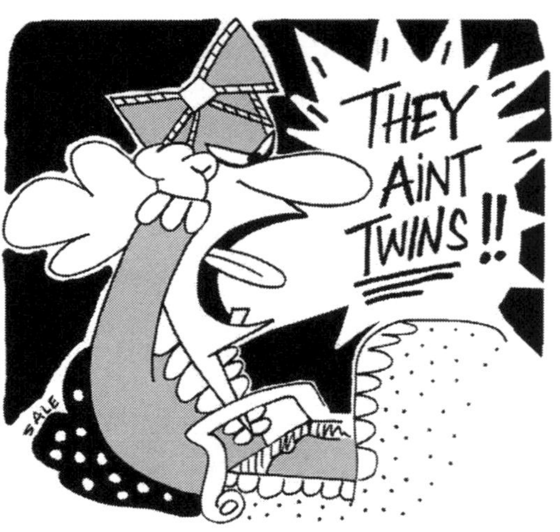

That's a 2-headed baby!!

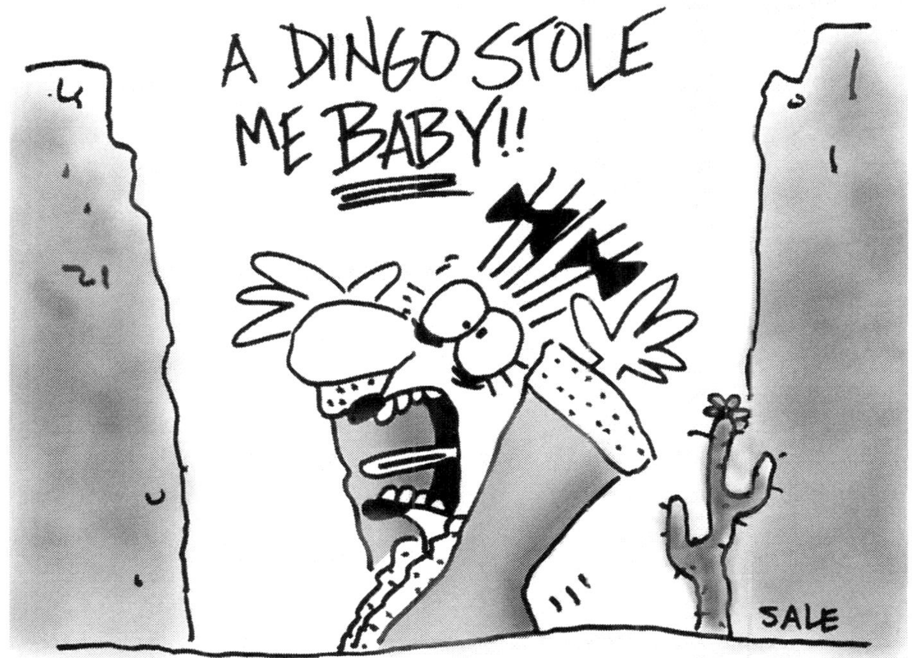

Edwina Pokey's Meryl Streep impersonation was the stuff of legends.

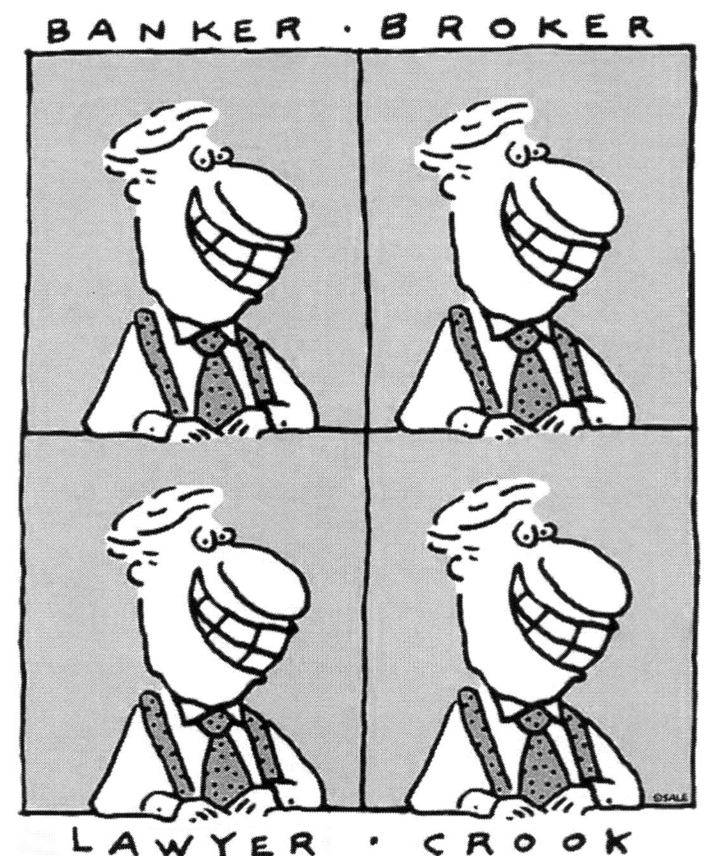

BANKER · BROKER
LAWYER · CROOK

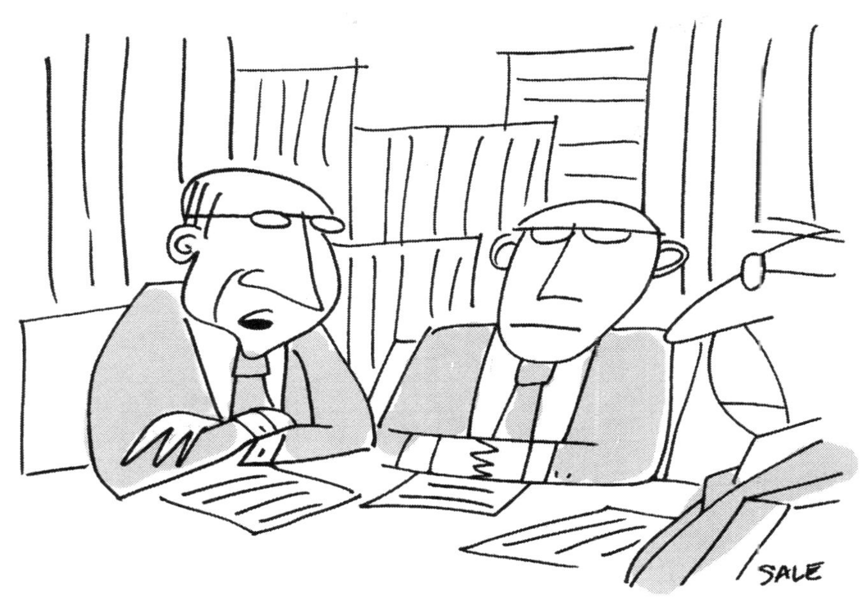

"We all agree that honesty is a policy,
but is it our policy?"

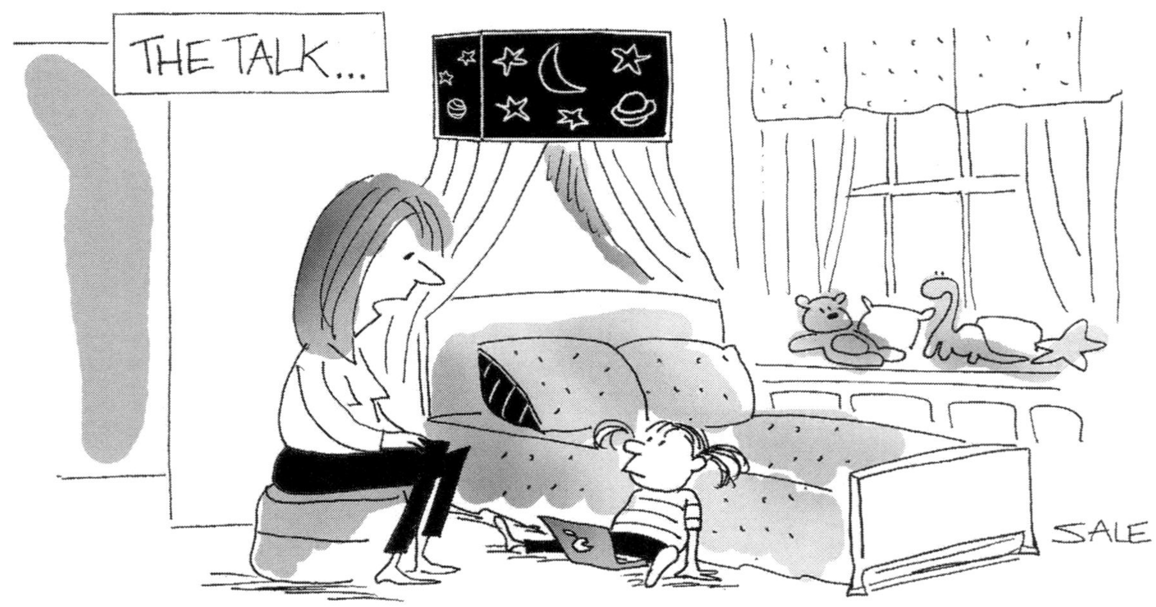

"Boys are different from girls in many significant ways, and as you meet more of them, you'll discover that gay men are God's gift to women."

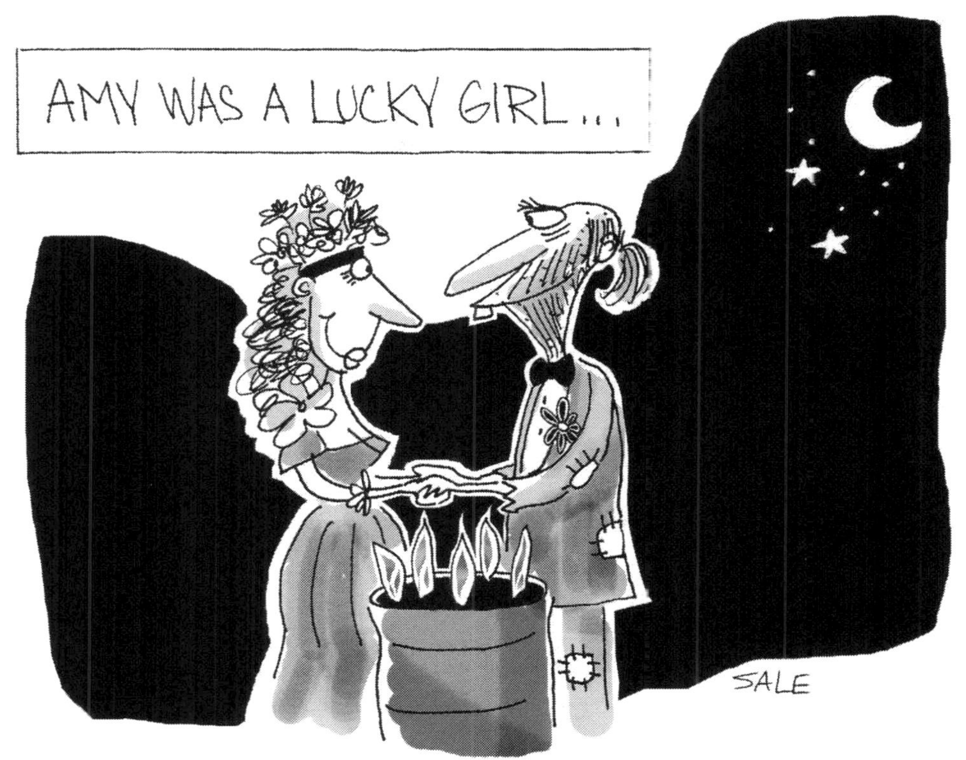

*Her family and friends loved Emmett and never
once gave her a hard time about being hobosexual.*

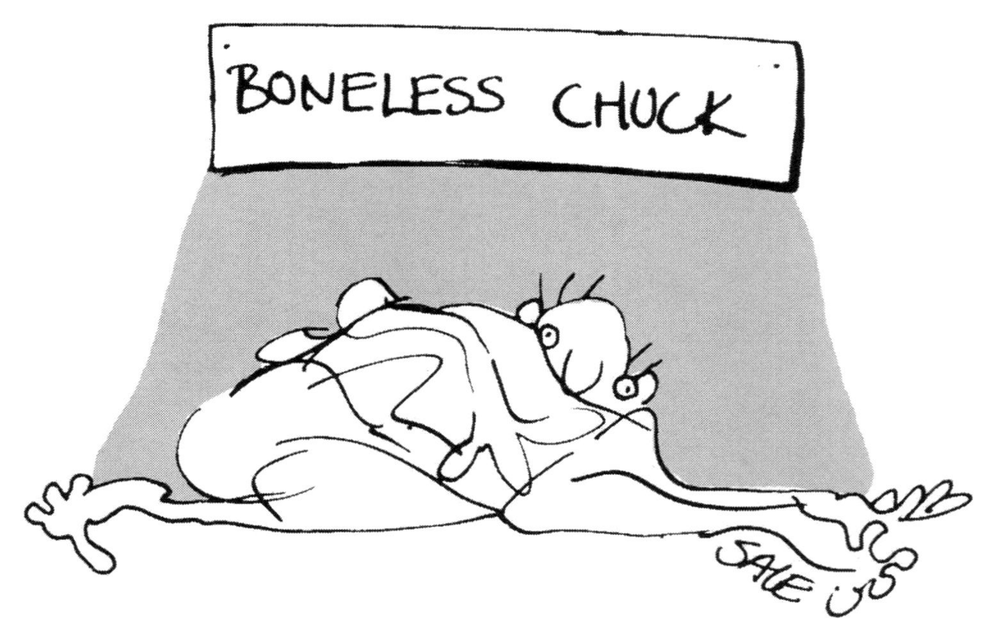

BONELESS CHUCK

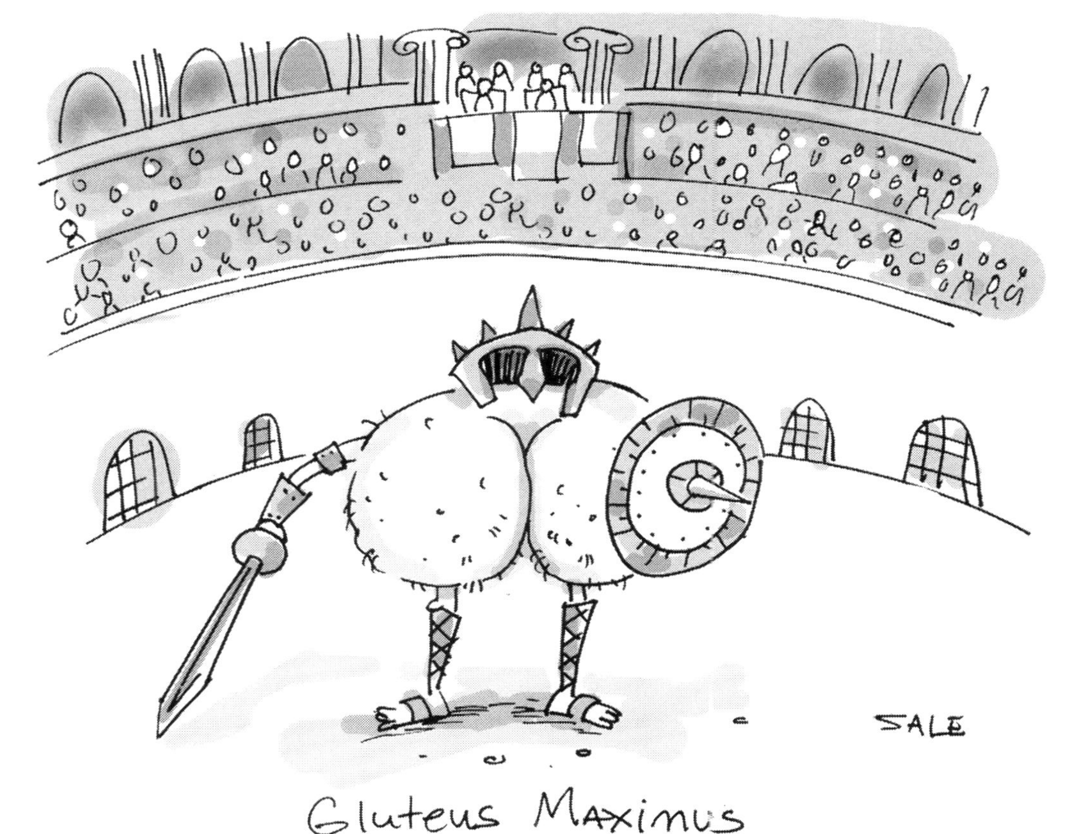

Gluteus Maximus

Life attracts all kinds of **characters...**

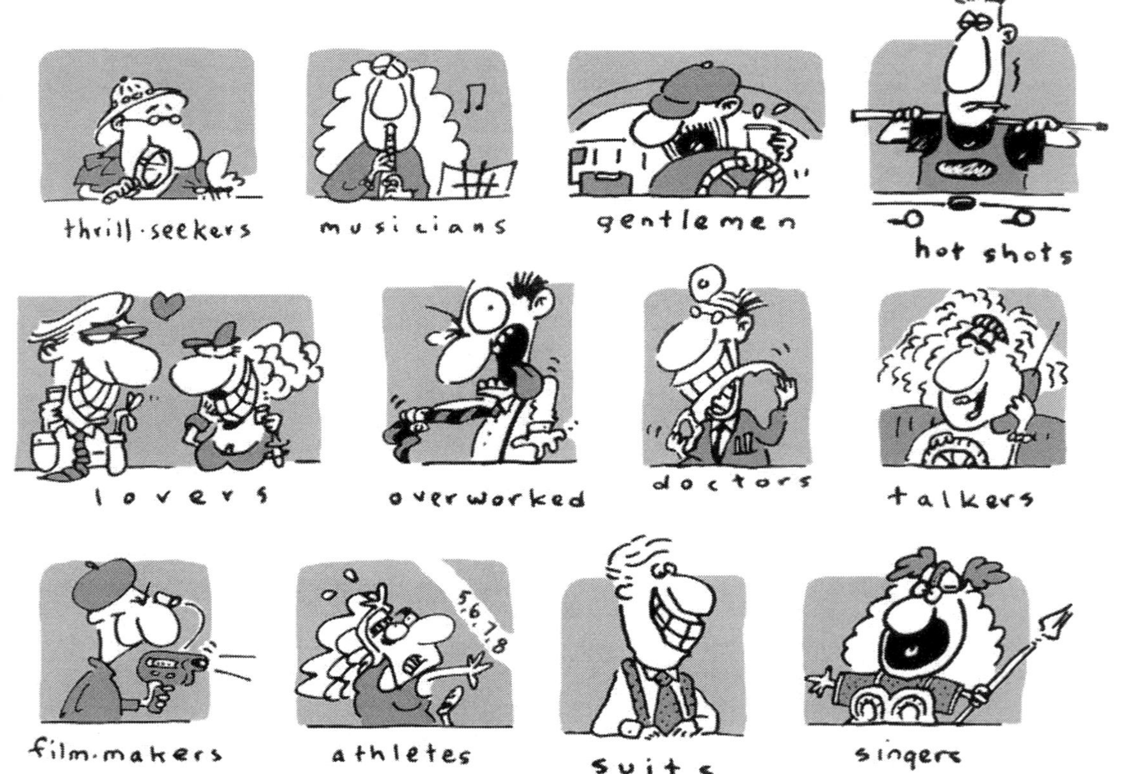

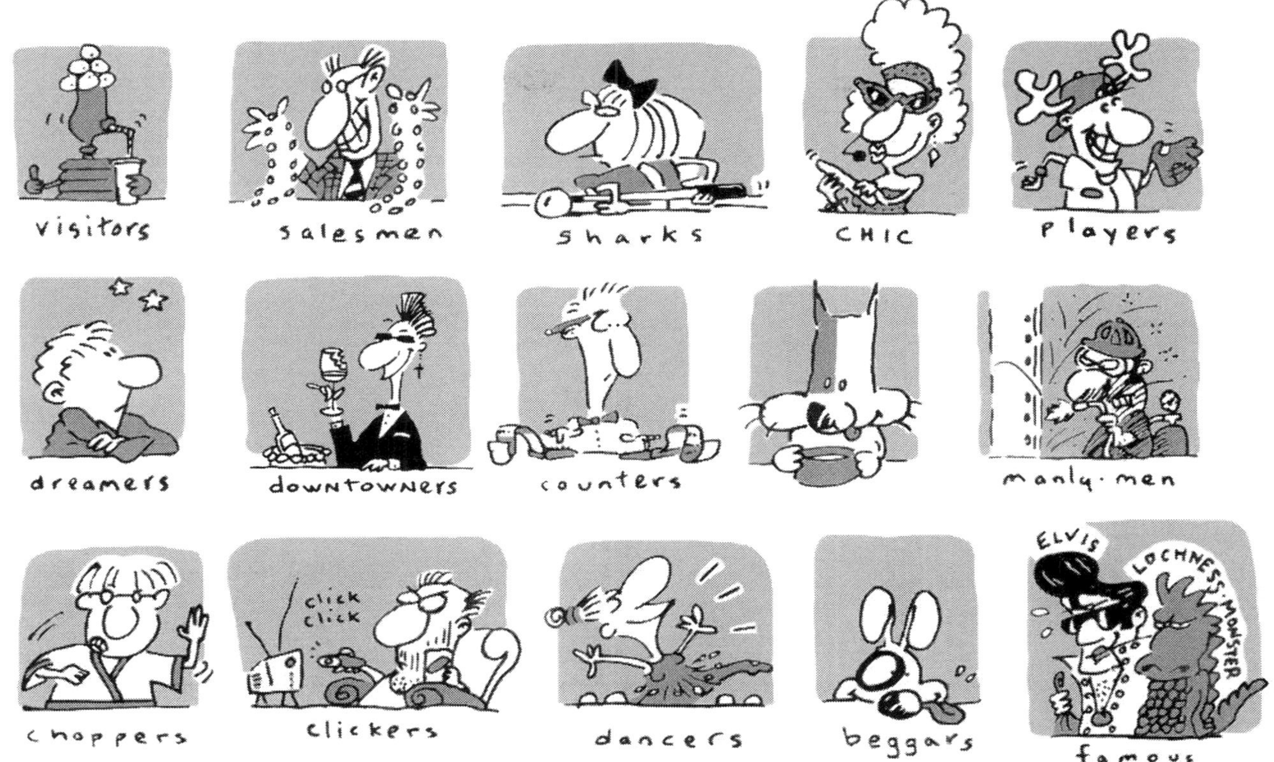

visitors
salesmen
sharks
CHIC
players
dreamers
downtowners
counters
manly·men
choppers
click click
clickers
dancers
beggars
ELVIS
LOCHNESS·MONSTER
famous

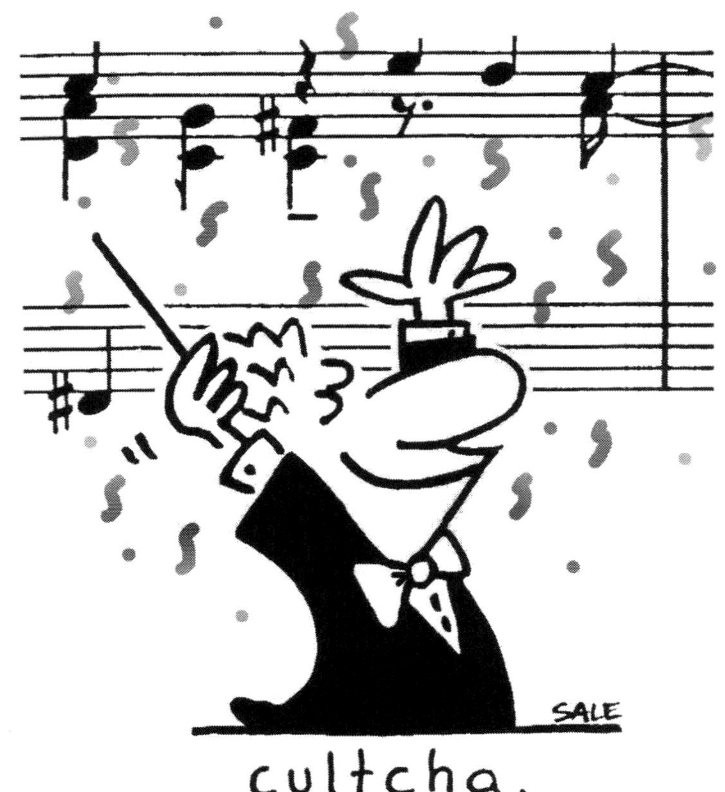

cultcha.

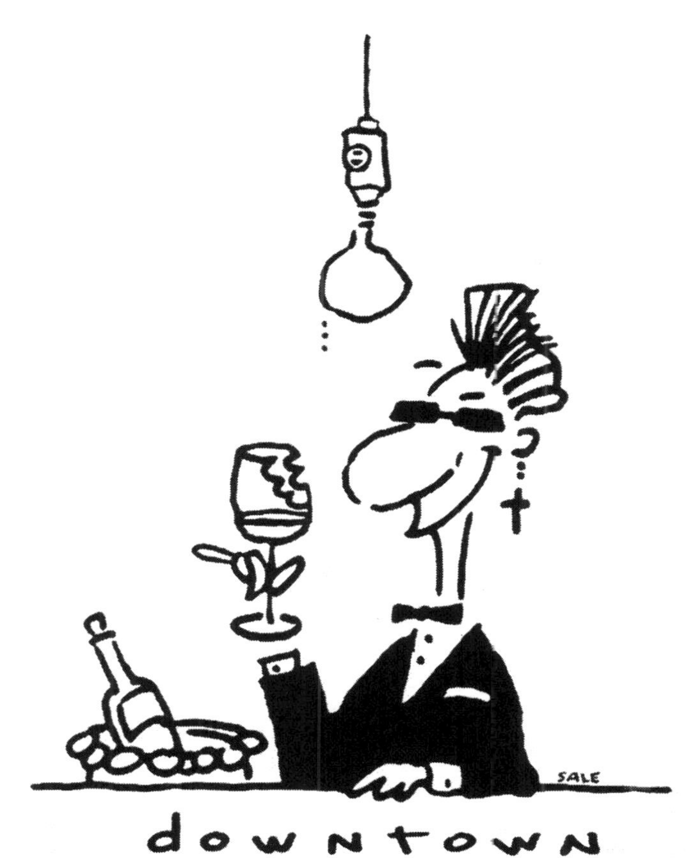

downtown

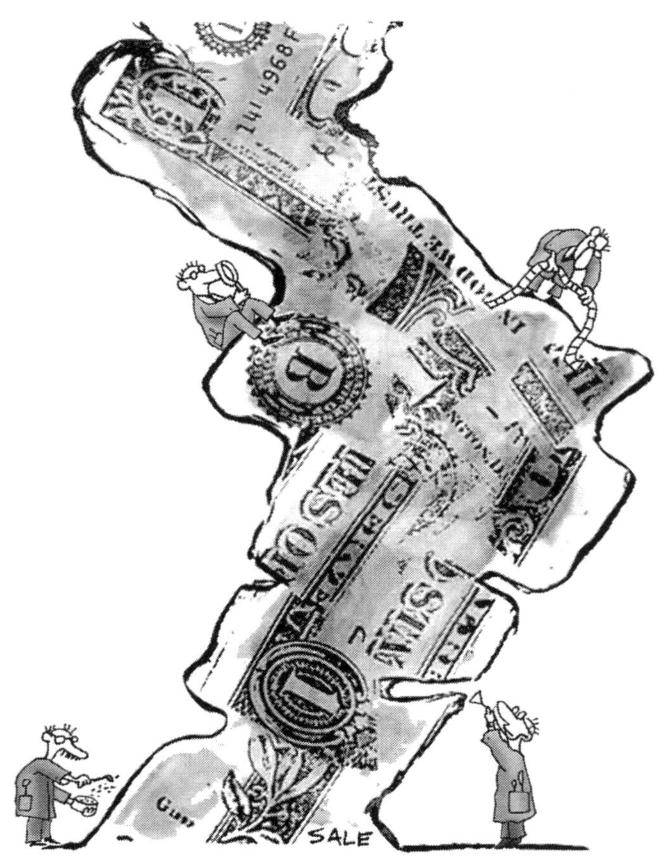

SALE

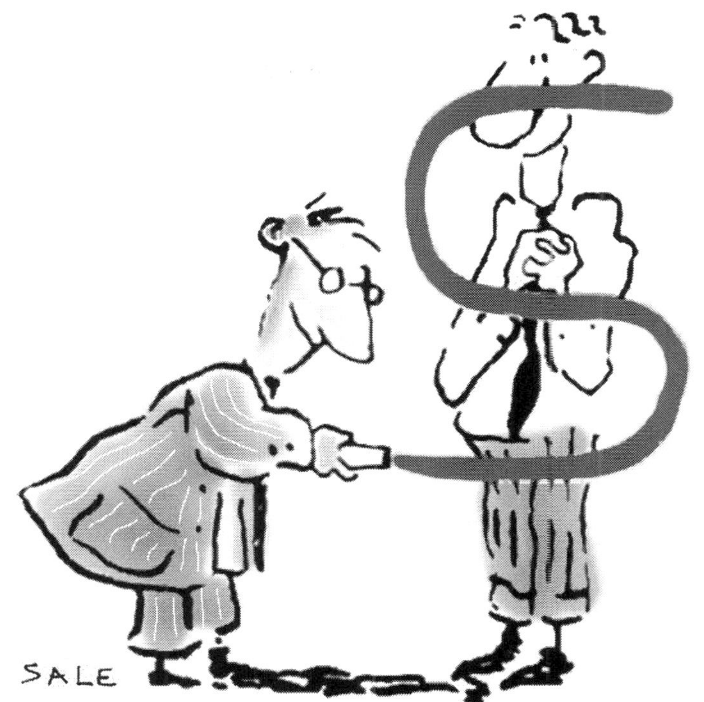

You're worth more than you think.

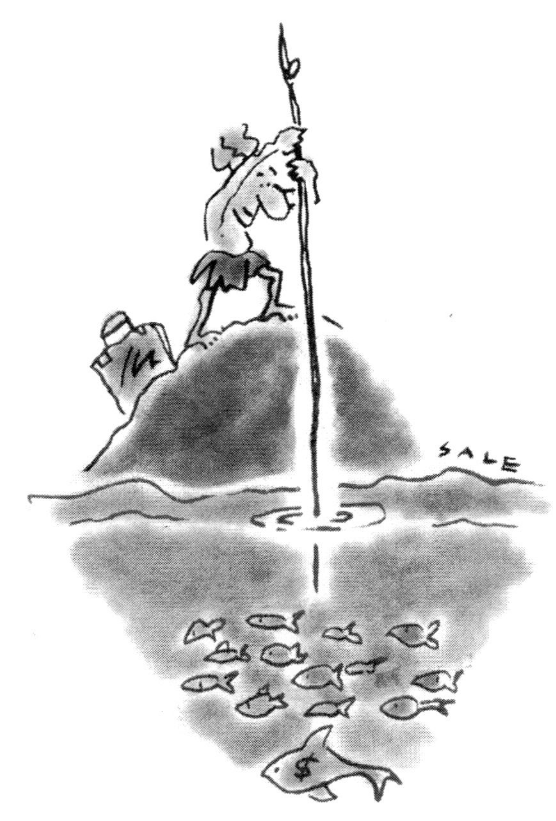

SALE
$

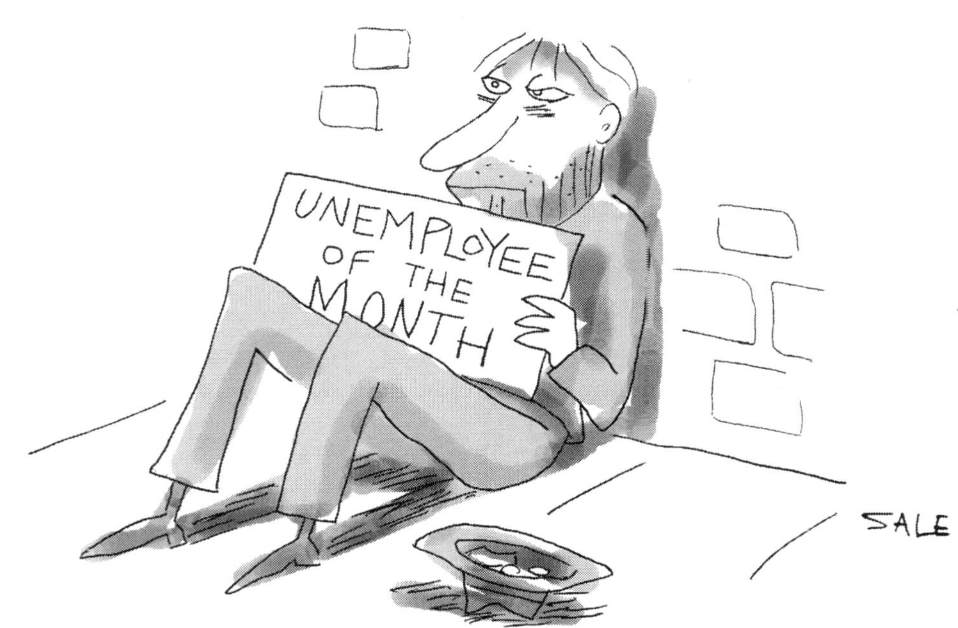

UNEMPLOYEE OF THE MONTH
SALE

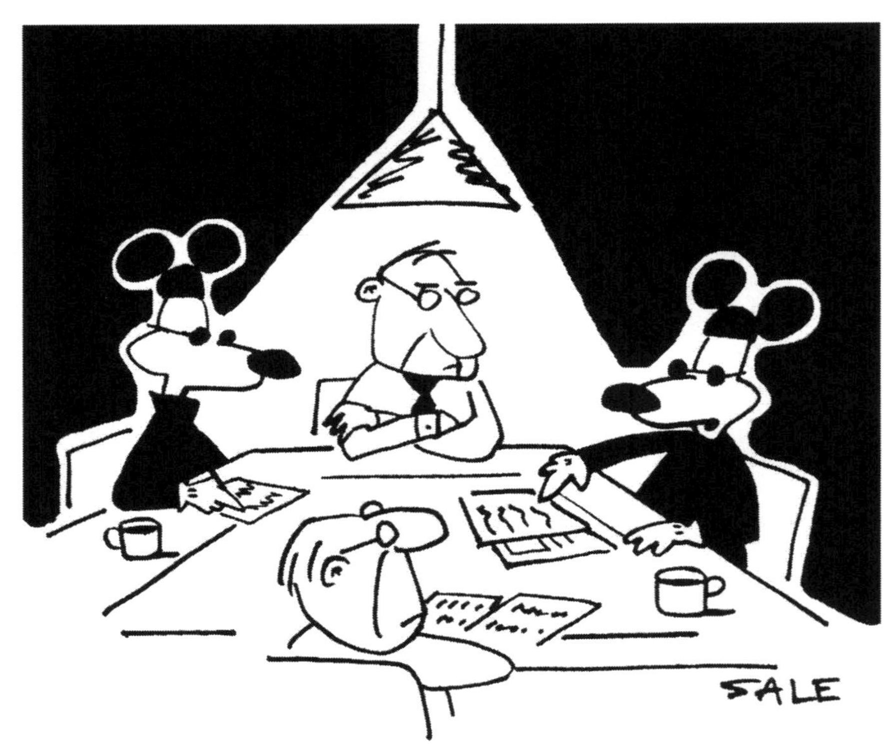

In the back rooms and corridors of power,
mice and men lay their plans.

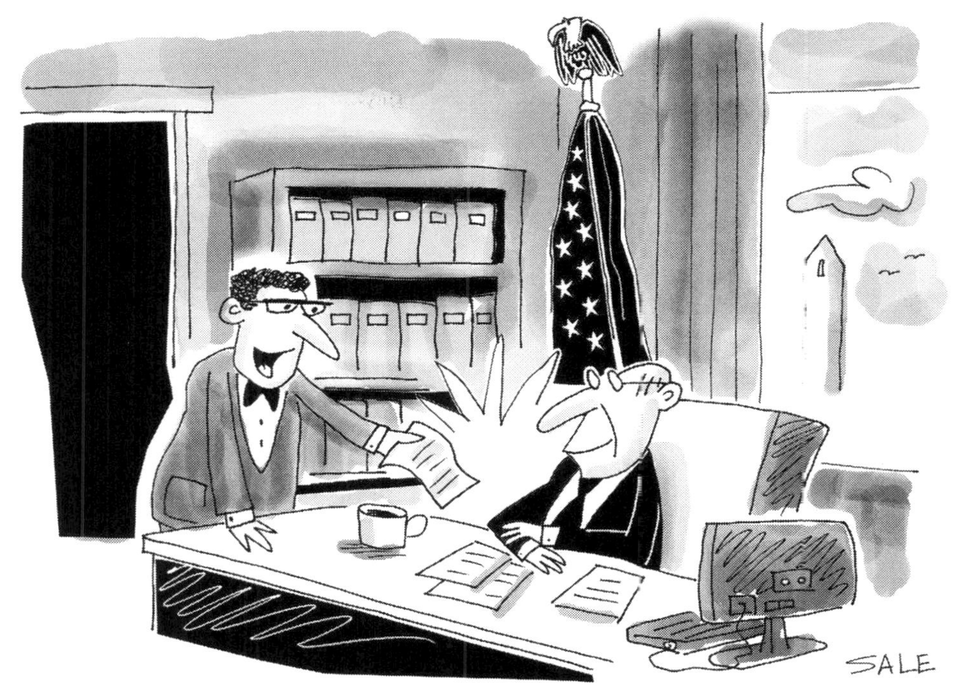

"This week's campaign donor list has arrived, Senator,
along with your instructions on how to vote."

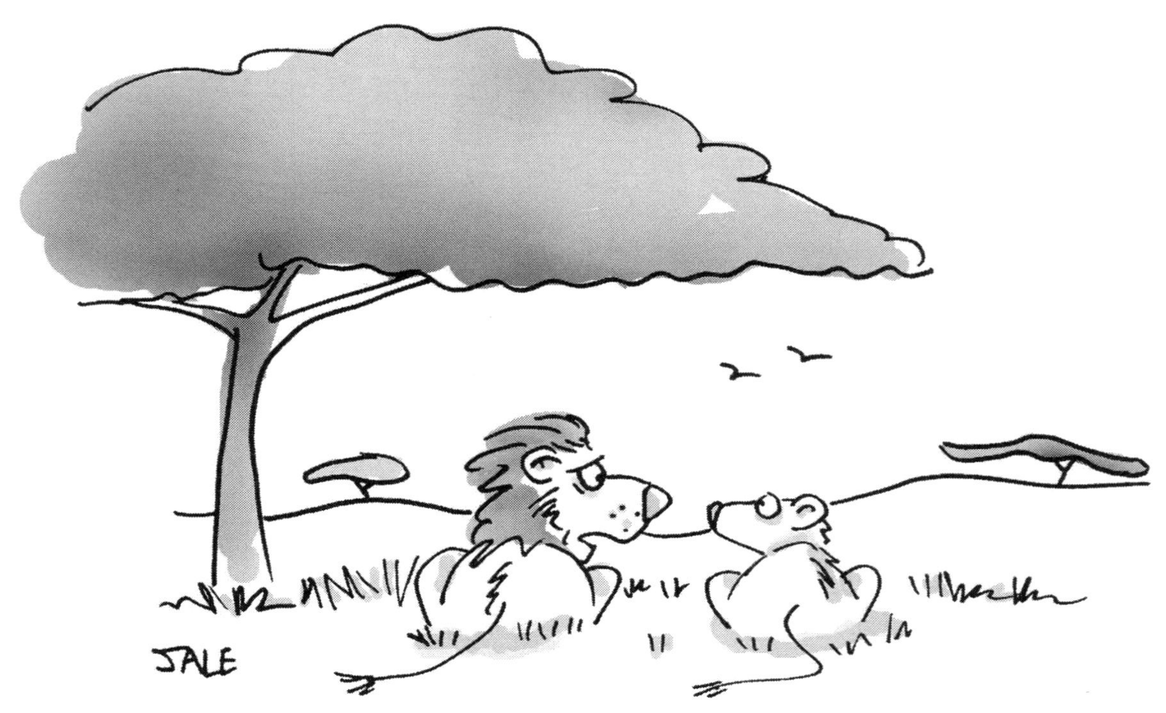

"Some days I'm terrified of being fearless."

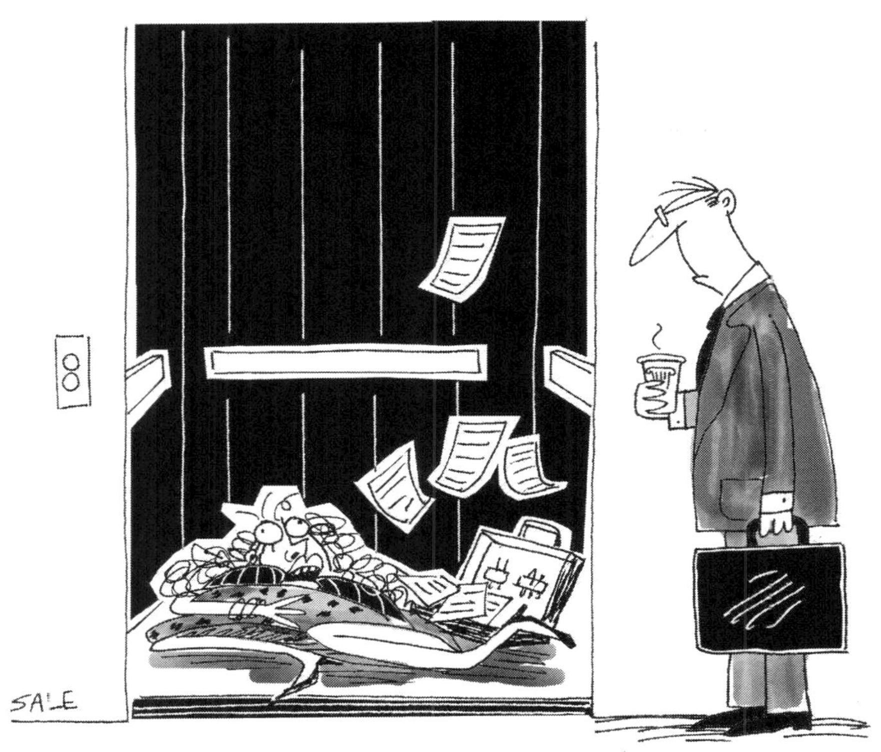

At 8:48 a.m. Monday morning, Carla's collection of fears, neurosis and negative self talk crushed her like a walnut.

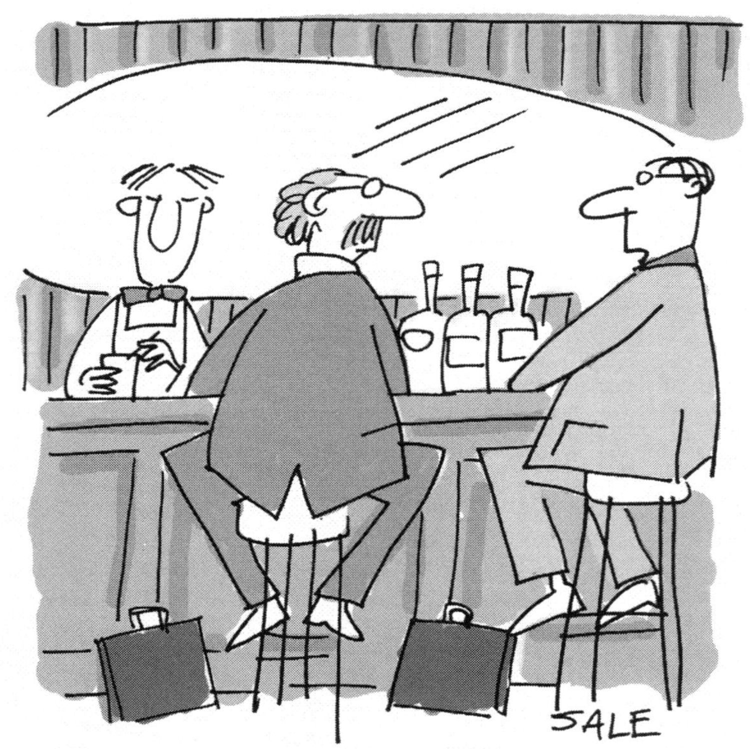

"*Call me old fashioned, but I miss the good old days of pay phones, power rock and pubic hair.*"

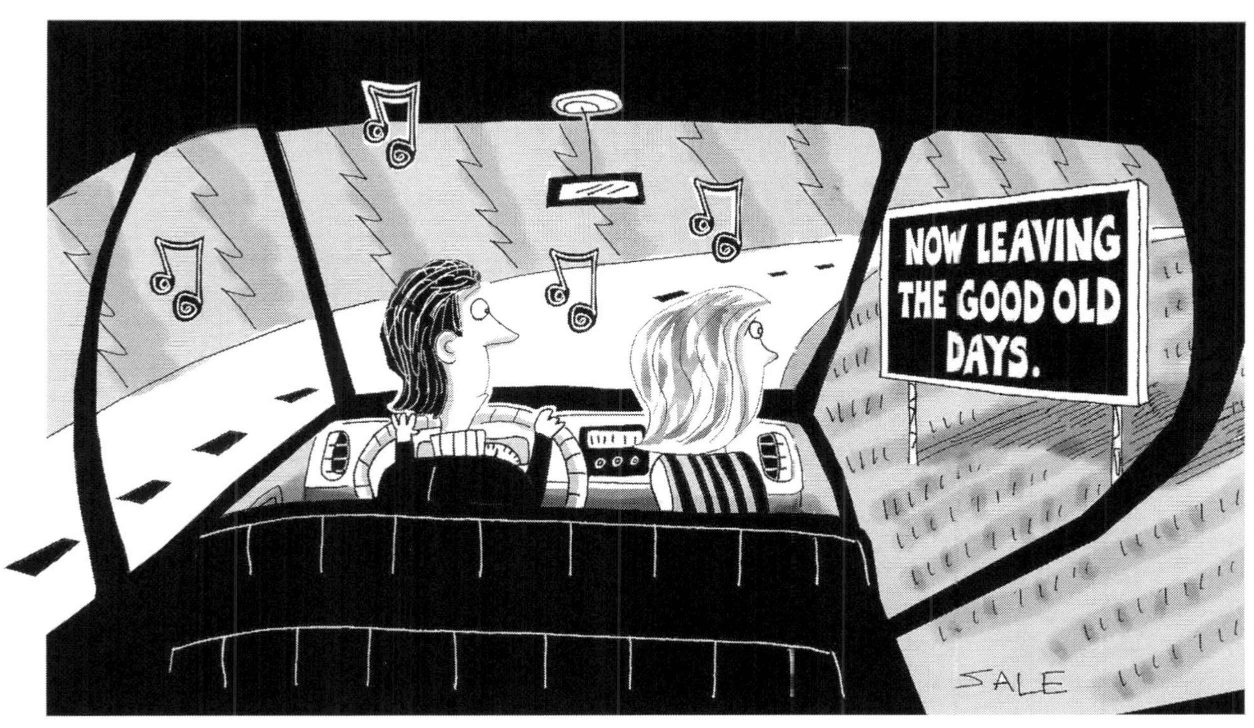

NOW LEAVING
THE GOOD OLD
DAYS.
SALE

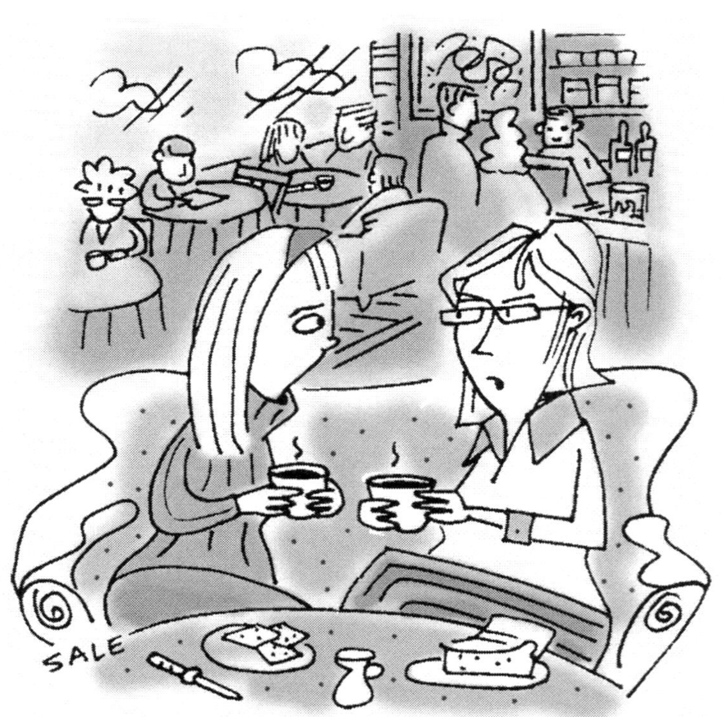

"Richard and I found a very affordable vacation package on Craigslist. We're spending the holidays in 1974."

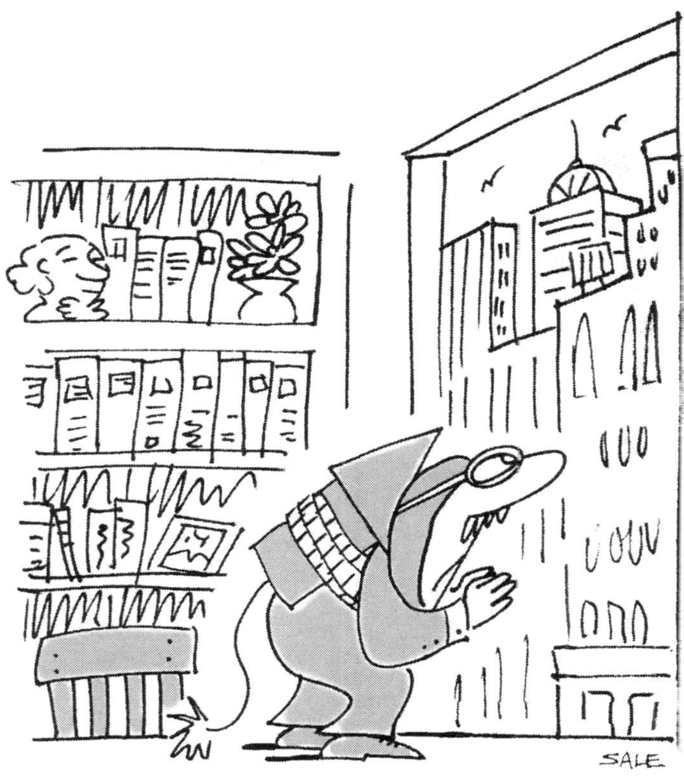

After serious thought and consideration, Brisby concluded that his first instinct was correct—running away was the answer.

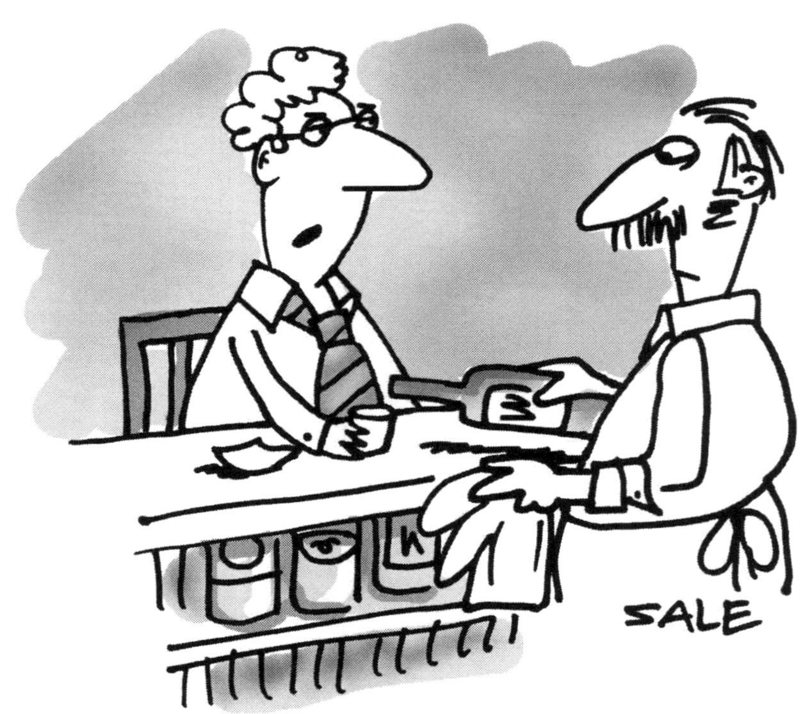

"*The wife and I had to postpone our divorce since neither of us can qualify for another mortgage.*"

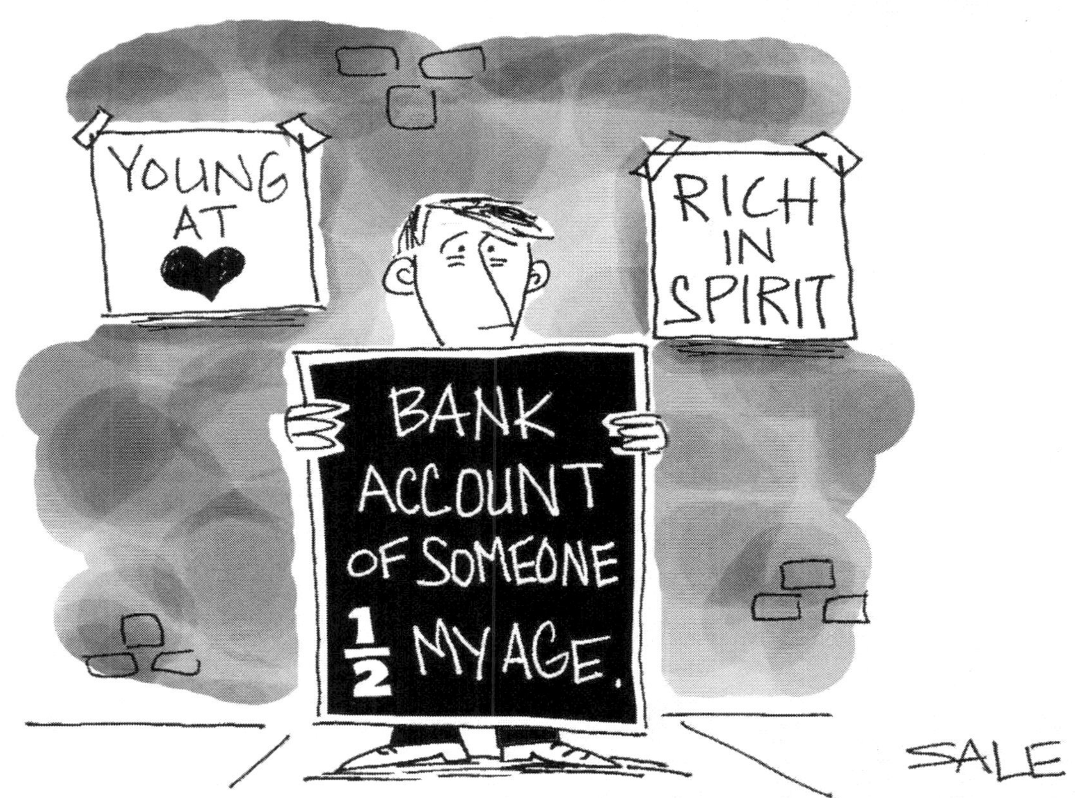

YOUNG AT ♥
RICH IN SPIRIT
BANK ACCOUNT OF SOMEONE 1/2 MY AGE.
SALE

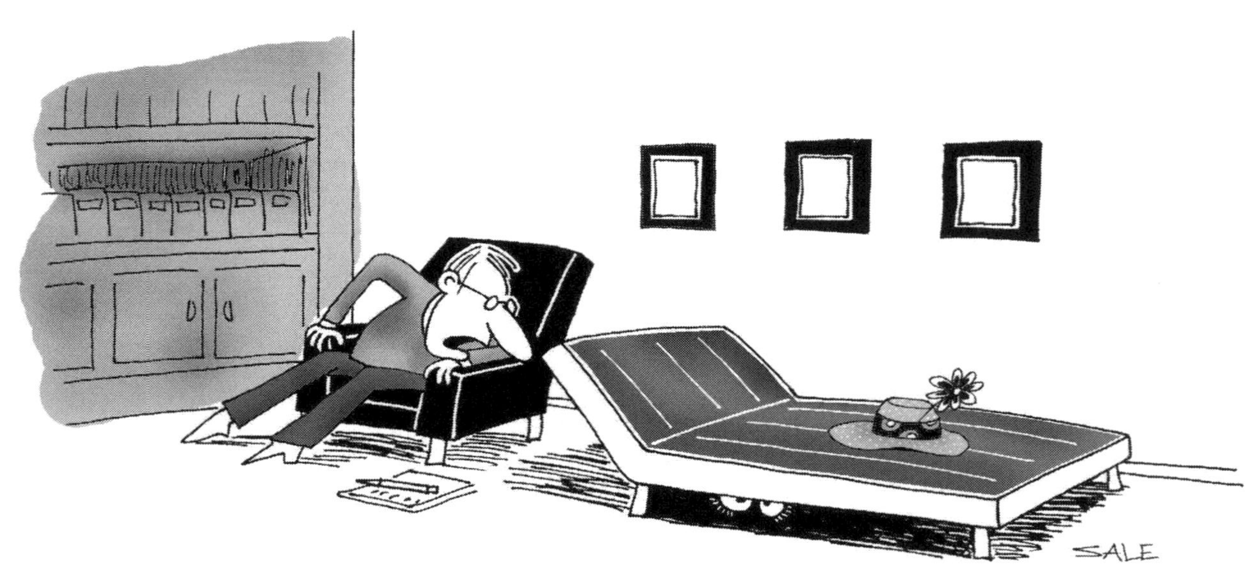

"*If it was easy Mrs. Sugarman, everyone would be well-adjusted.*"

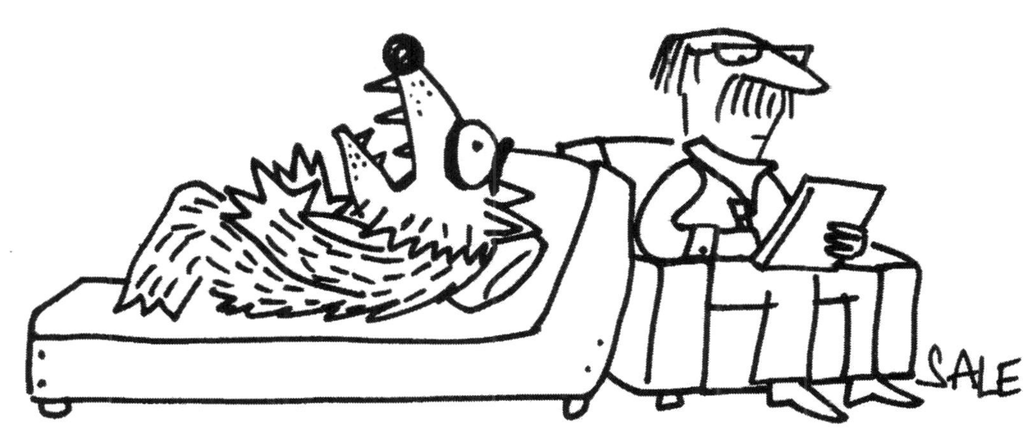

"*You gotta help me, Doc, the wife caught me
wearin' the sheep clothes again.*"

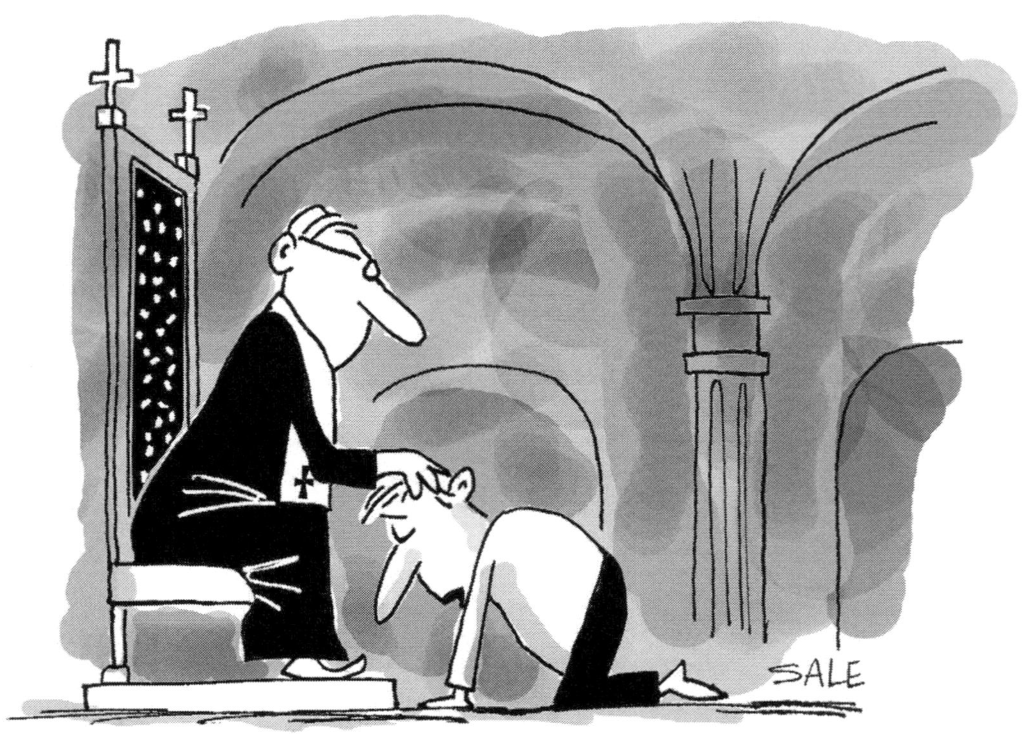

"Forgive me father for the things I've done for a Klondike Bar."

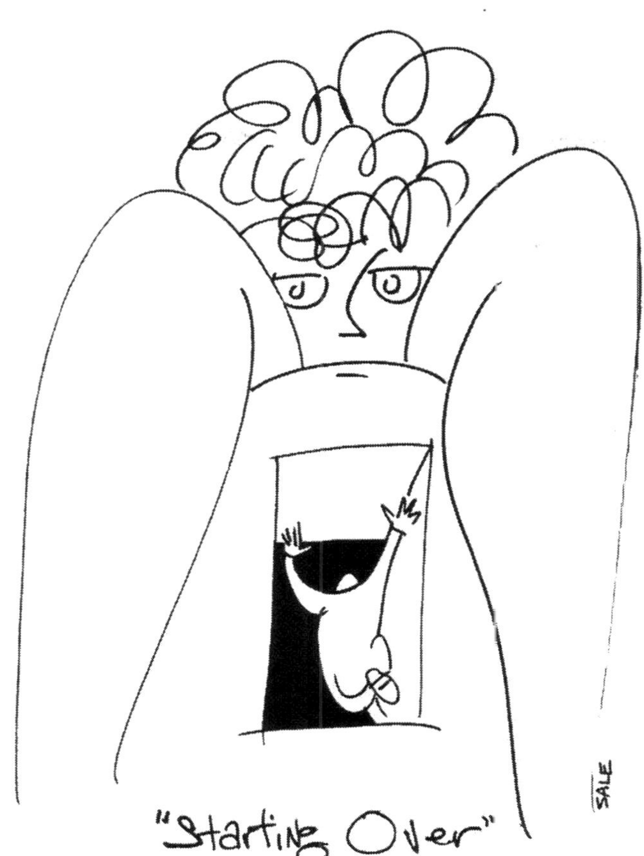

"Starting Over"

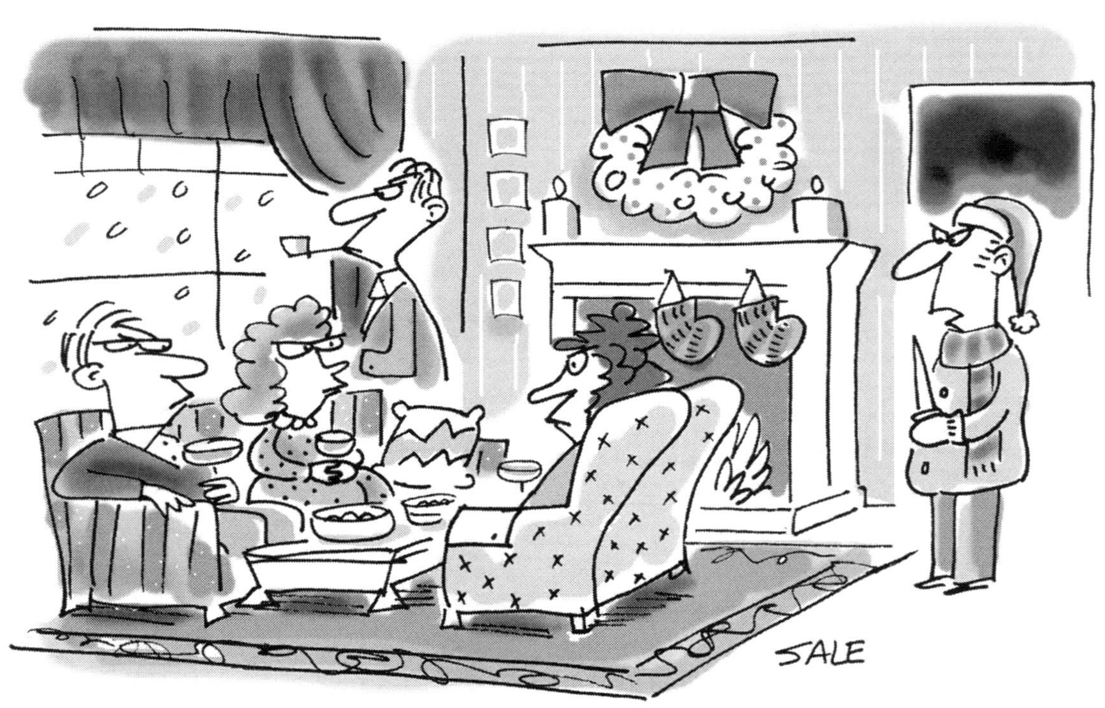

"Who wants to step outside and cut this tension with a knife?"

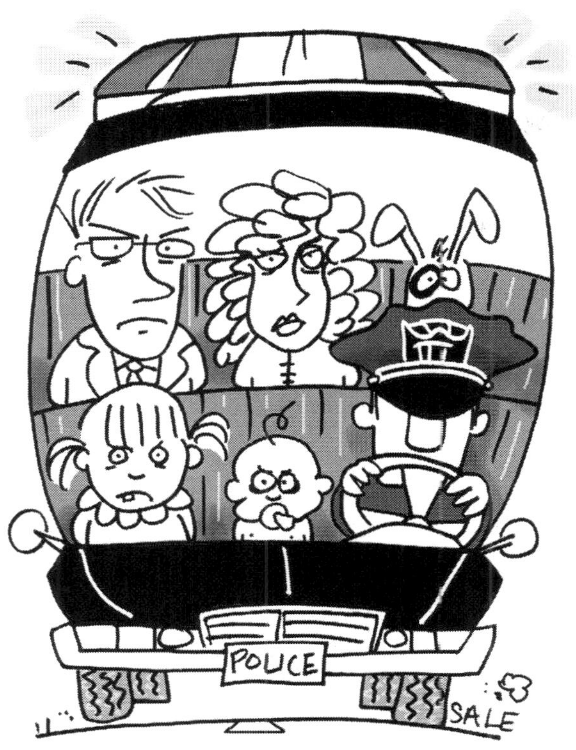

*You can't choose your family. But, you can
choose to turn them in for a reward.*

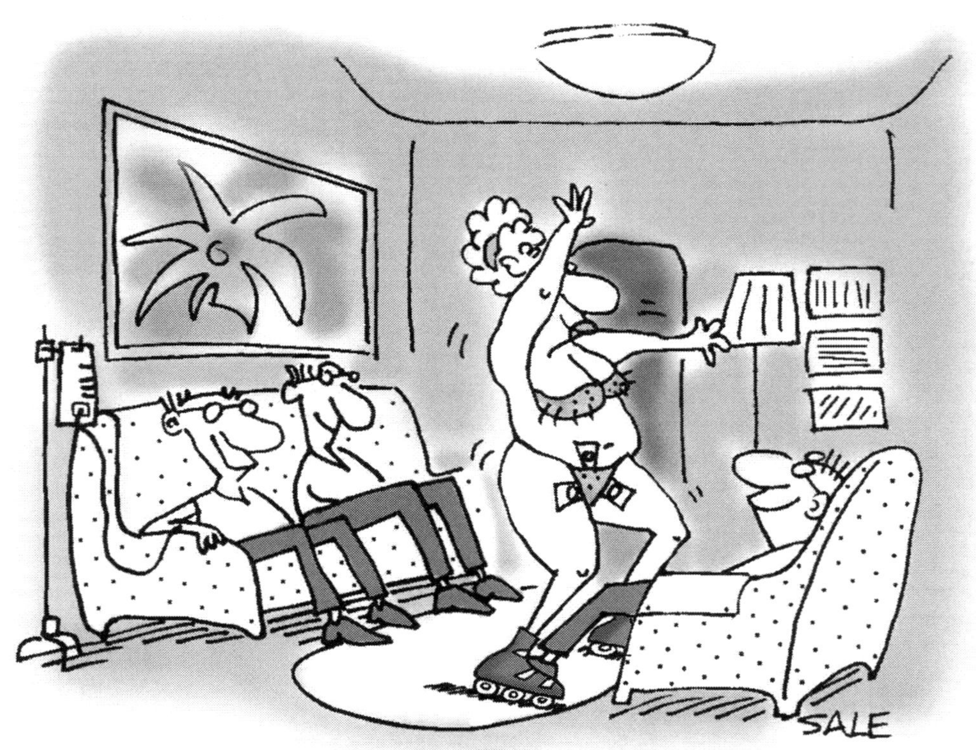

*Grandma Keller's home-based business, Feels On Wheels,
made her a celebrity at the Senior Center and earned her
AARP Entrepreneur of the Year.*

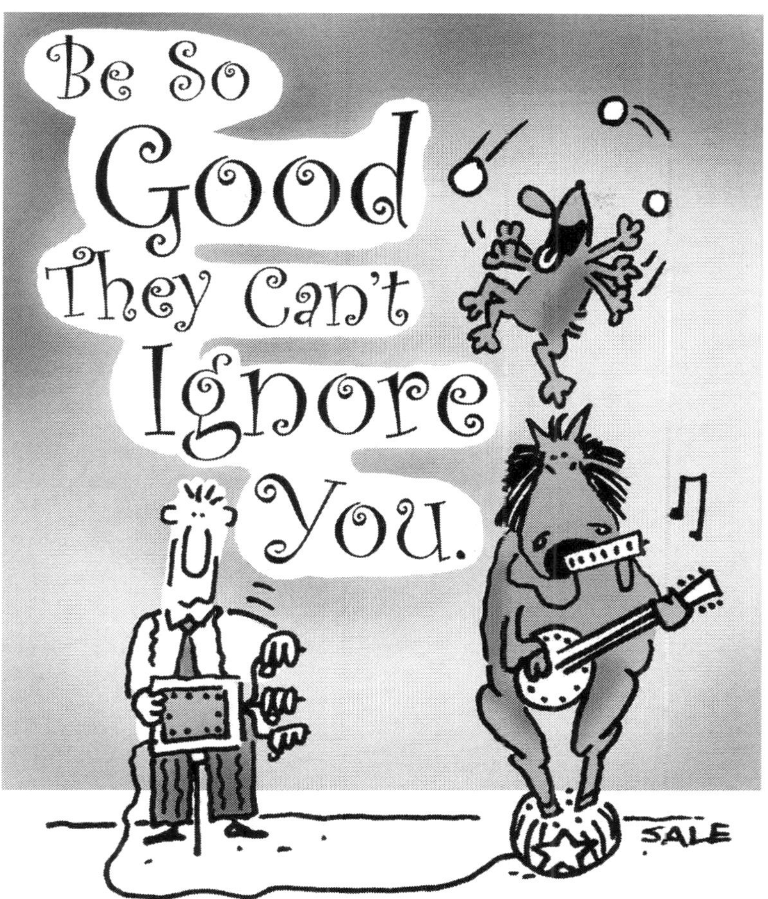

Be So Good They Can't Ignore You.
SALE

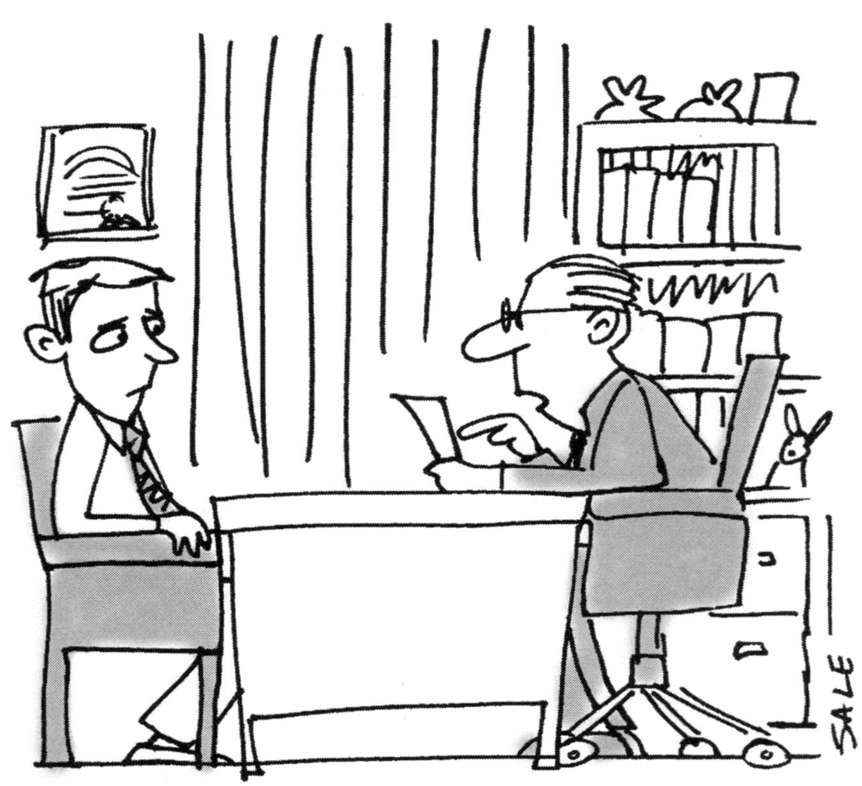

"Adjusted for the recession and factoring in your youthful attributes, your Myers-Briggs test results indicate you'd make a fine scarecrow."

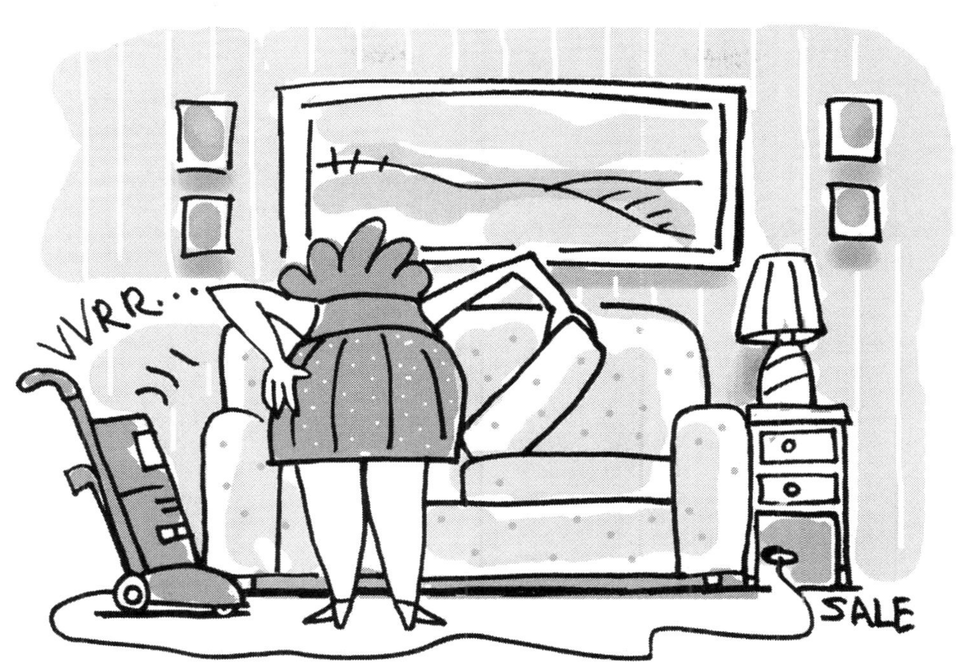

*"Son-of-a-gun...Honey, come here quick!
I found your street cred!"*

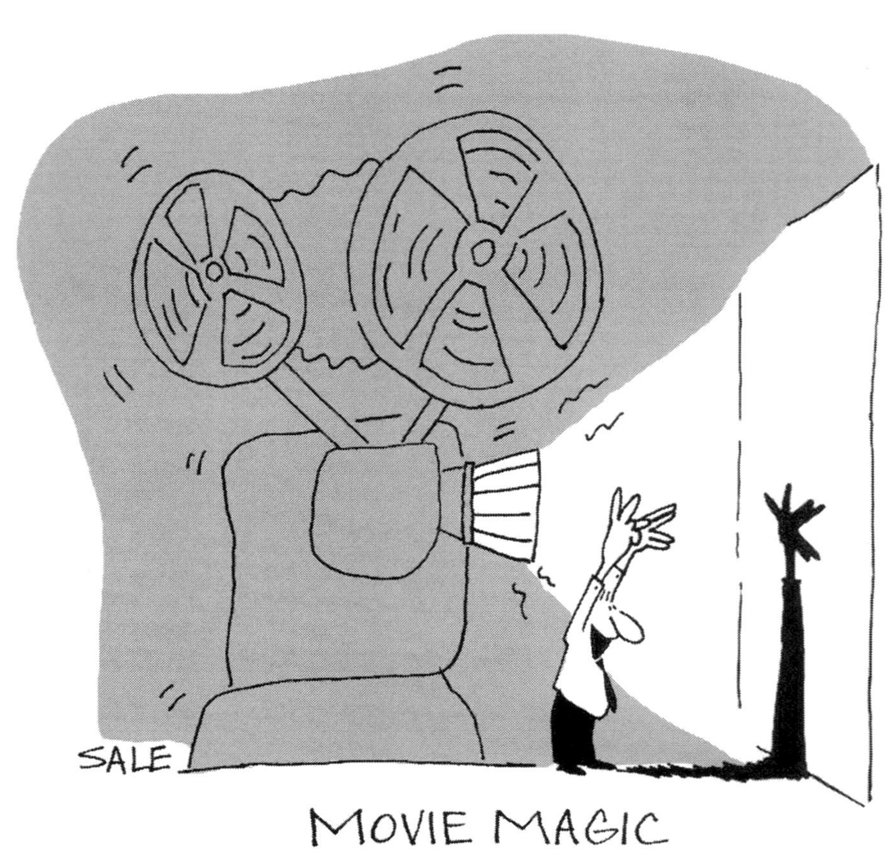

MOVIE MAGIC

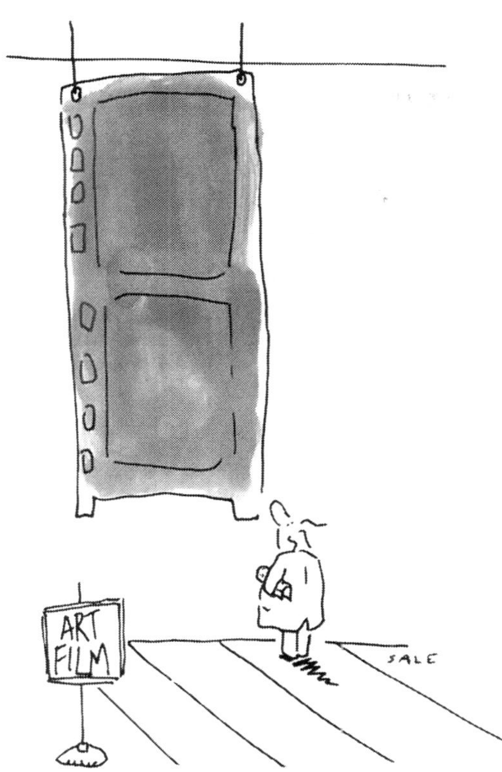

ART
FILM
SALE

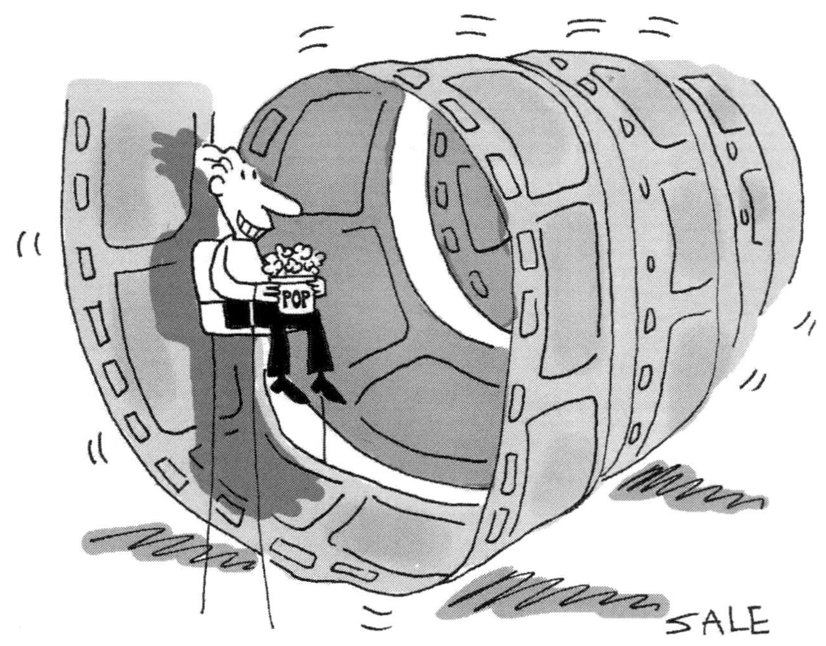

Private Screening.

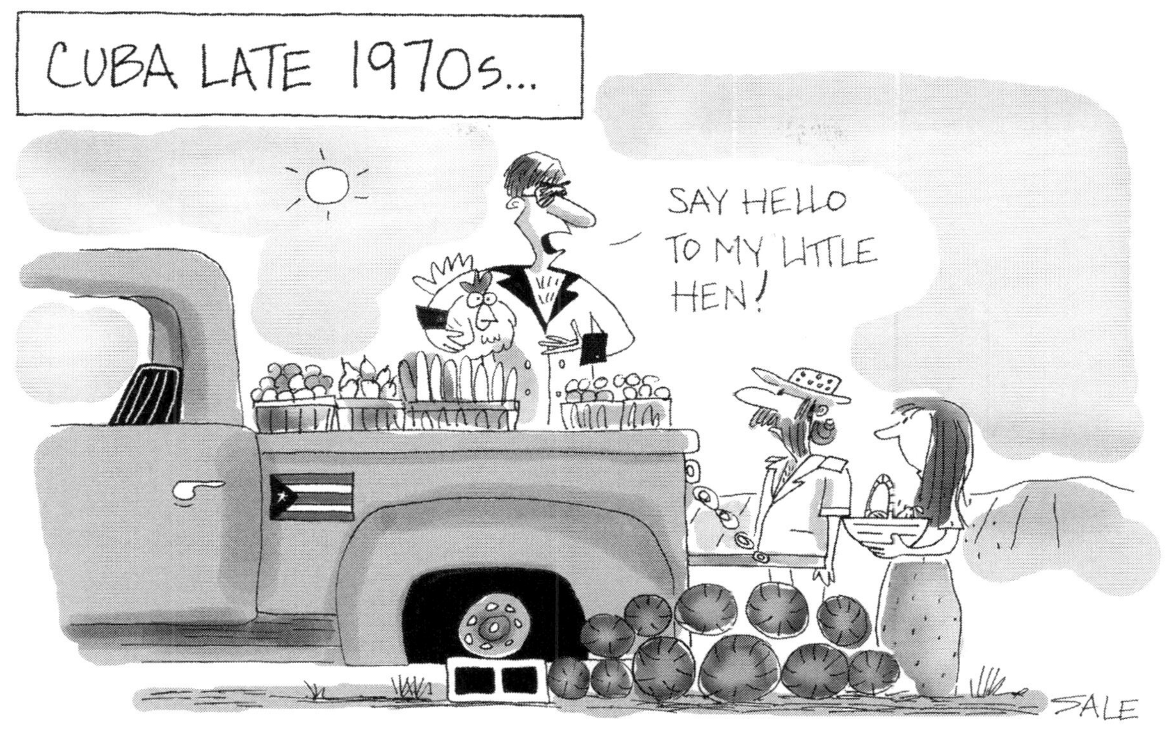

Before pursuing a life of crime, Tony Montana worked at his family's business on Old Havana Road adjacent to Fidel's Moustache Mug Emporium.

America's Most Wanting.

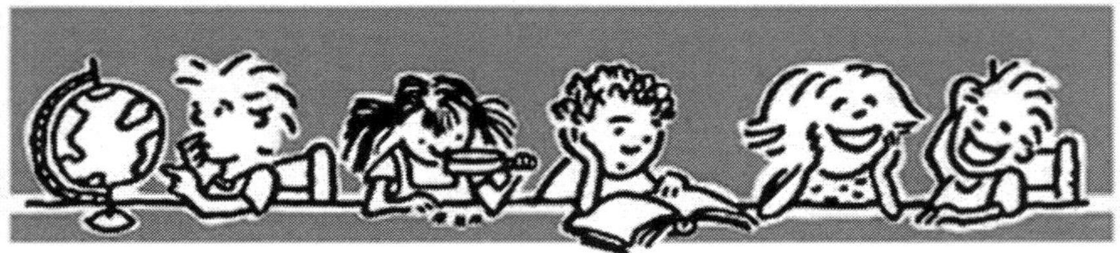

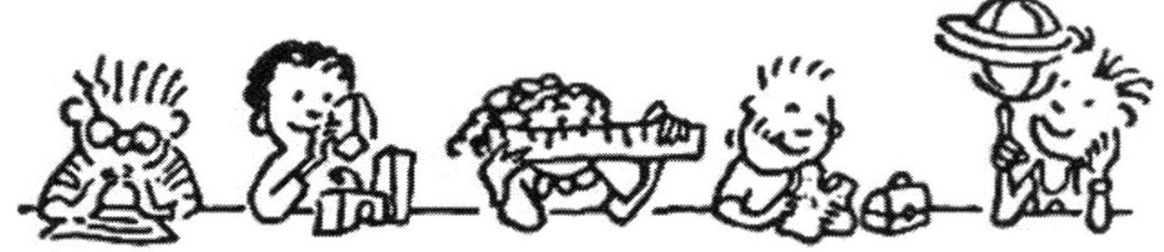

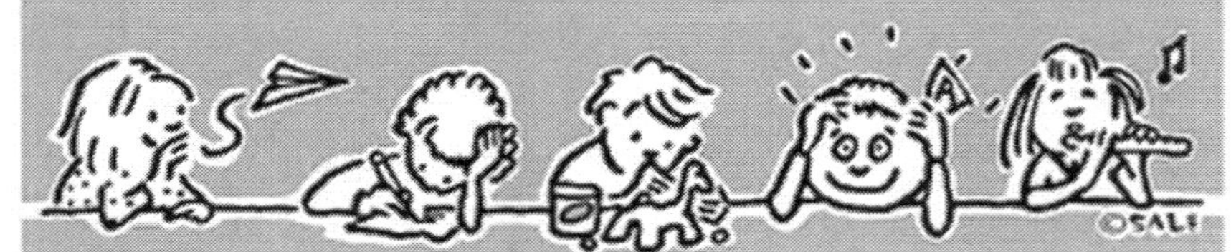

Good Kids. Smart Kids. Our Kids.
Love. Encourage. Support. Protect. Teach them.

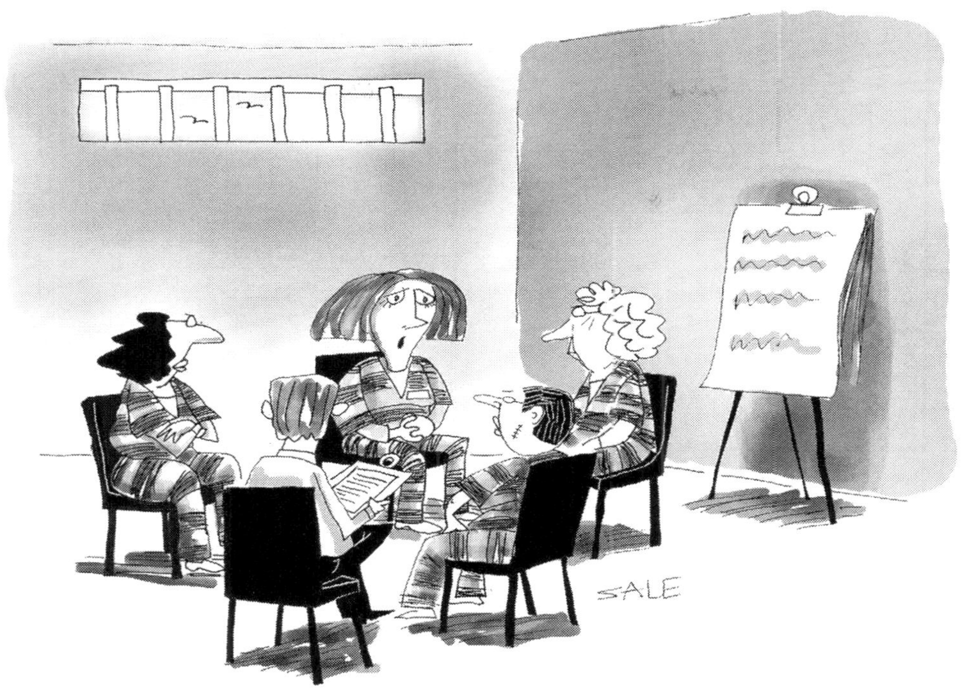

"Hello, my name is Ms. Dunbar. I'm a school teacher.
I stole supplies from my home to bring to class."

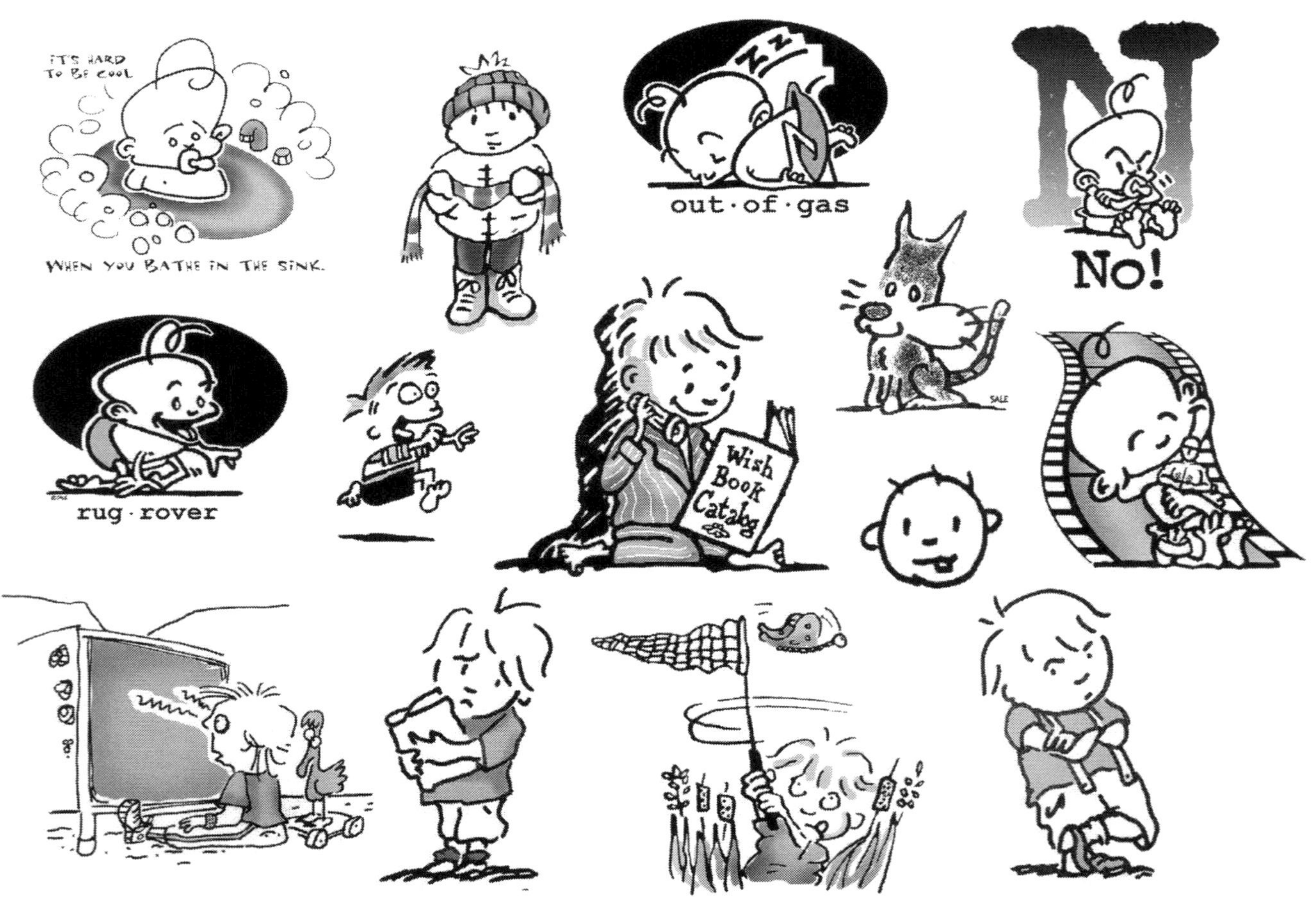
IT'S HARD
TO BE COOL
WHEN YOU BATHE IN THE SINK.
out·of·gas
N
No!
rug·rover
Wish
Book
Catalog

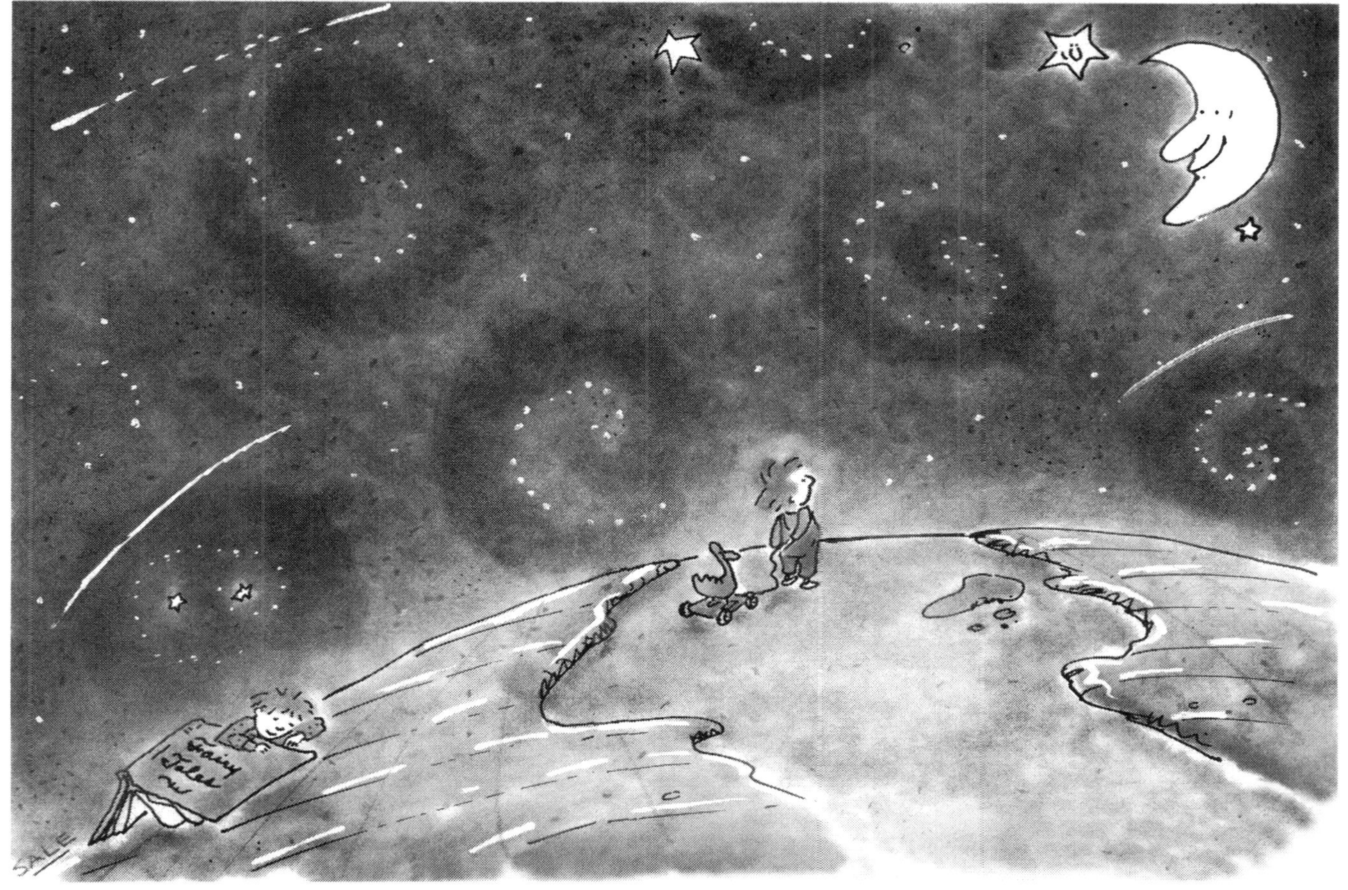

Fairy Tales
SALE

Classic New York T-Shirts

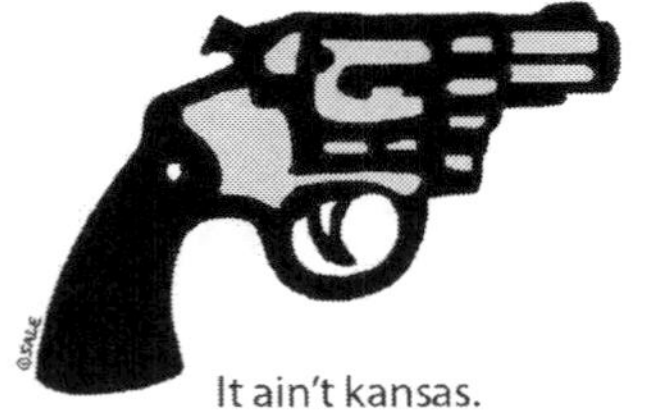

It ain't kansas.

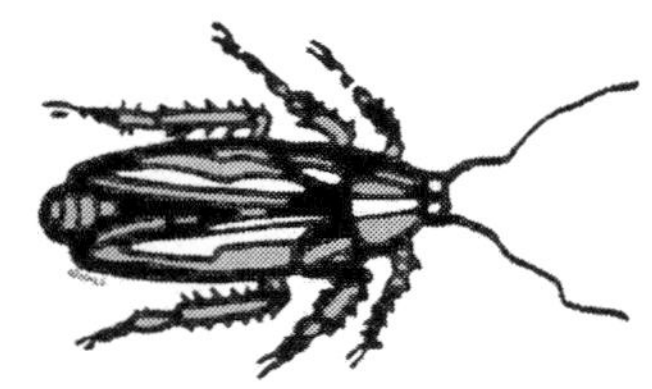

Actual size.

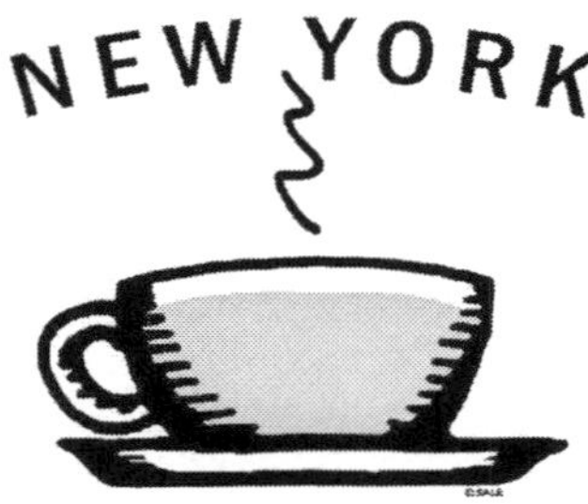

Open 24 Hours.

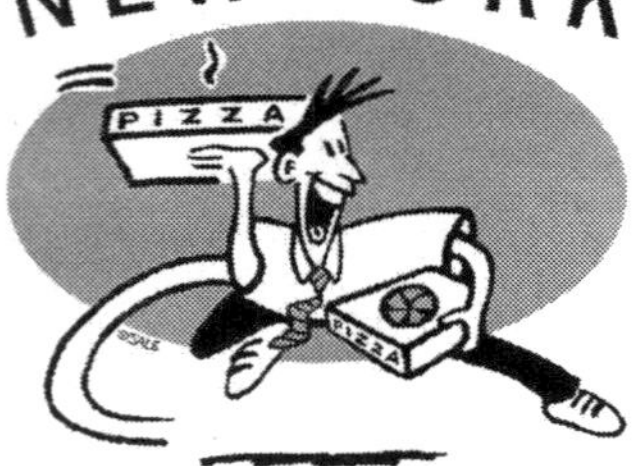

Where the pizza will arrive before the police.

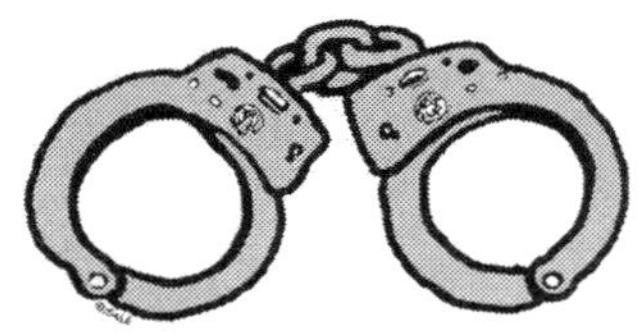

Assume the position.

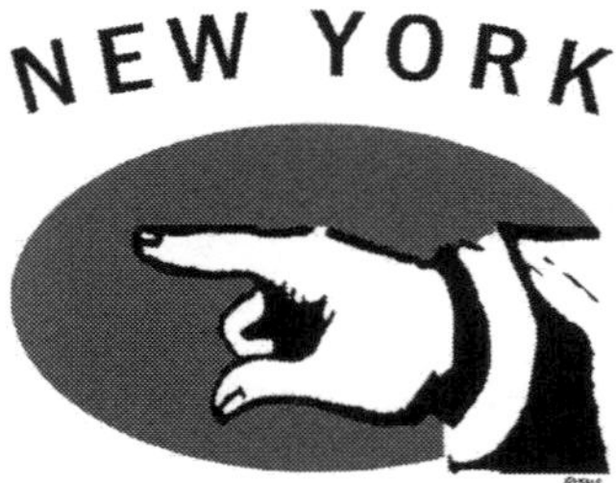

You talkin' to me?

These designs and many more are available on shirts and other items at: grahamsale.com

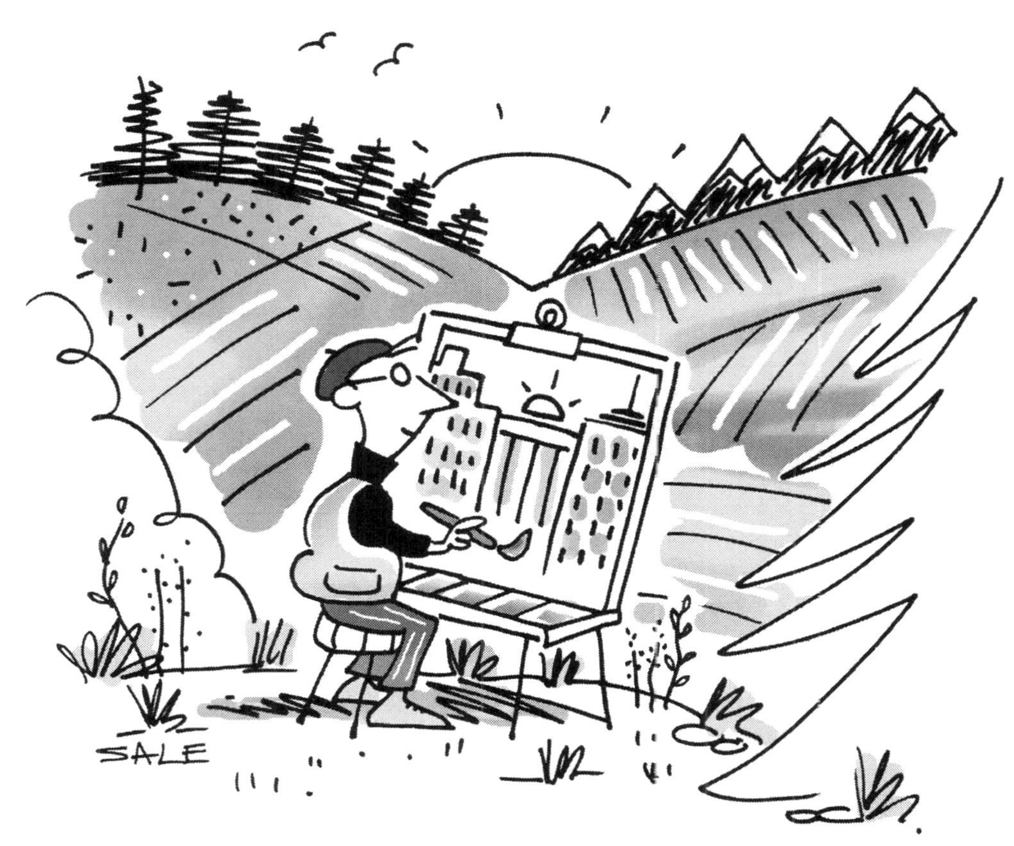

Once a New Yorker...

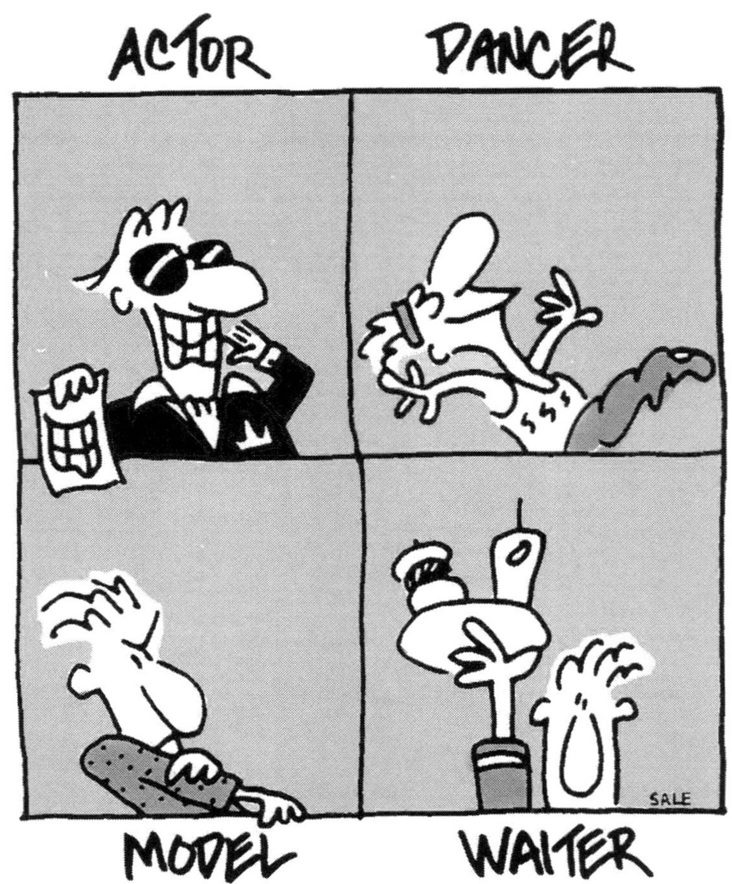

ACTOR
DANCER
MODEL
WAITER
SALE

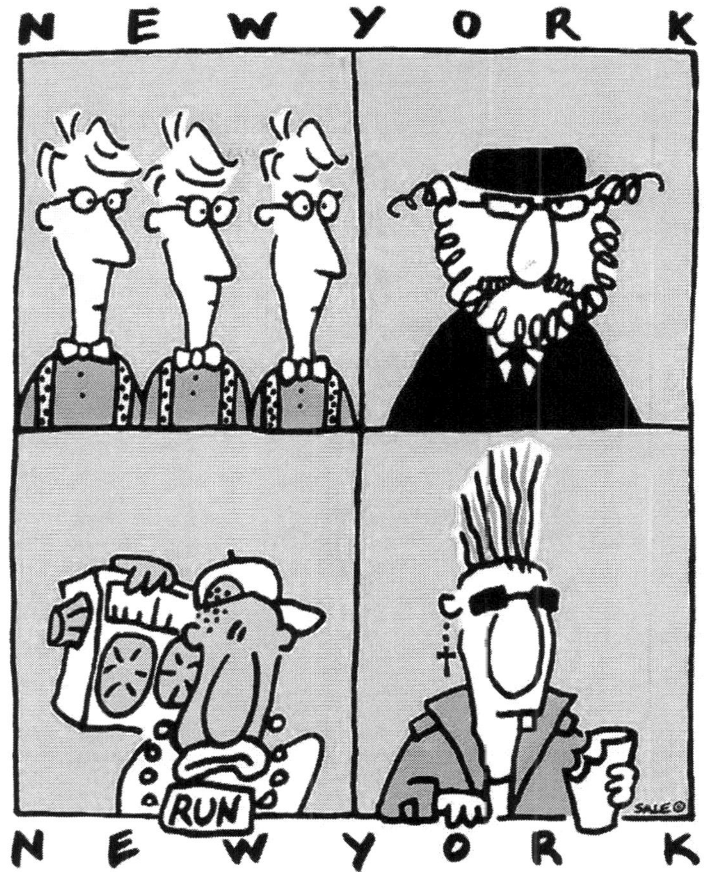

N E W Y O R K
RUN
NEW YORK
SALE

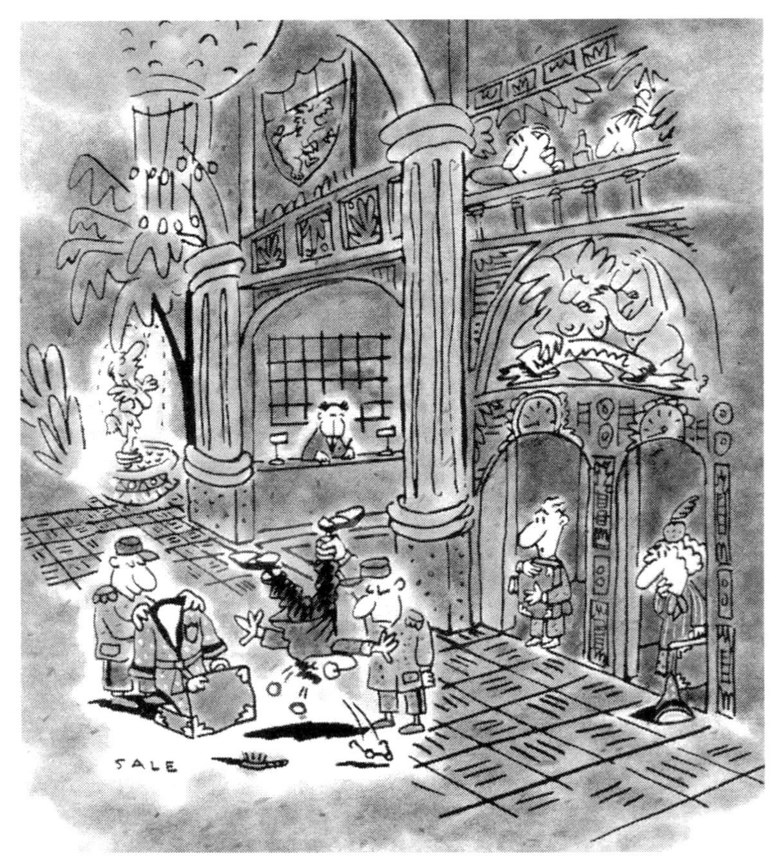

Busted

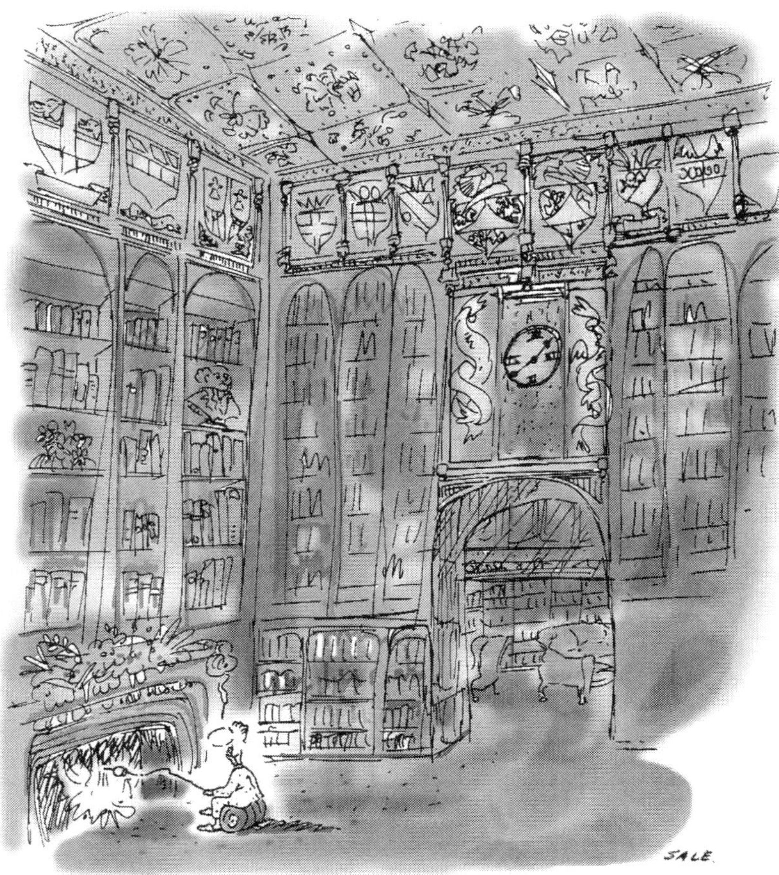

Roughing it.

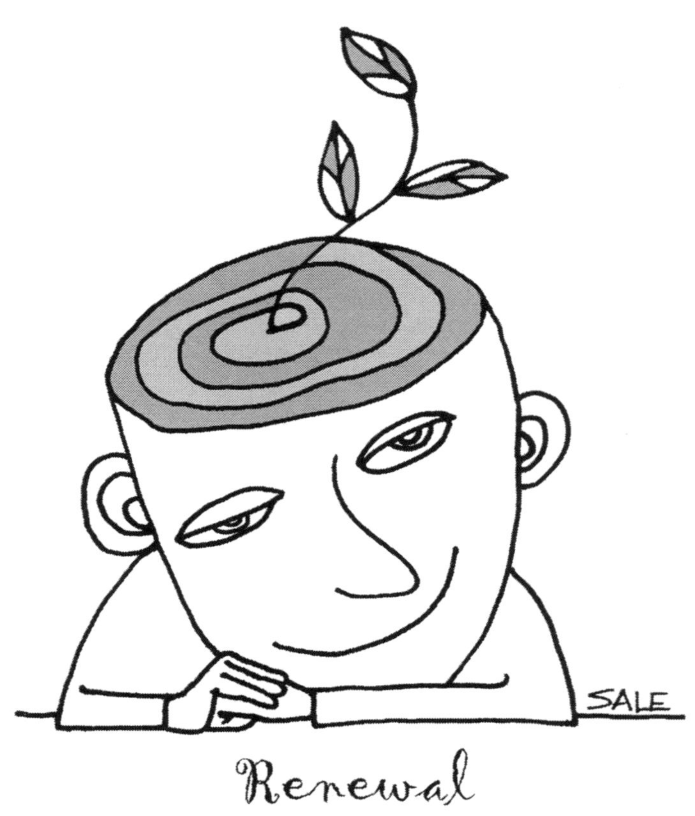

Renewal

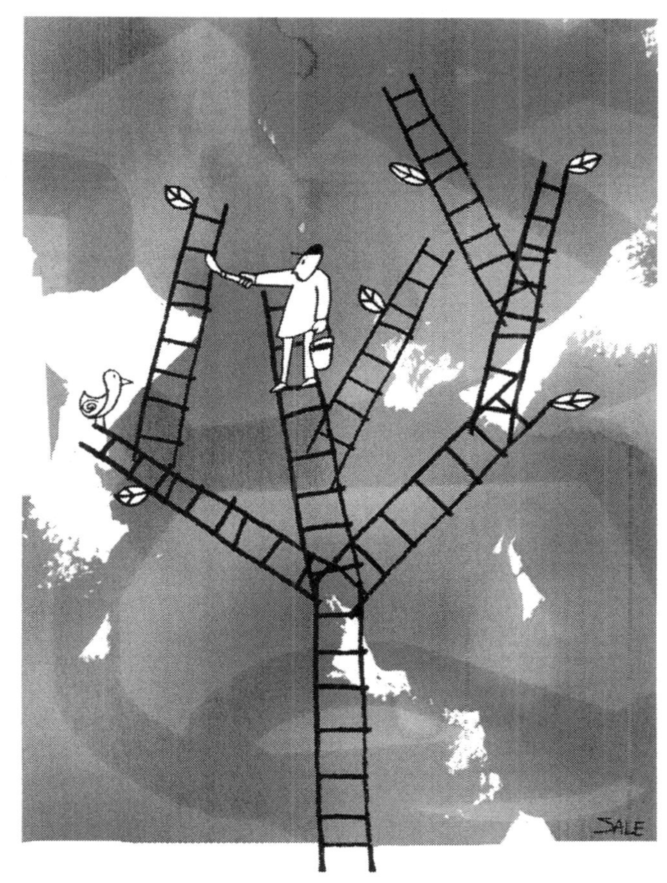

Keep designing your journey.

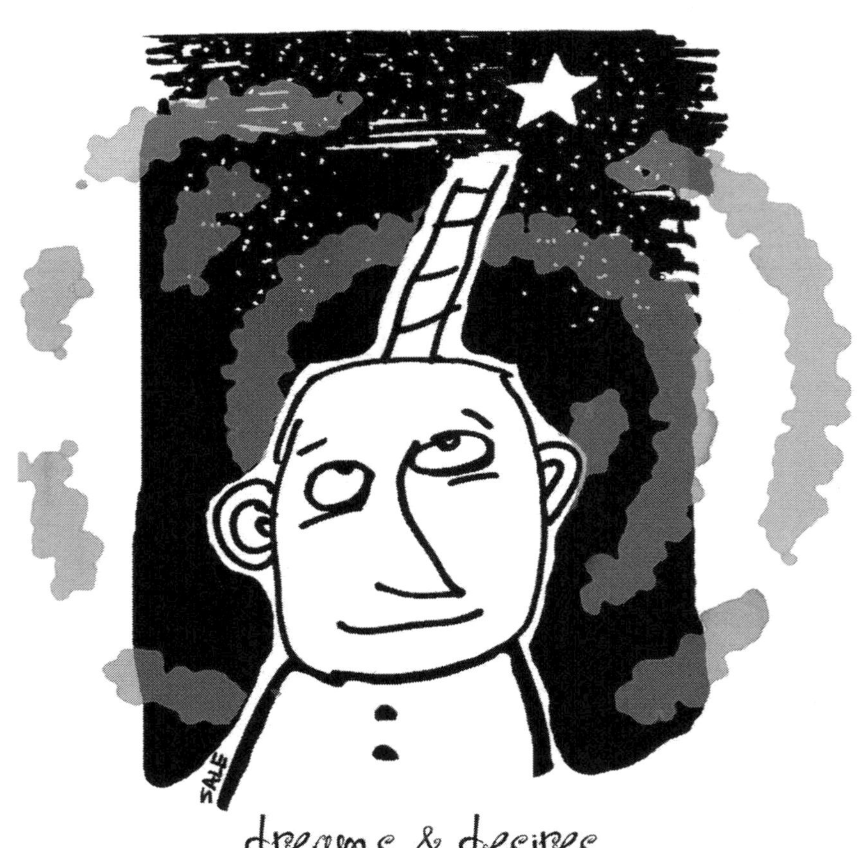

dreams & desires

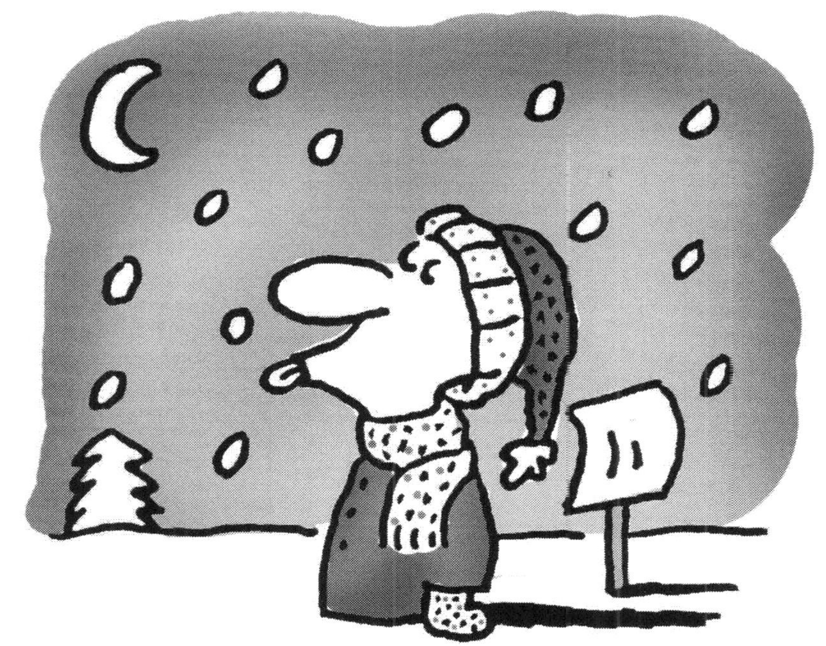

SIMPLE JOYS

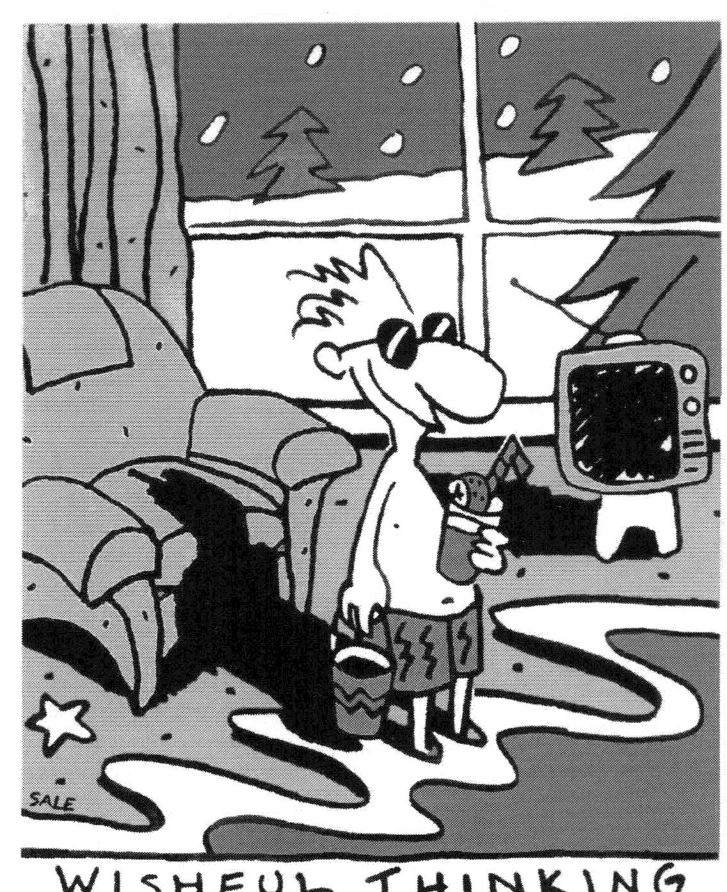

WISHFUL THINKING

UNDER·THE·WEATHER

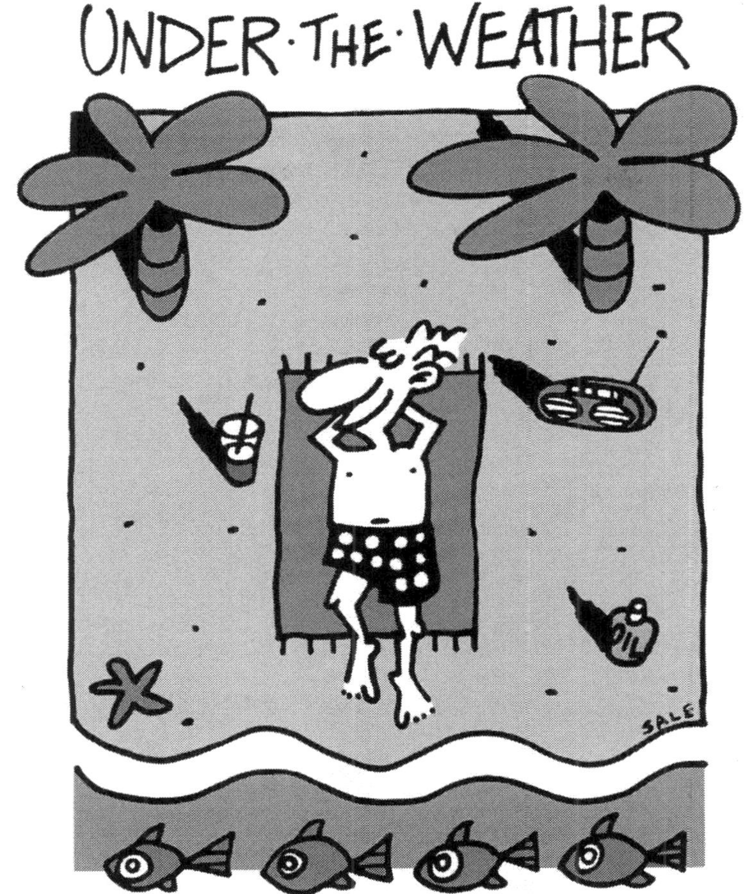

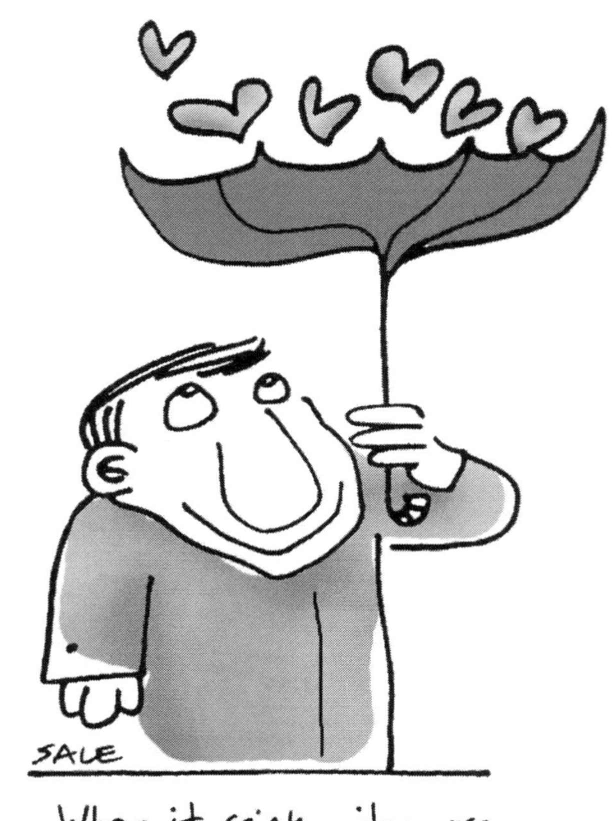

When it rains — it pours.

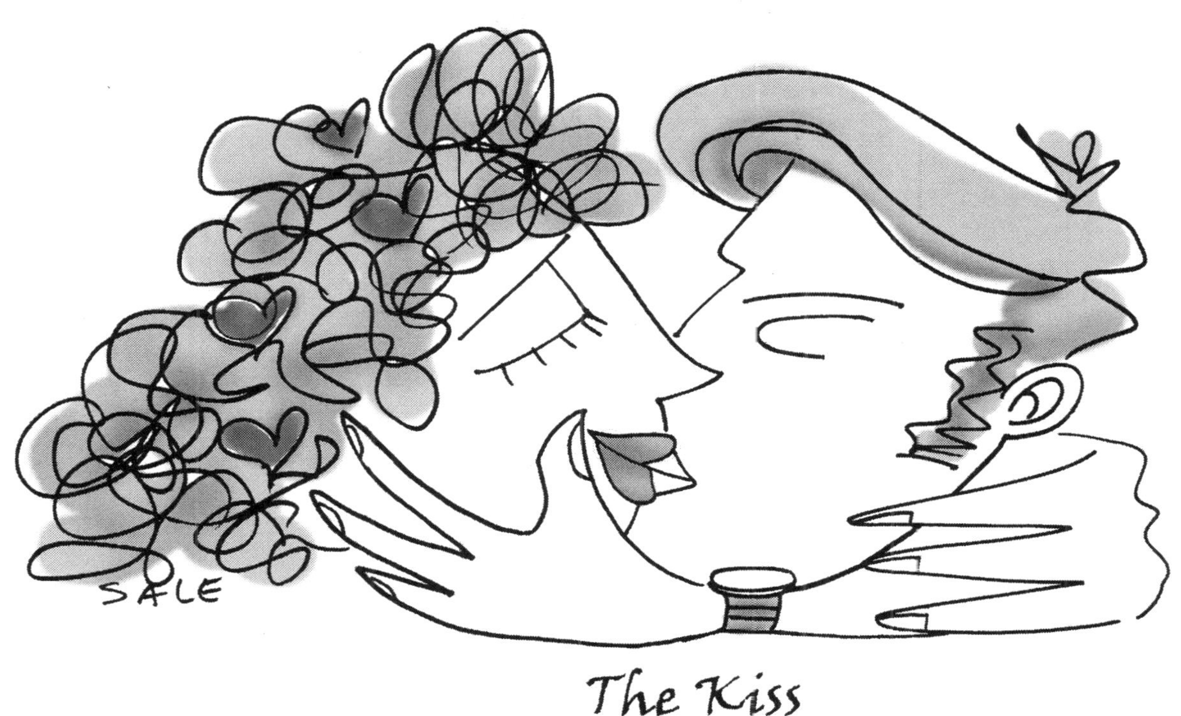

The Kiss

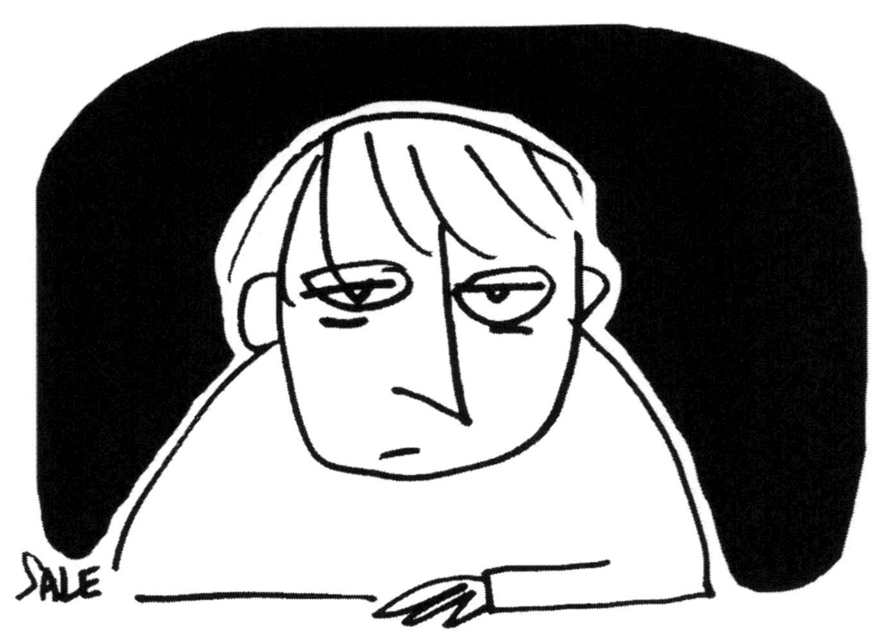

Millard caught a virulent strain of life
for which his convivial nature was no match.

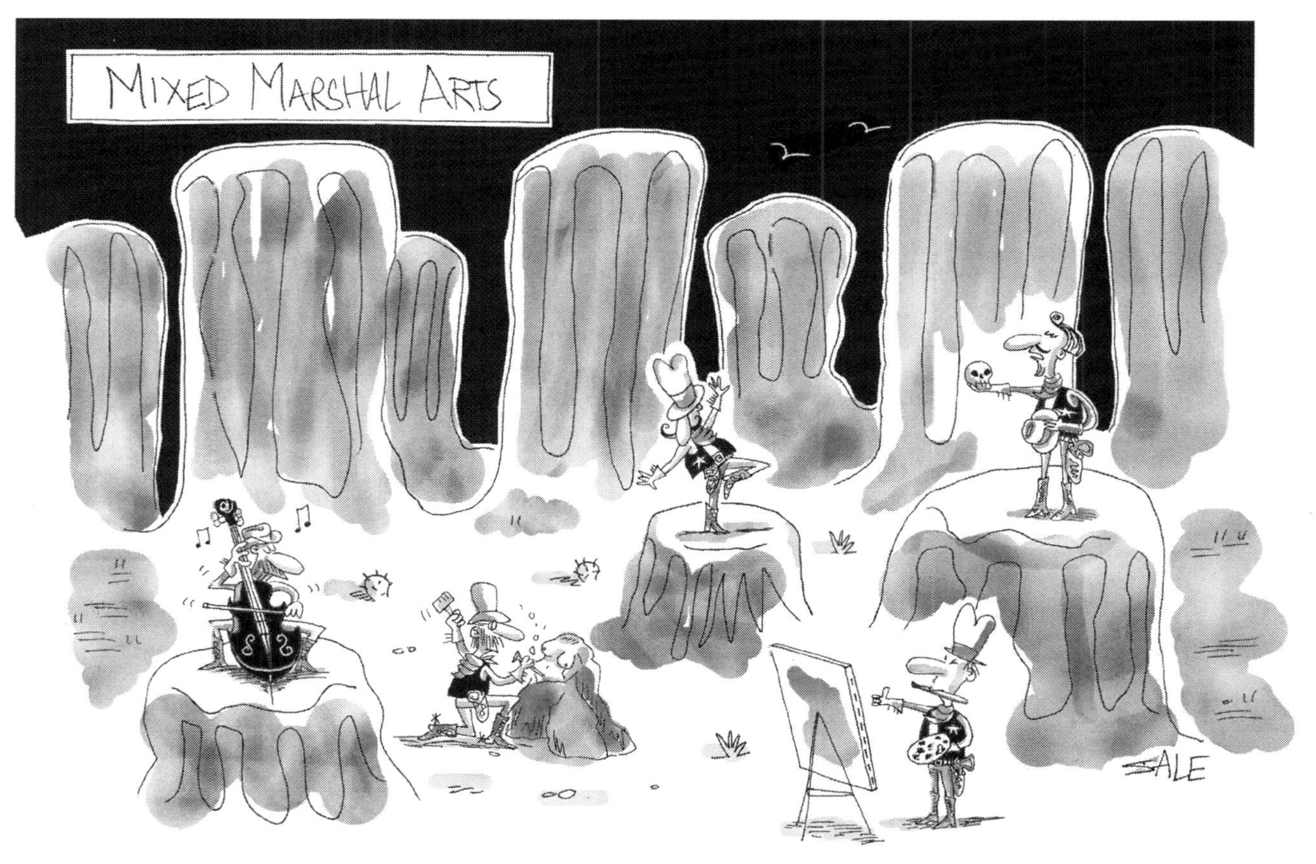

MIXED MARSHAL ARTS
SALE

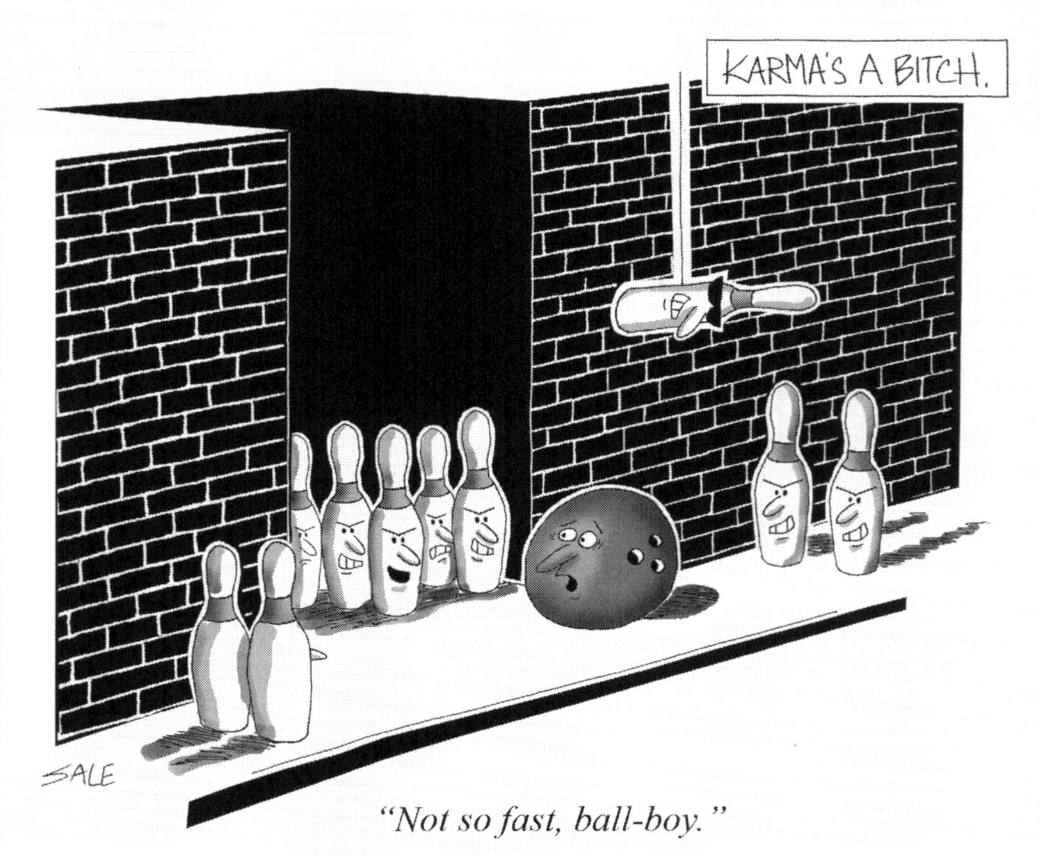

"*Not so fast, ball-boy.*"

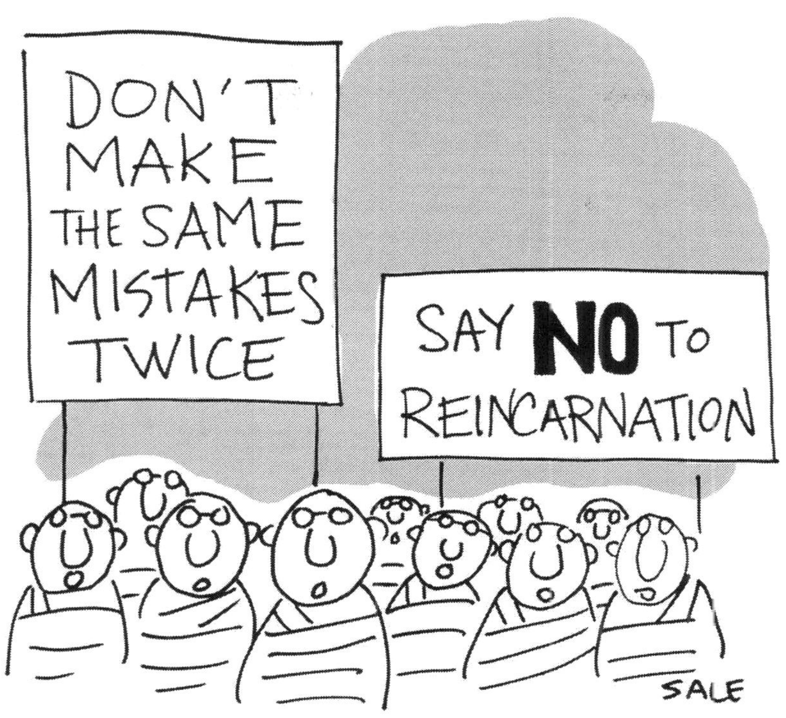

Reformed Buddhists

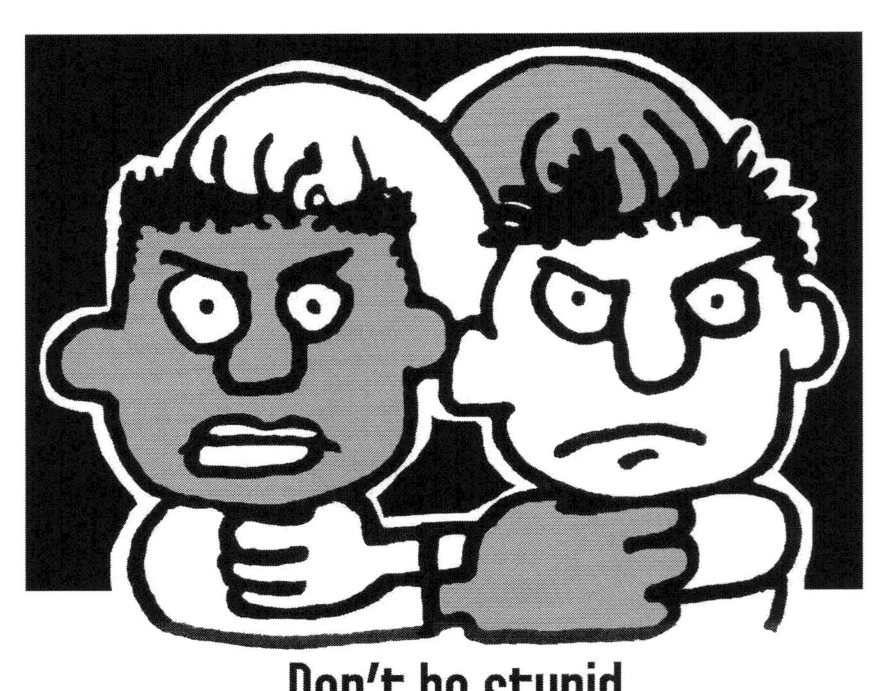

Don't be stupid.

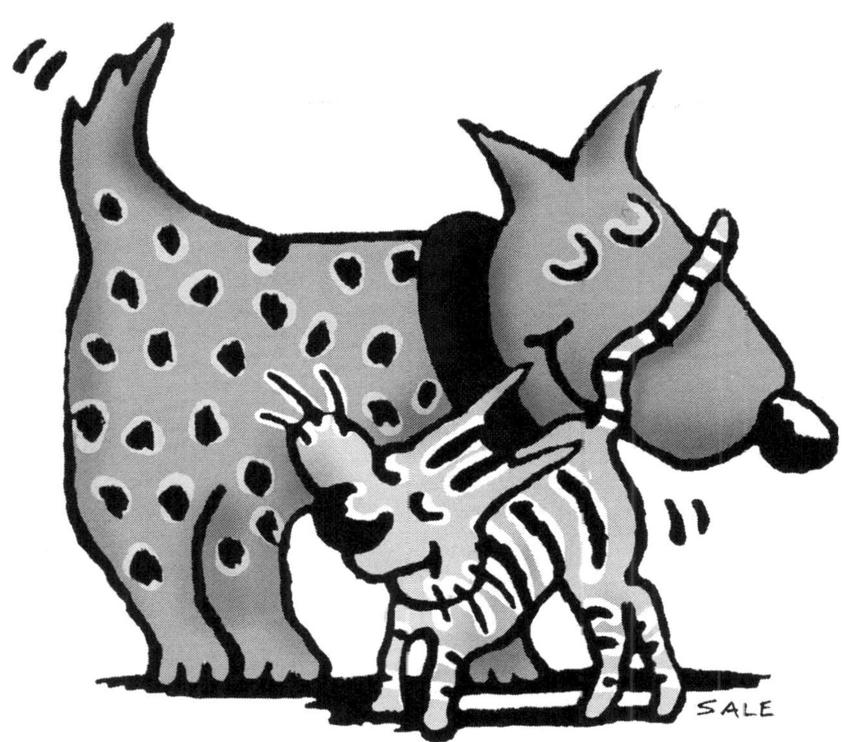

Dysfunctional hate. Try it.

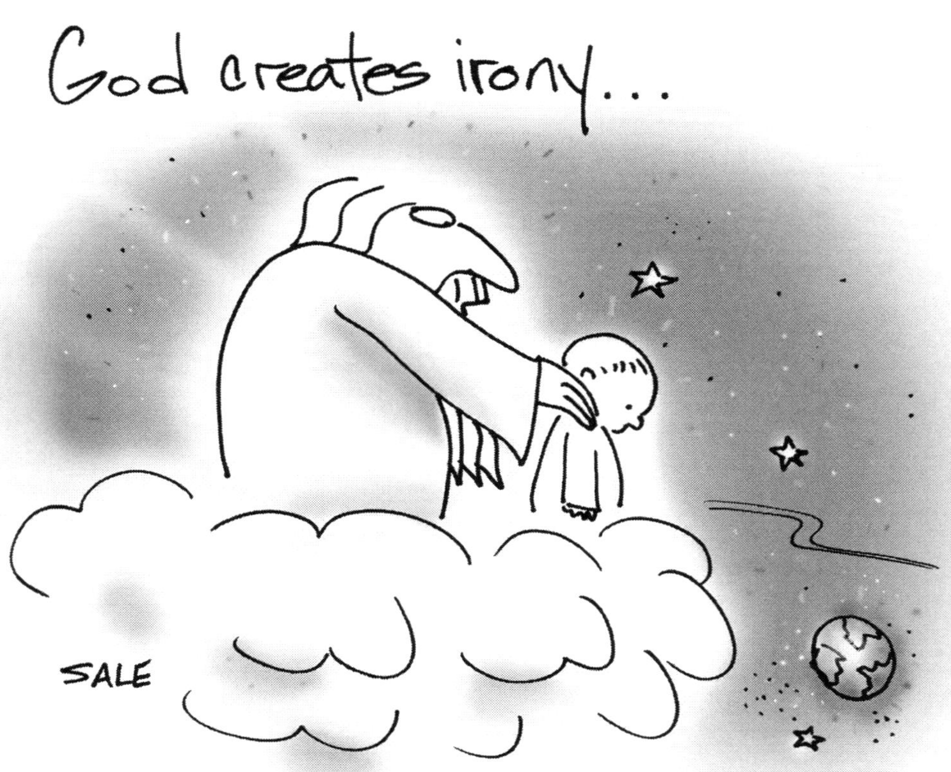

"*I know they are a rough bunch, Son, but...*
what doesn't kill you will make you stronger."

The Recession Hits Heaven.

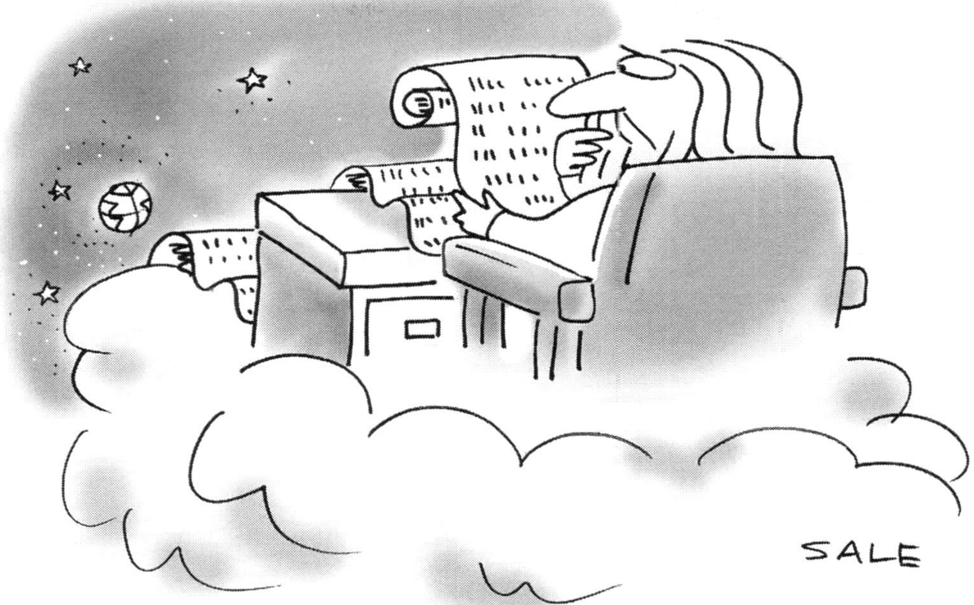

With a soaring deficit and the high cost of energy, God is forced to review his policy of opening a window whenever closing a door.

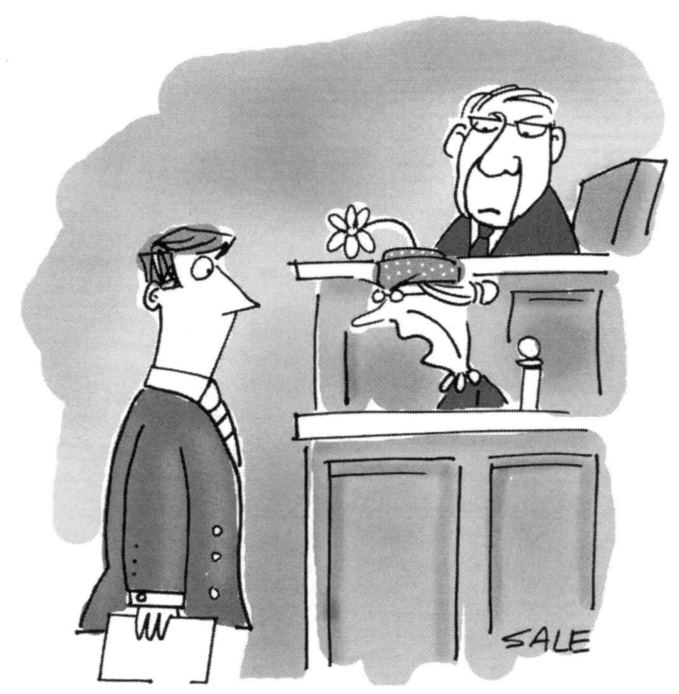

"*There's nothing the matter with my memory, buster. I can remember when a Brazilian was someone who came from Brazil.*"

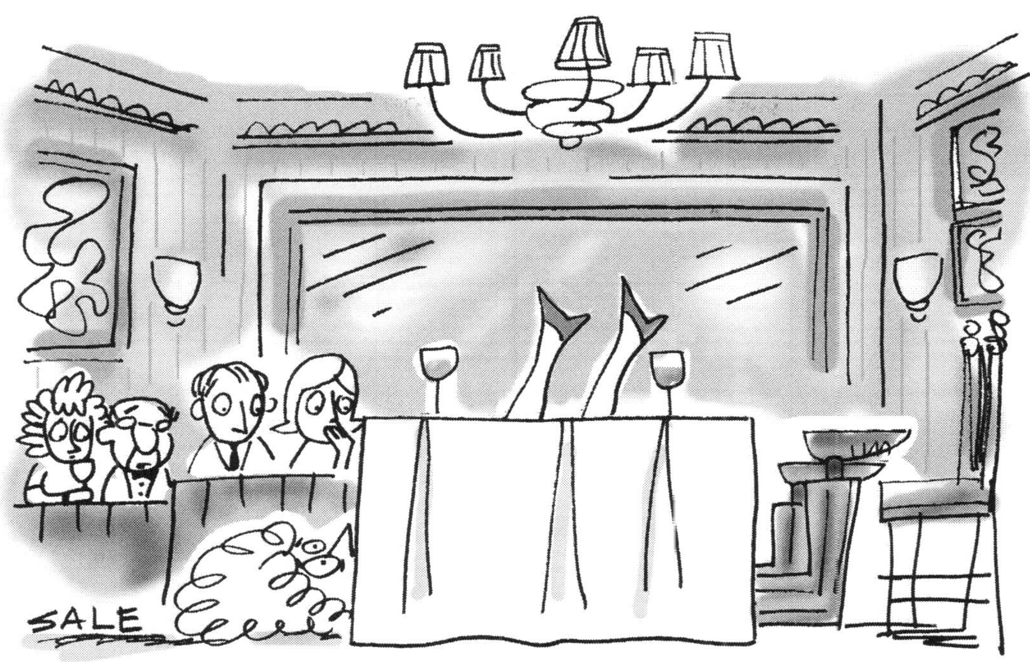

Marge Lewis found she had mixed feelings when a well-meaning customer, who saw her choking, rushed to her aid and mistakenly performed the hymen lick instead of the Heimlich maneuver on her.

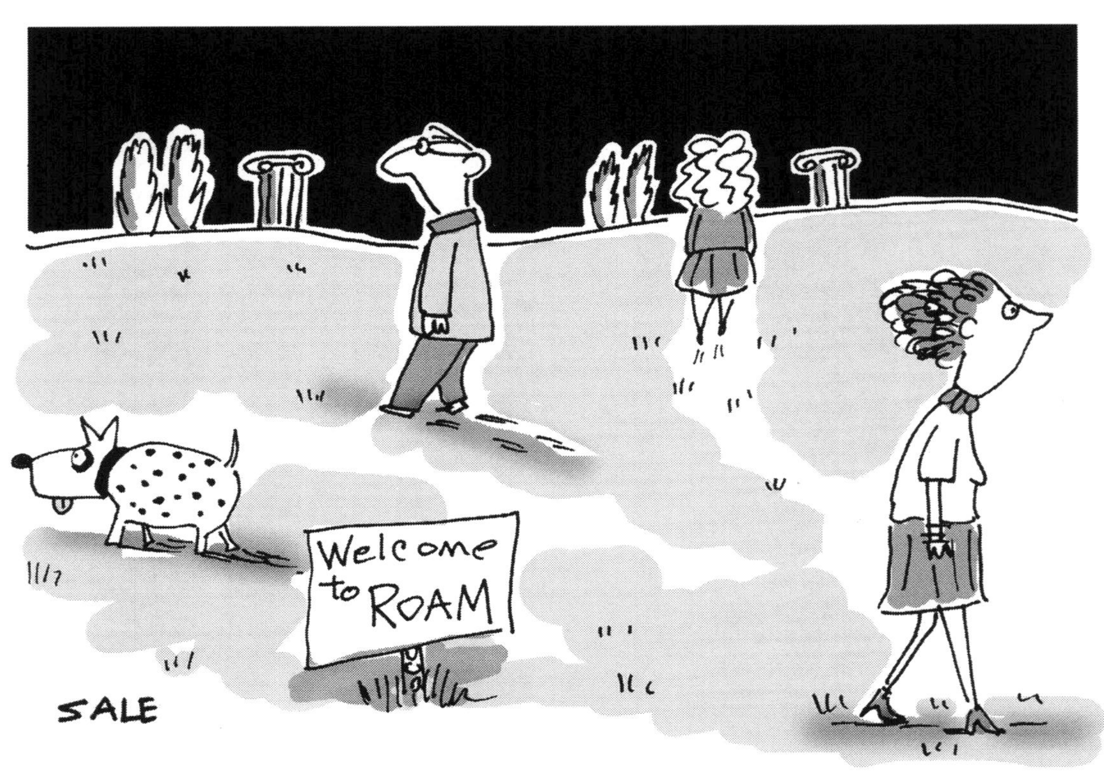

When in Roam...

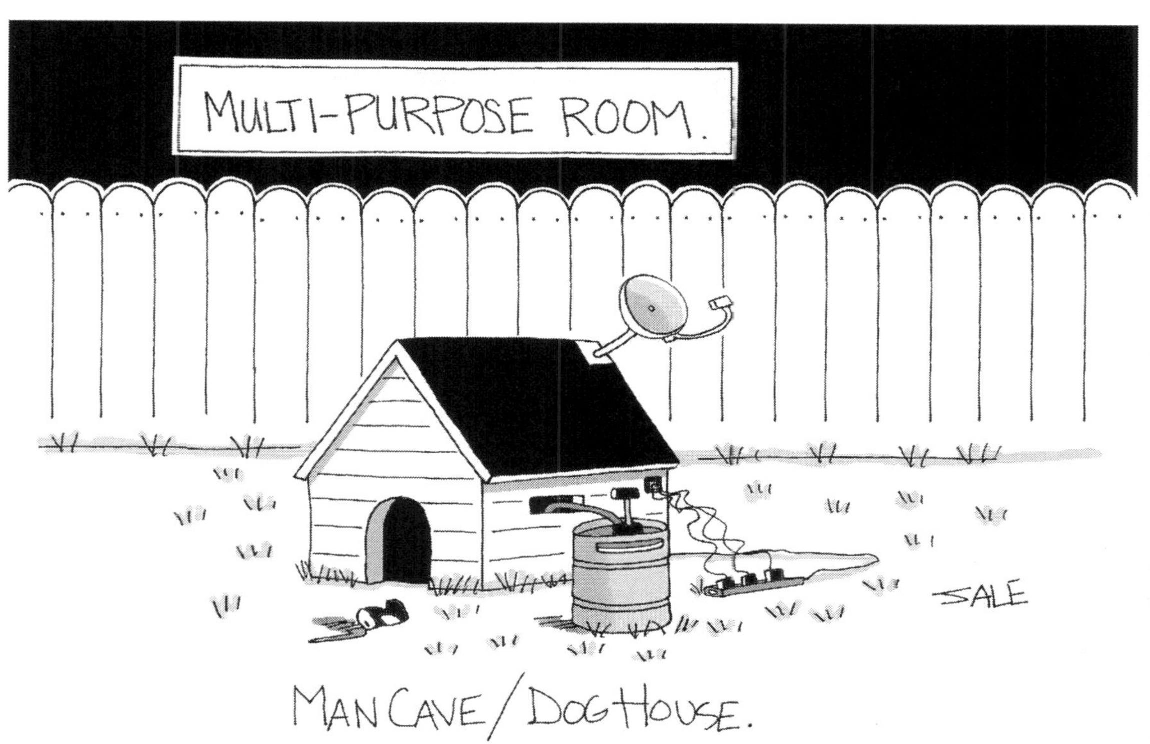

MAN CAVE / DOG HOUSE.

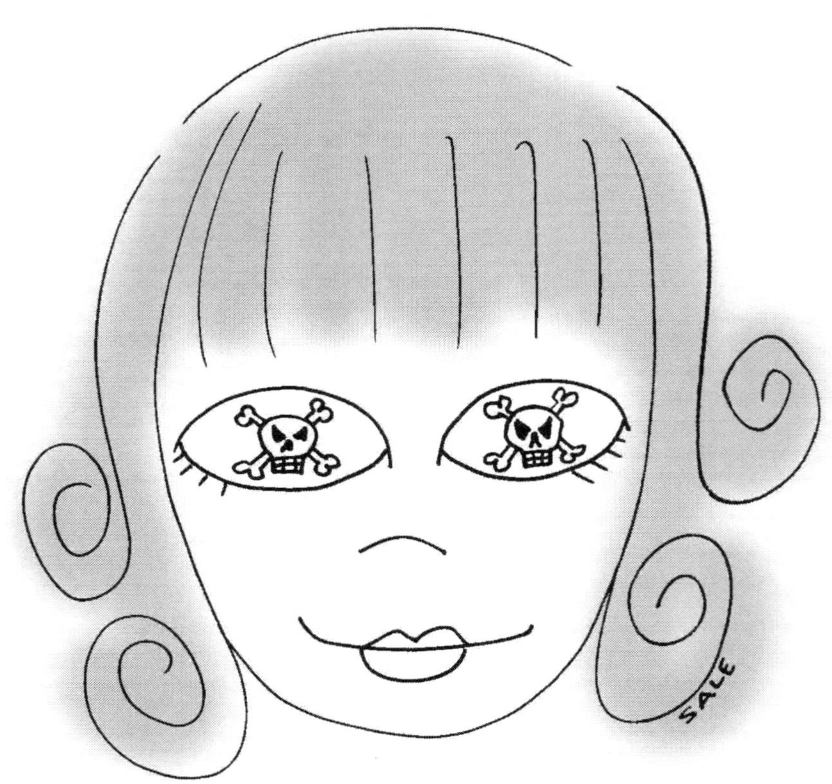

*She said everything was fine, but something
in her eyes lead him to believe otherwise.*

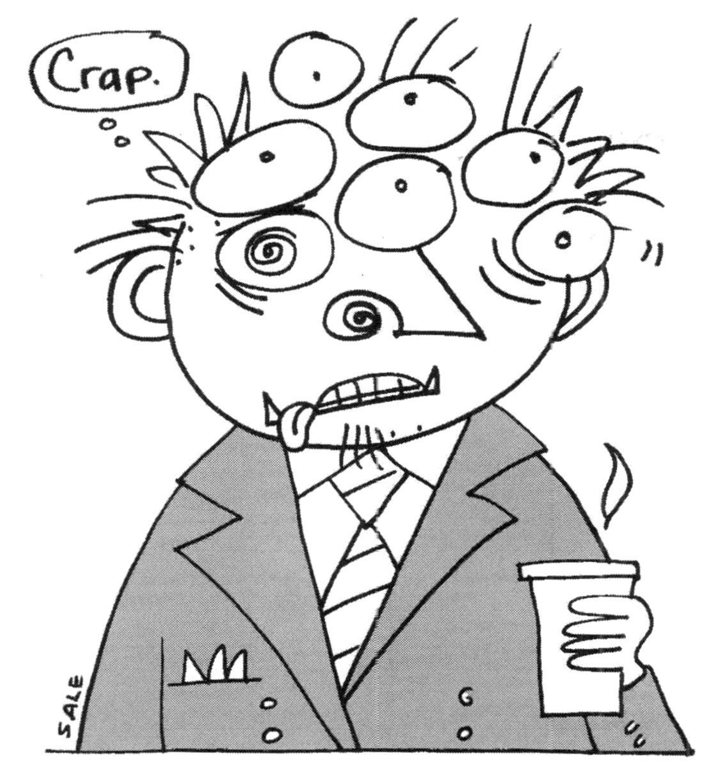

Kenny was so focused on getting his winter flu shots that his cooties vaccination totally slipped his mind.

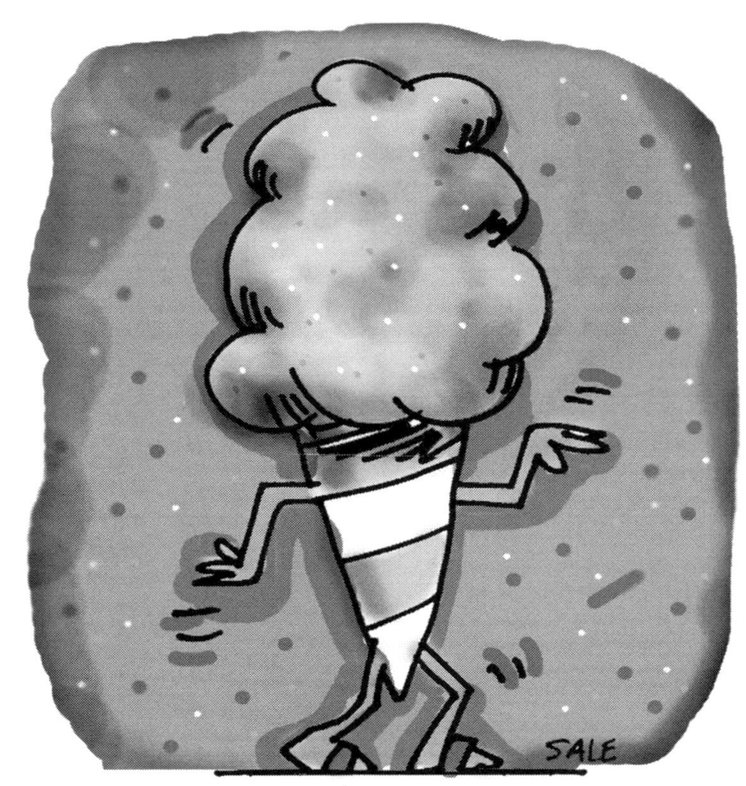

Egyptian Cotton Candy.

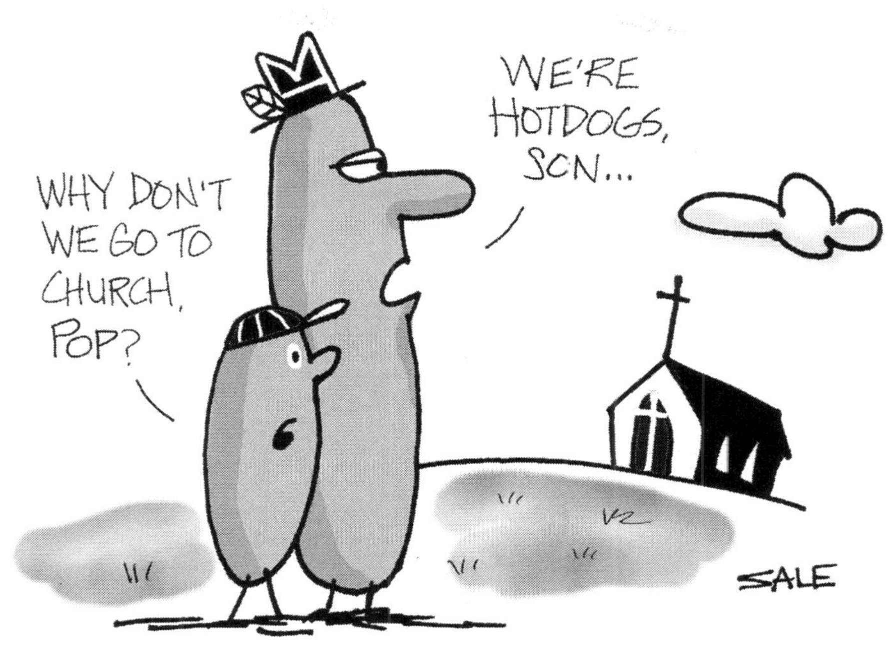

"The less you know about our creation the better."

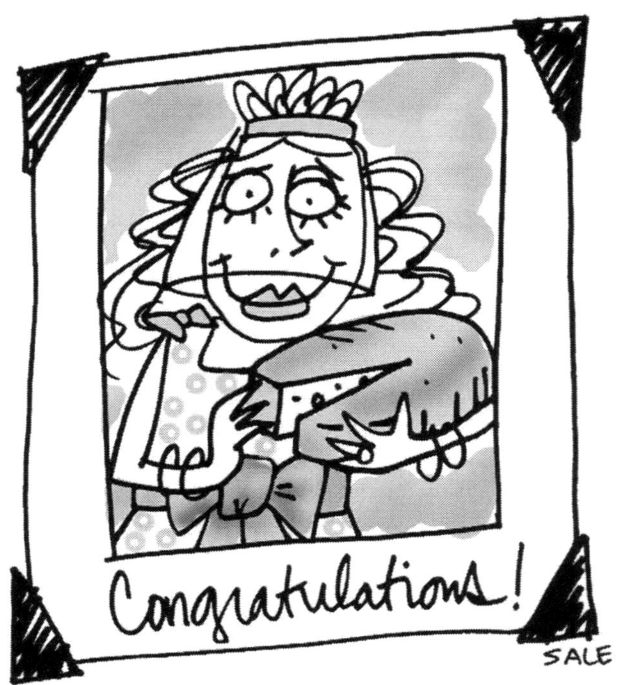

*The happiest day in Linda's life was the day
it became legal to marry cheese.*

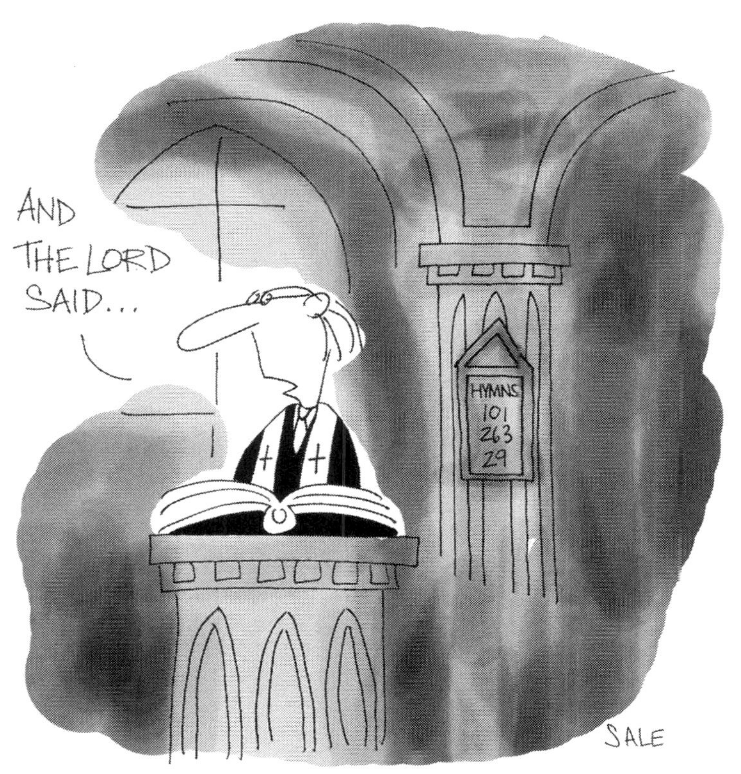

"Blessed are those who resist being schmucks."

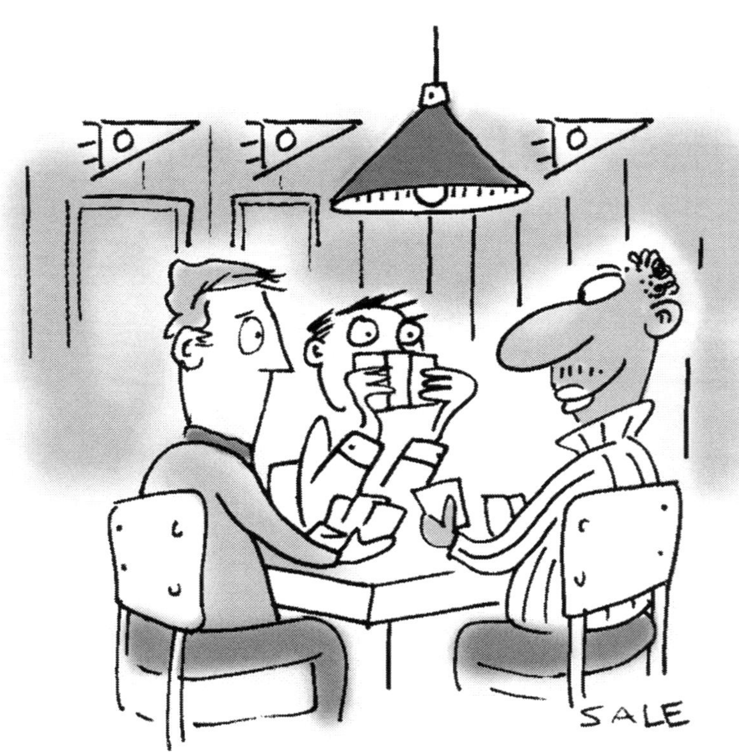

*Jamal loved to freak out the other players
by playing the race card*

Stereotypes

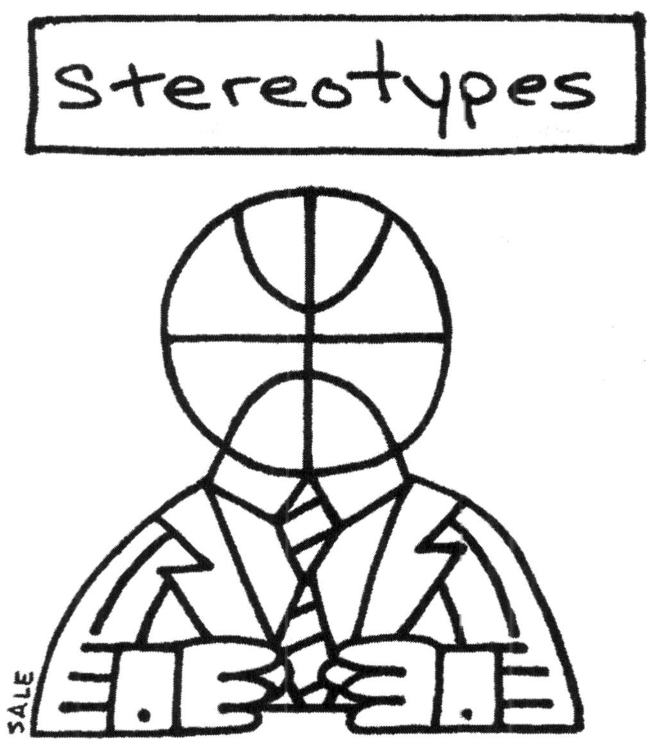

For his whole life, people just assumed
Wilson played basketball.

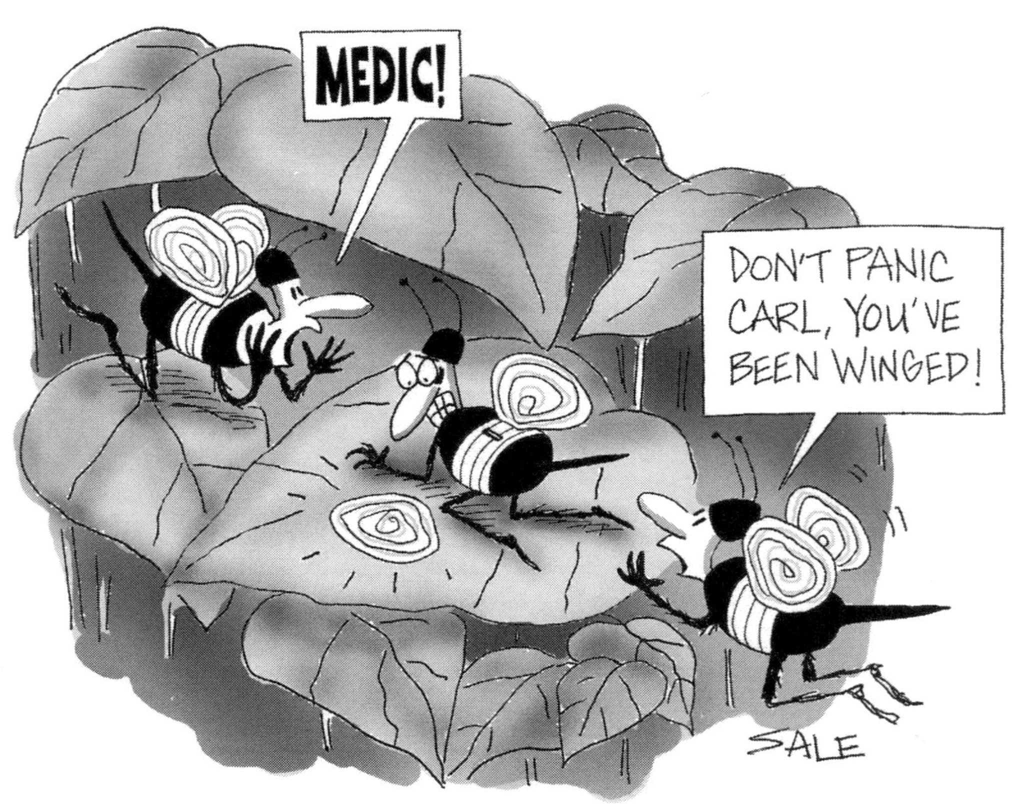

(No insects were hurt in the drawing of this cartoon.)

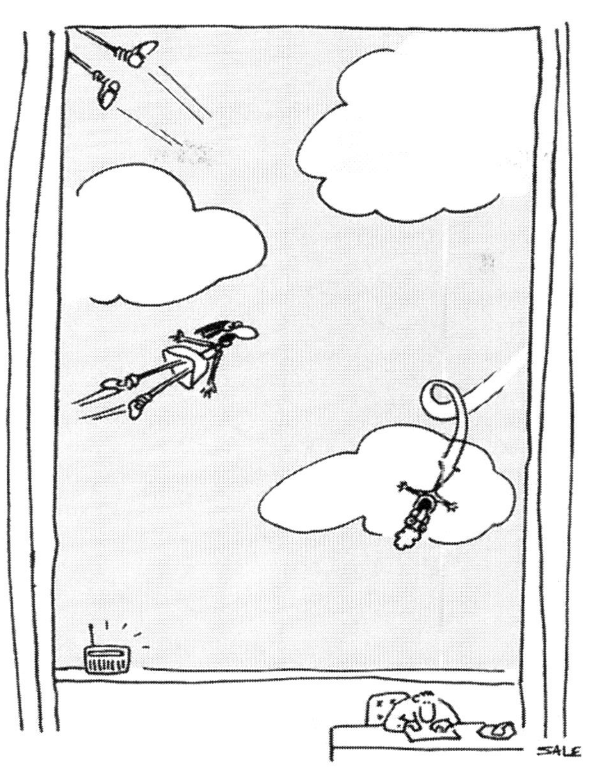

"*...With winds gusting up to 70 mph, the National Weather Service has issued an anorexic alert.*"

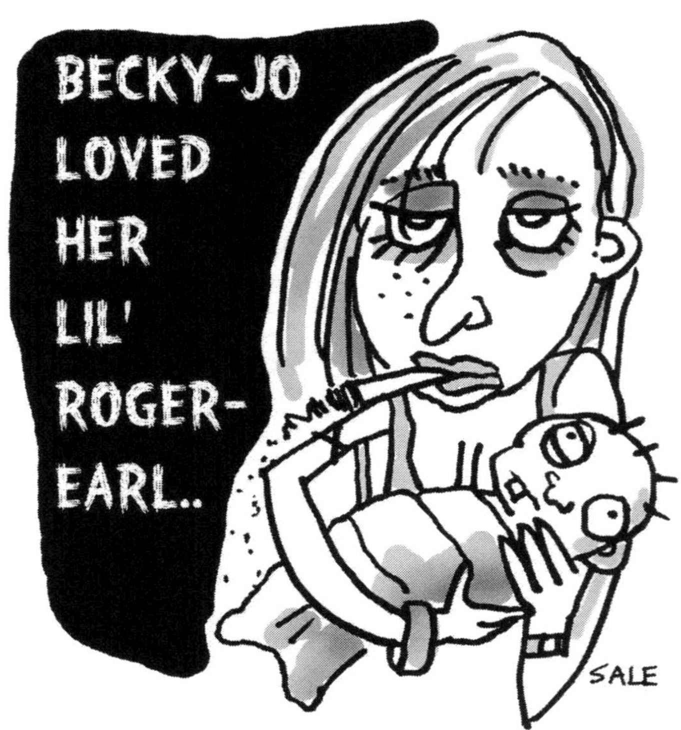

But there were days she questioned her congressman's insistence that she become a single mother.

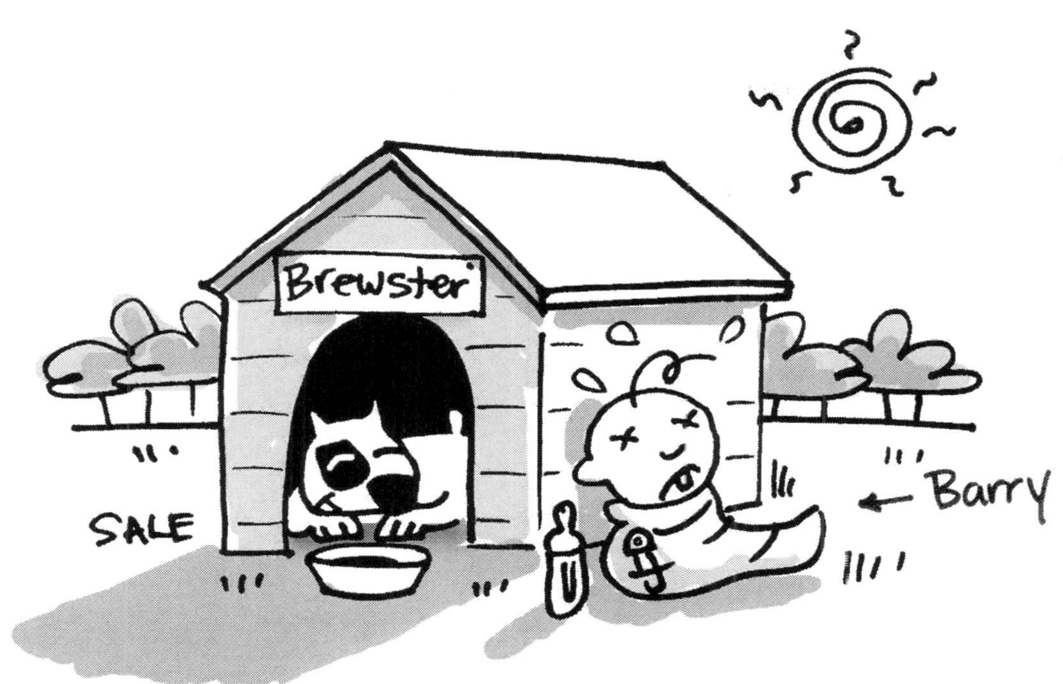

For Bonnie Greenblatt, it turned out that having a pet was not actually good practice for having a child—just ask Barry Greenblatt.

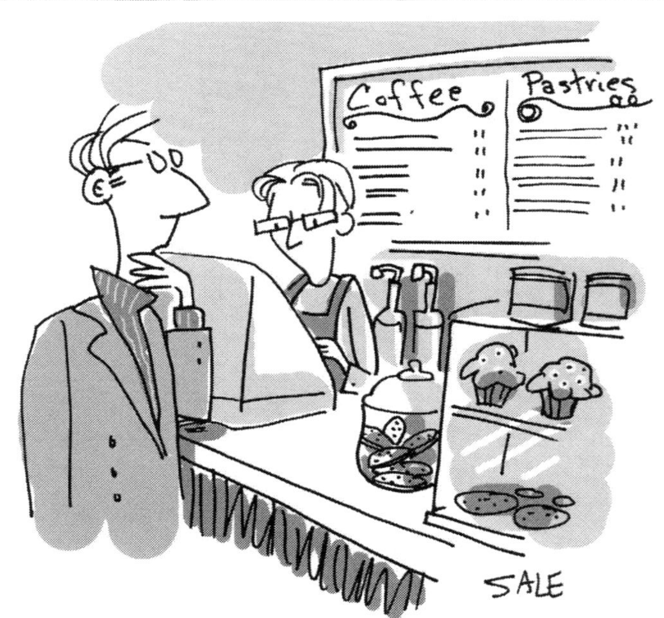

*I'll have a cafe mocha-vodka-Paxil-marijuana-latte
to go and recreational size it, please.*

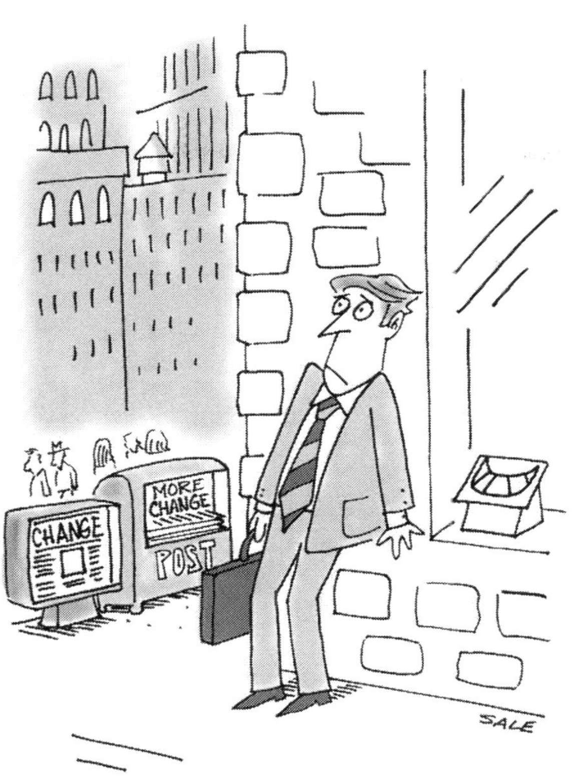

In a world full of change, Ted Whiteman never knew from day-to-day if he was the predator or the prey.

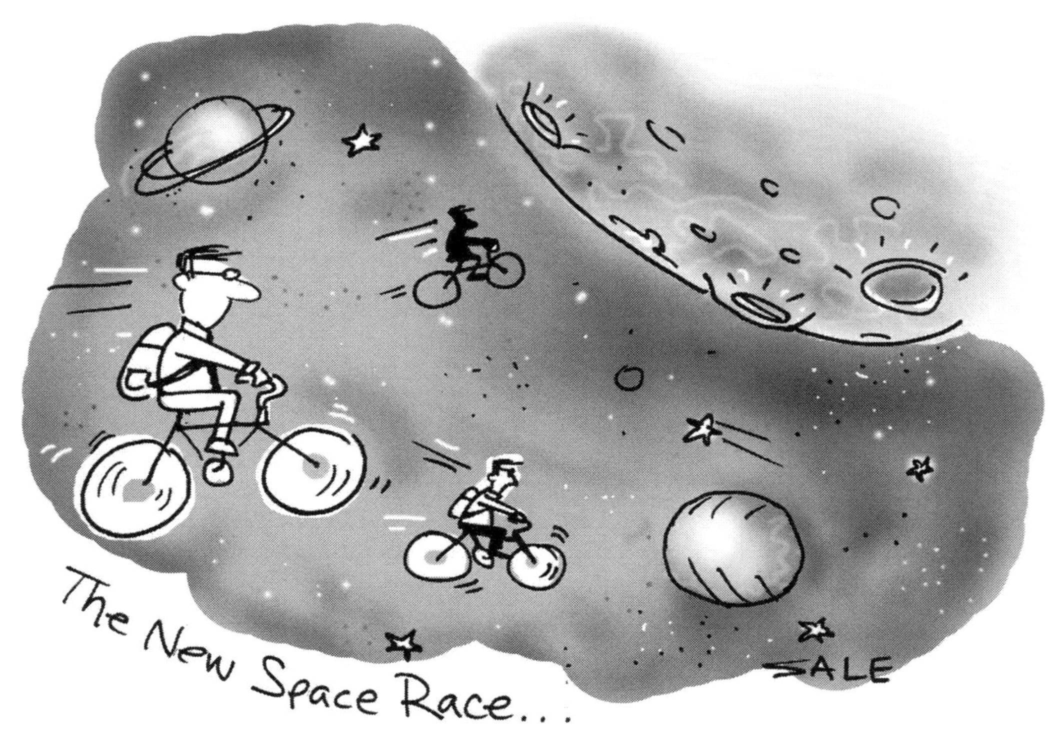

Evangelical Christians, Latter Day Saints and Jehovah's Wittnesses race to baptize the first extra-terrestial.

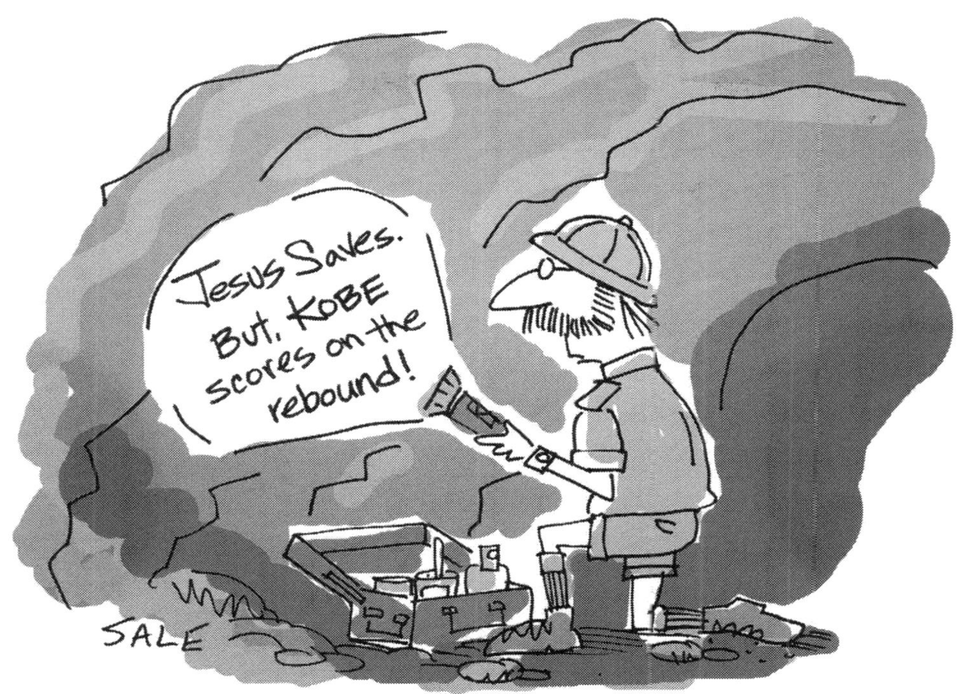

Advancements in forensic science brought religious scholars back to Jesus' tomb in search of answers.

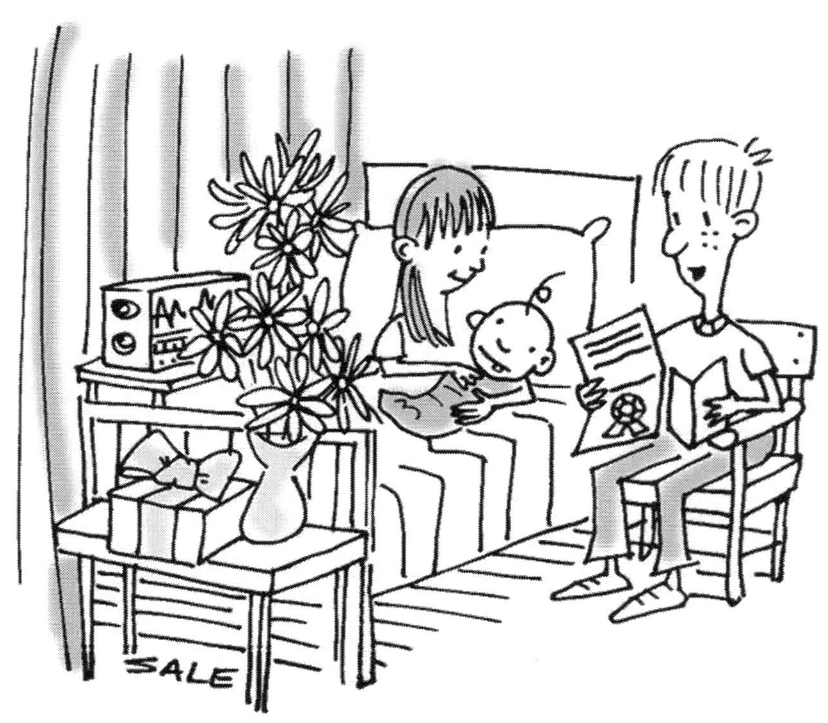

"Check it out honey, your parents set up a Rehab & Bail Bond Trust Fund for Timmy."

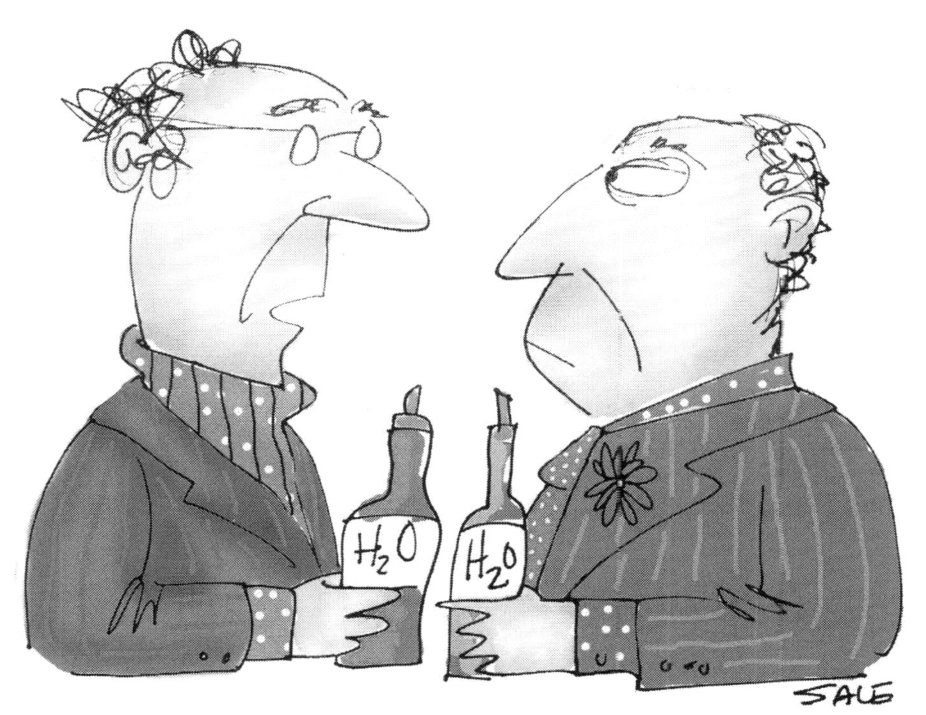

"*Remember the good old days when everyone loved a mime?*"

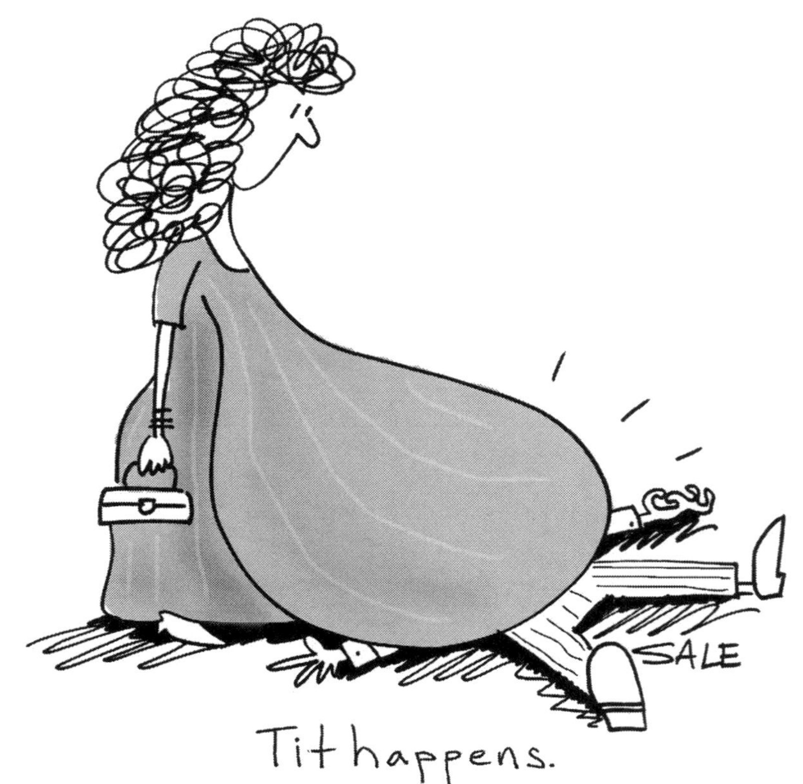

Tit happens.

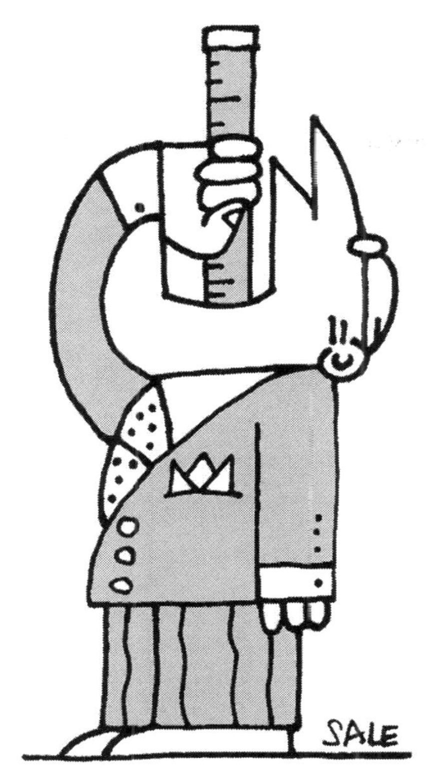

*Johnson had wondered for years
just how full of crap he was.*

11:59PM APRIL 14TH

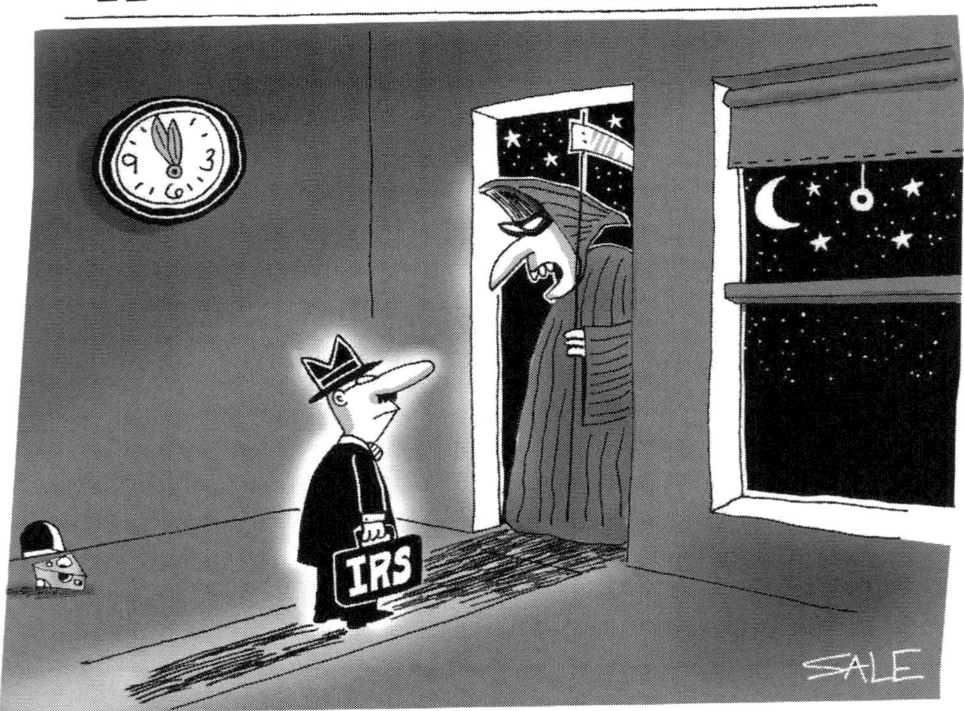

"Ready to kick some ass?"

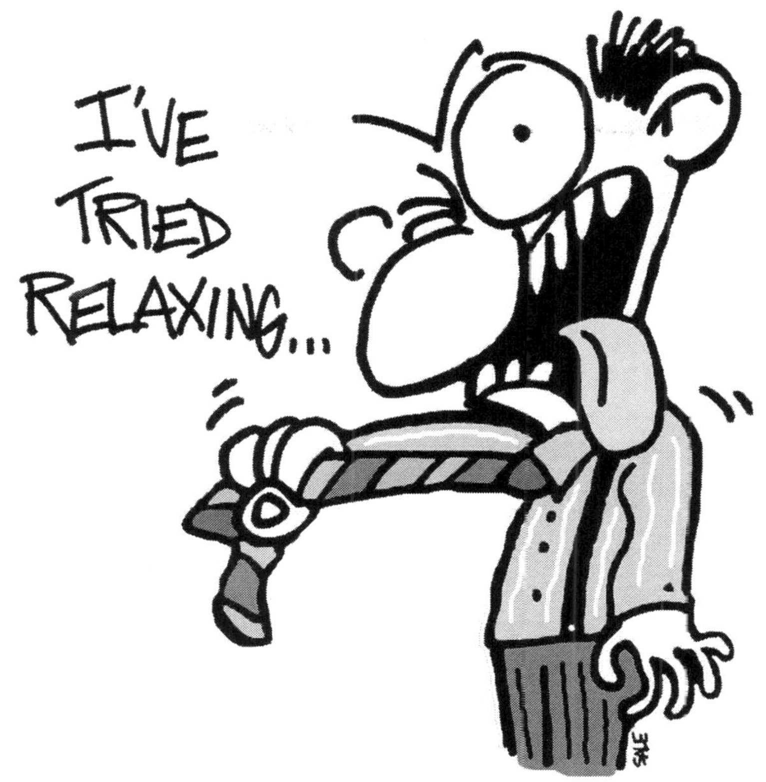

"But I've had more experience being tense."

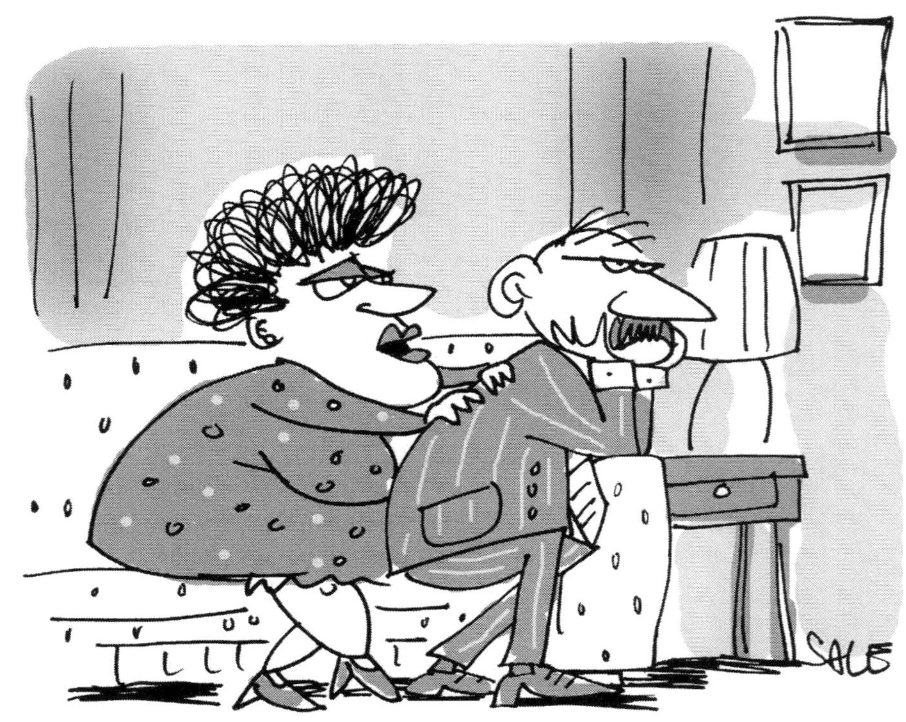

"*Honey, I'm not laughing at you - I'm laughing at the thought of everyone on my blog, twitter and facebook laughing at you.*"

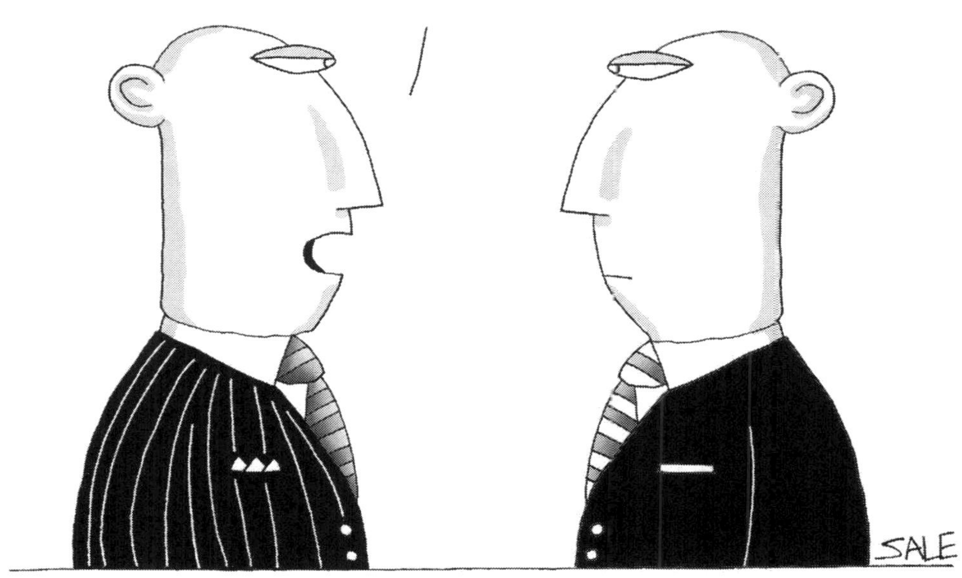

"*It made me sick.*"

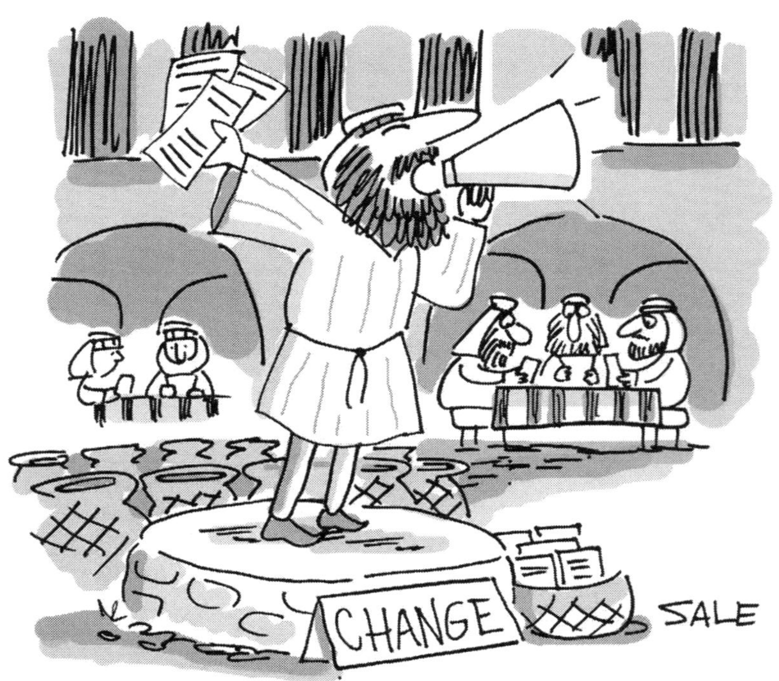

The day after Jesus' birth an announcement was made throughout the land for people to change their calendars from B.C. to A.D..

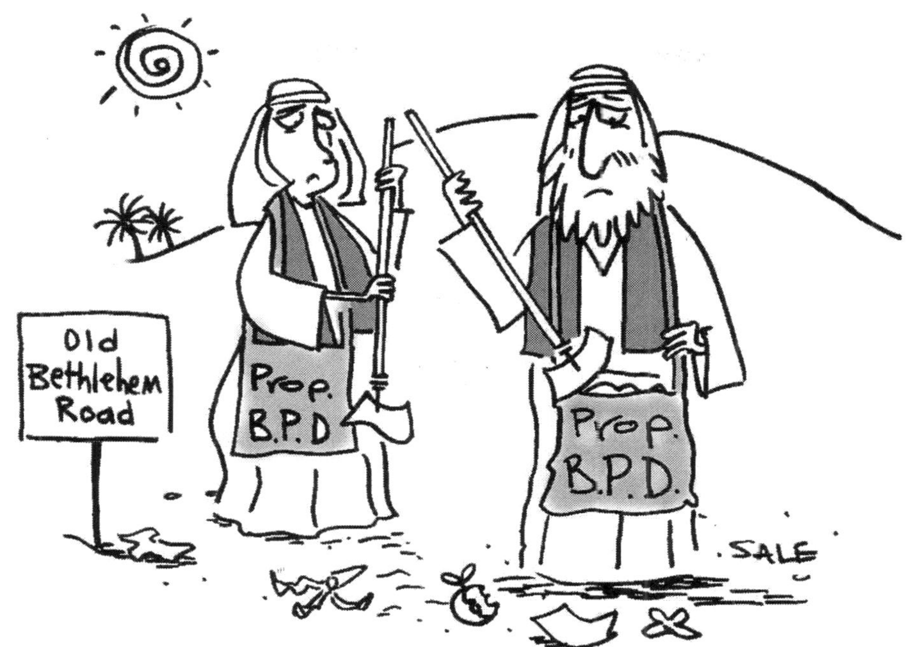

As first-time offenders, Mary and Joseph got off with probation, community service and parenting classes for keeping a child in a manger.

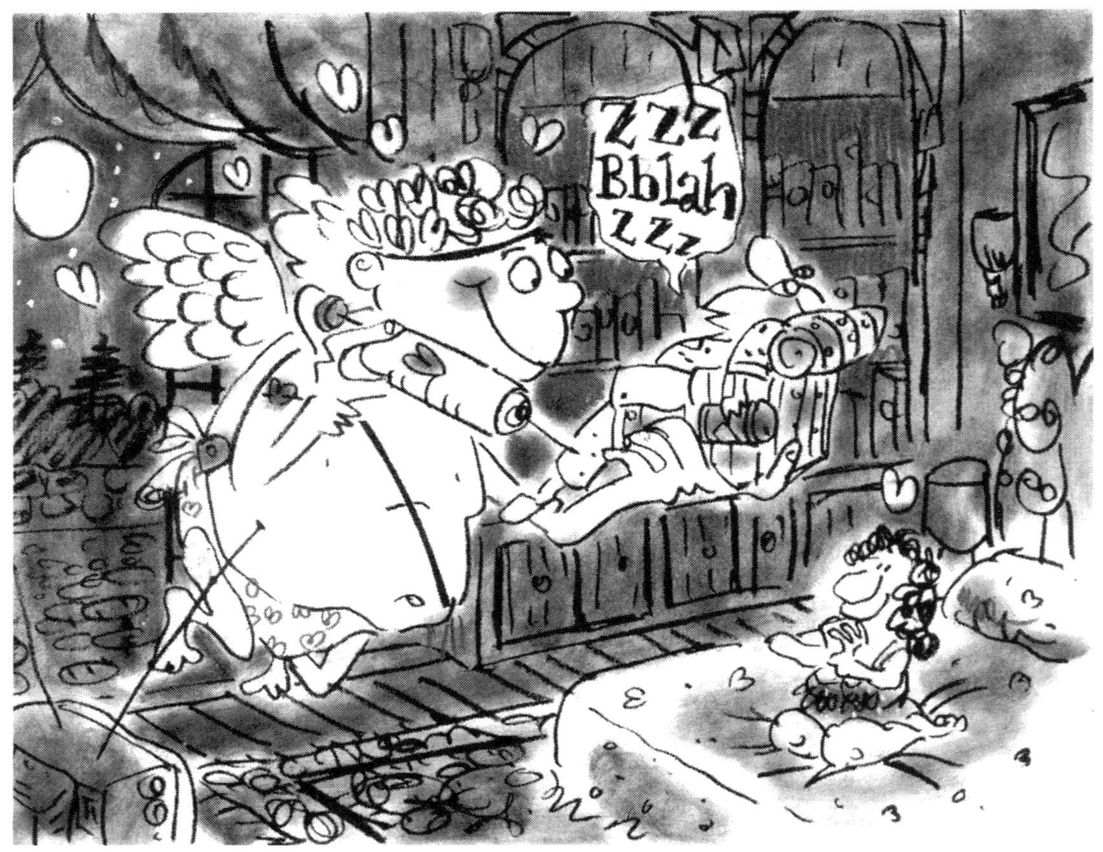
ZZZ
Bblah
ZZz

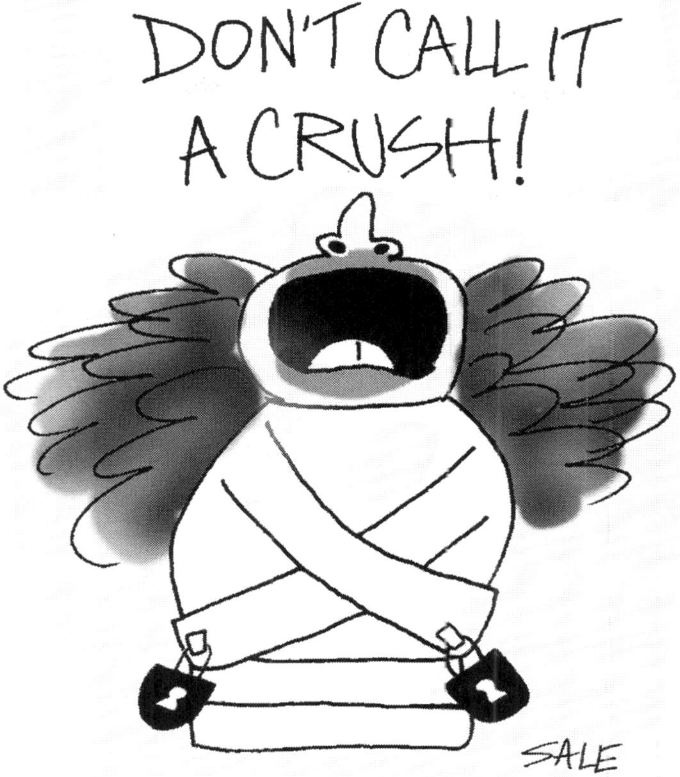

DON'T CALL IT A CRUSH!

SALE

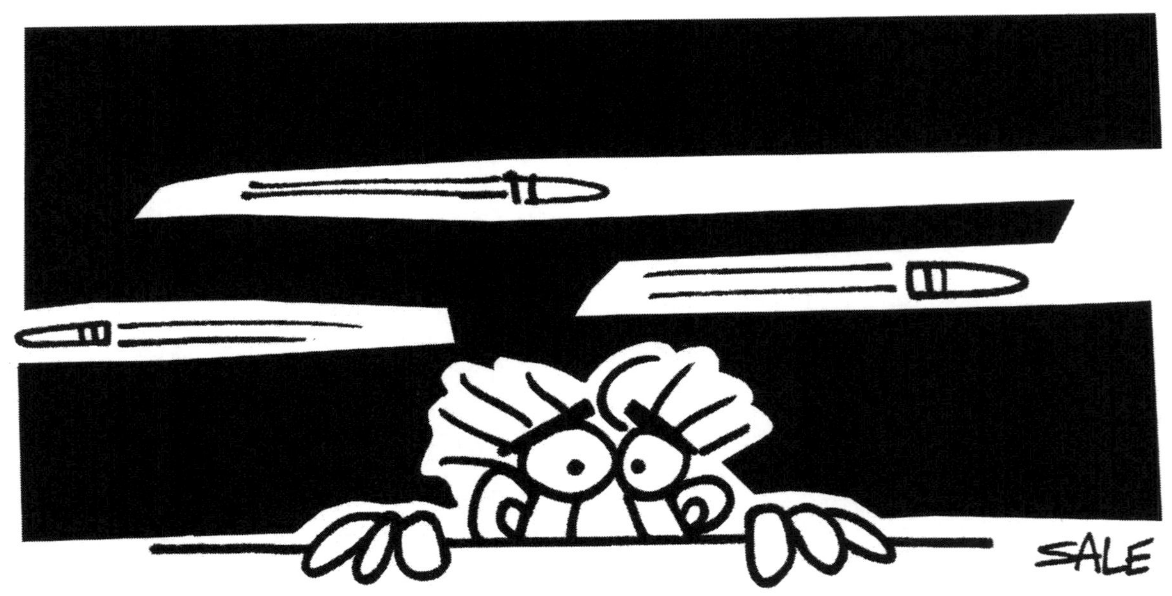

"*What doesn't kill you…confirms your suspicions.*"

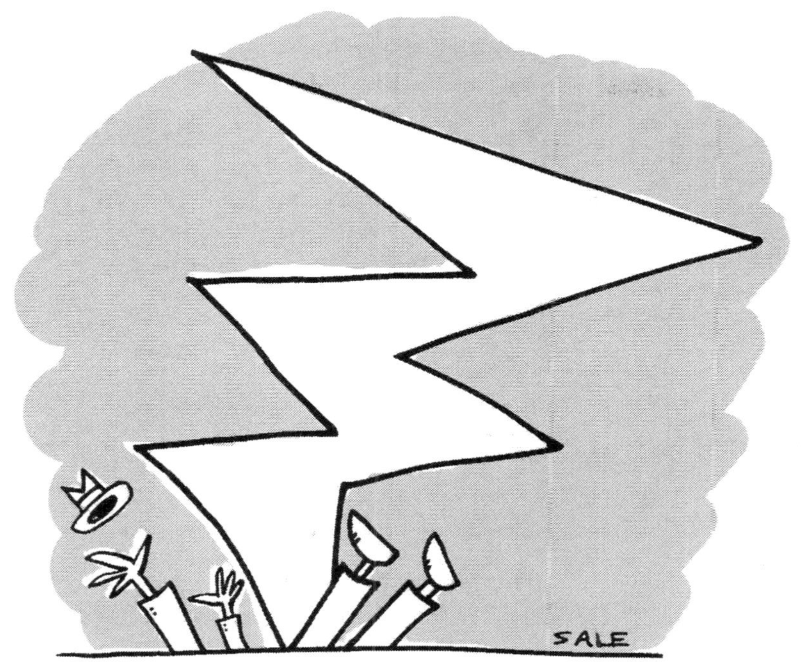

A lot of people owed Ken an apology. He wasn't just being paranoid, the Universe really was out to get him.

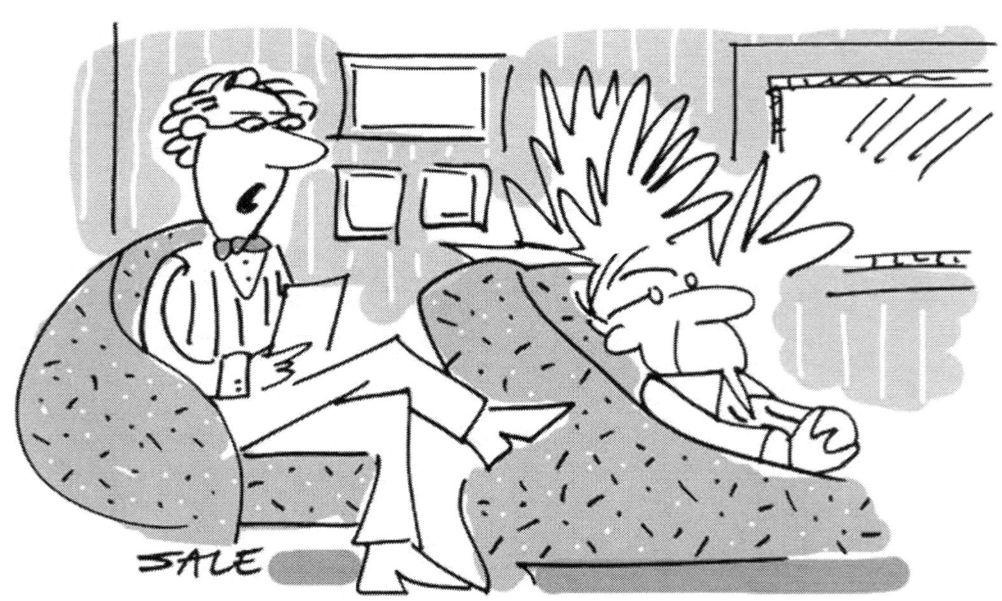

Mr. Peterson, Grace, Roy, Ira, Winston, Bobo, Sun-lee, Gustav... the bad news is you have multiple personalities; the good news is this gives you a tremendous advantage in this terrible job market.

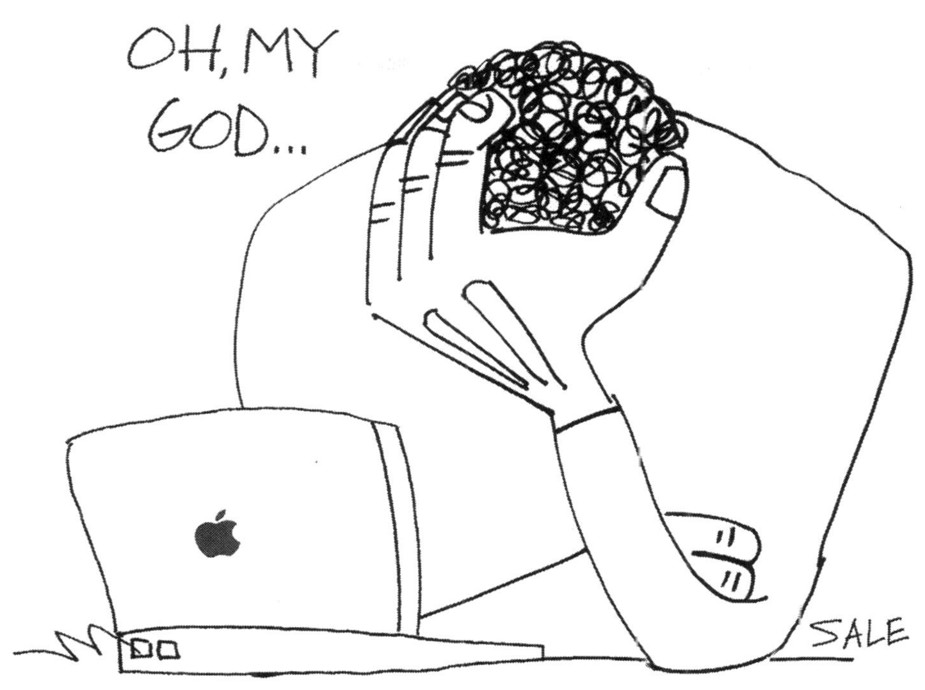

"I've been unfriended on FaceBook"

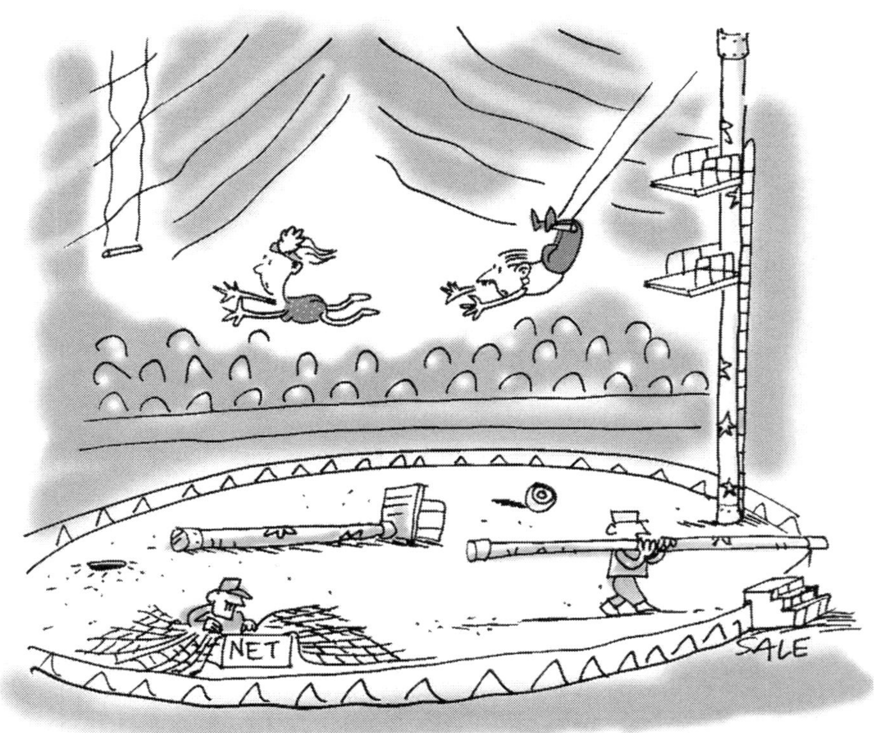

Jobs become obsolete—talent doesn't.

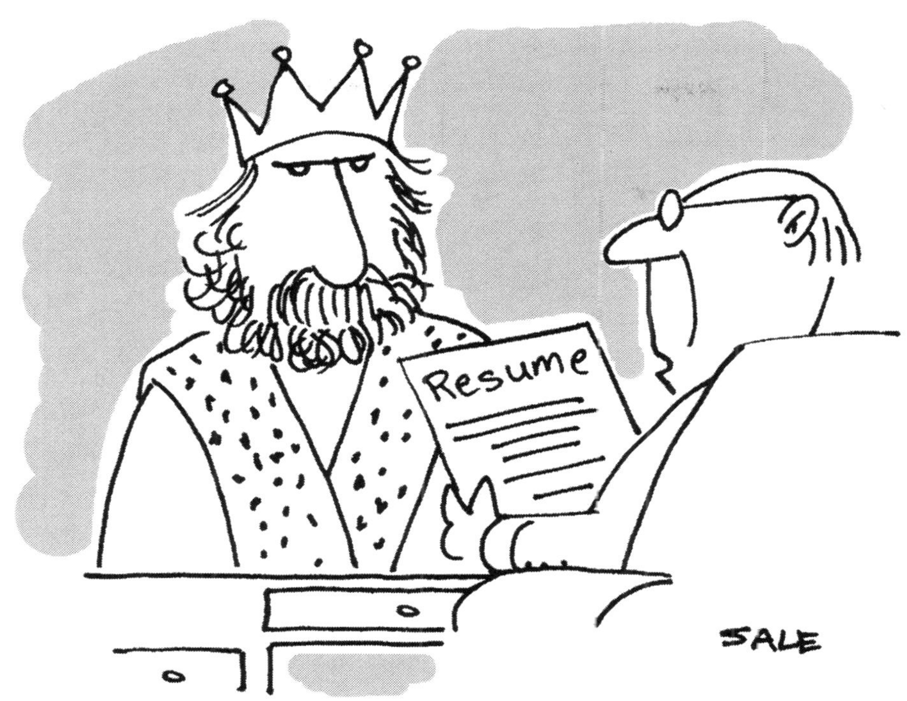

"It says here, Self-Employed, would you be more specific?"

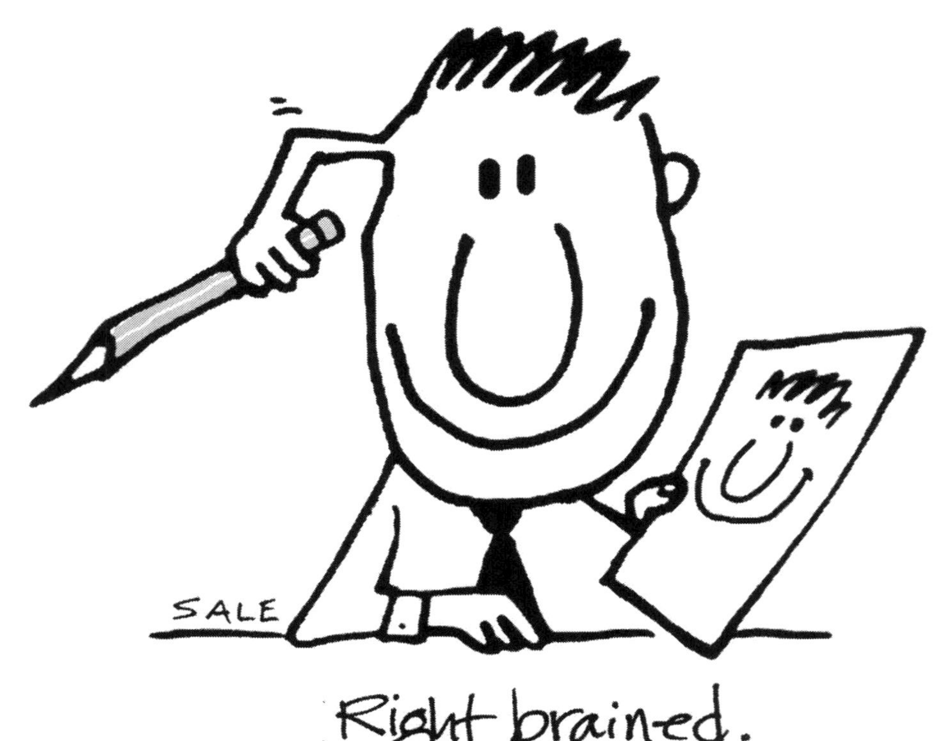

Right brained.

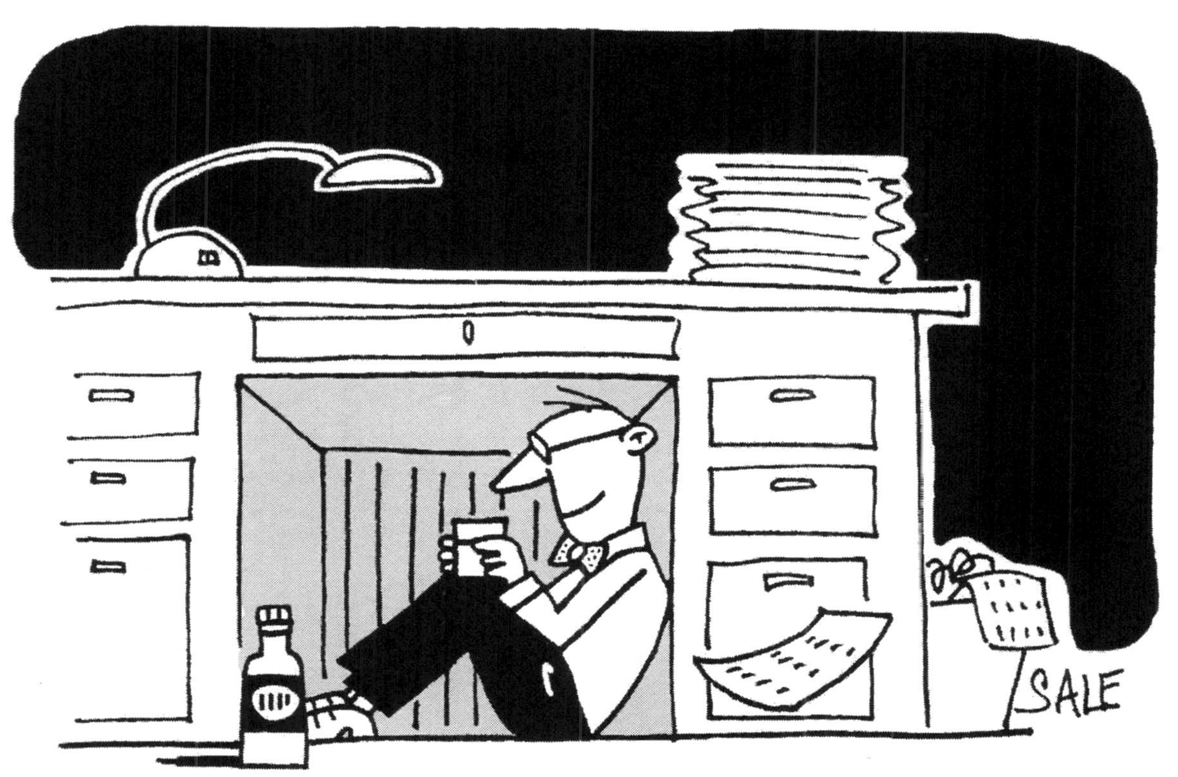

The best part of writing is drinking.

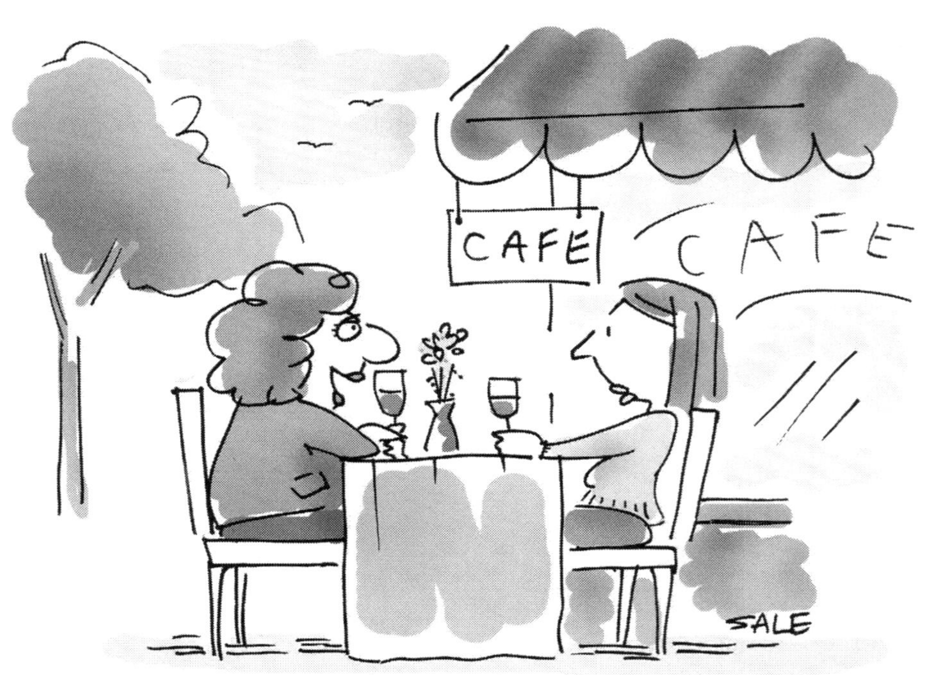

I checked Jerry into sex rehab for a tune-up.

God Blogs.

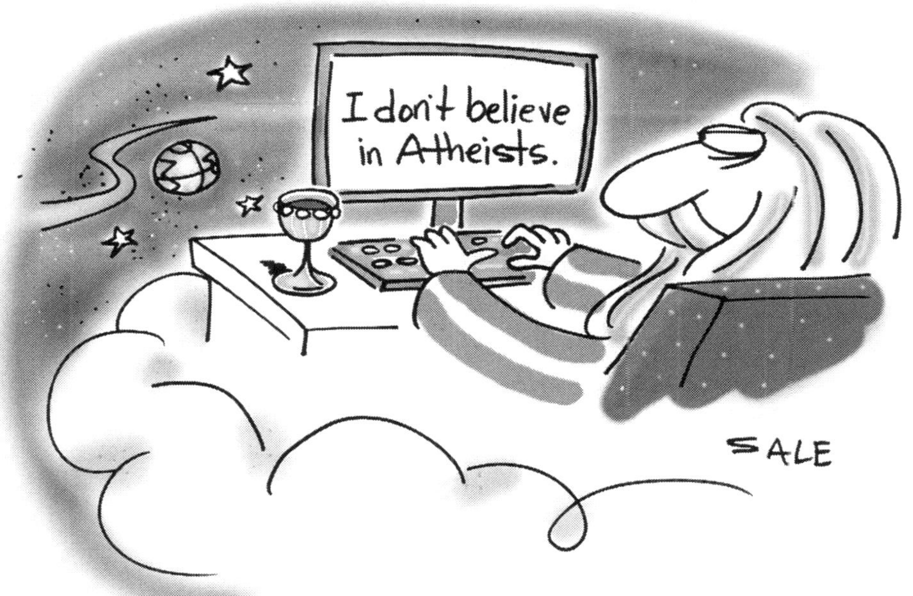

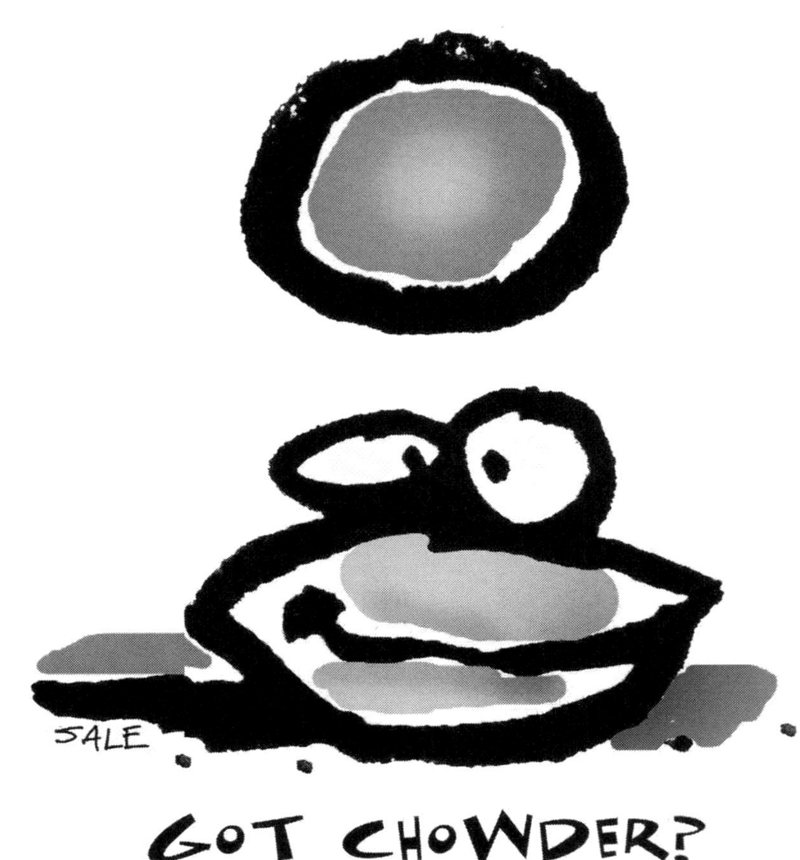

GOT CHOWDER?

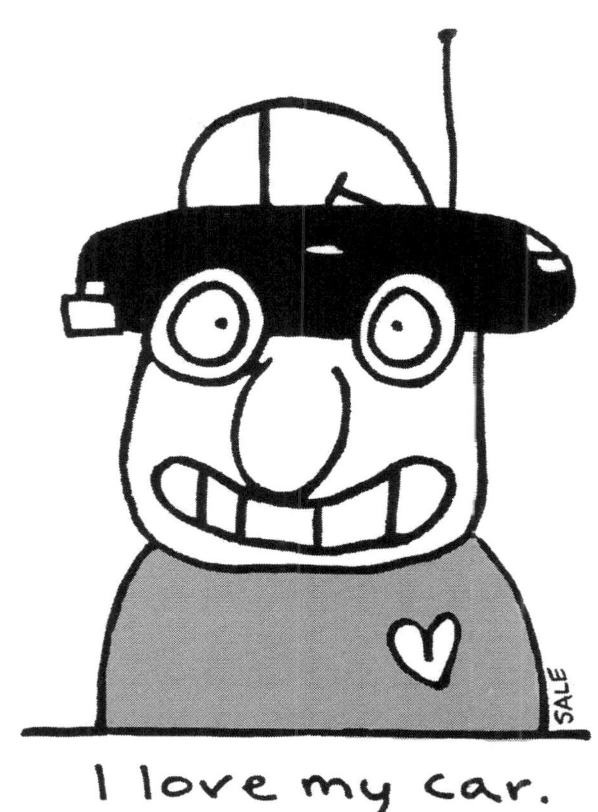

I love my car.

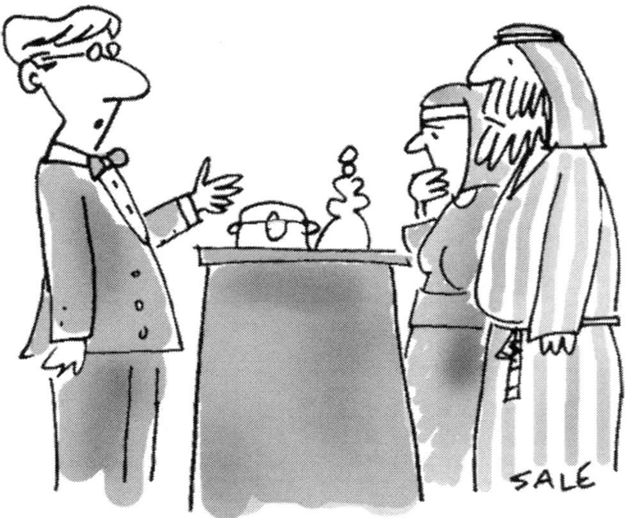

"Unfortunately, Frankincense and myrrh have very little value today. However, had you kept the set intact and not sold the gold for cash we'd be talking six or seven figures, maybe higher."

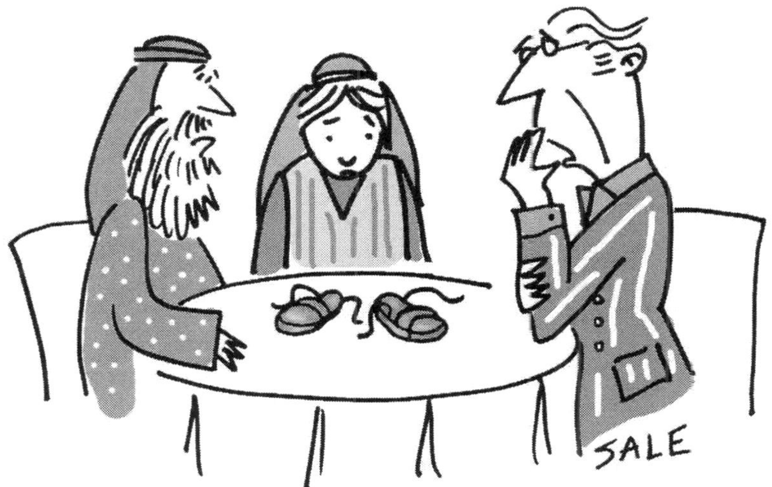

"Naturally, preserving a historic item increases its value, but good heavens, bronzing the Messiah's baby sandals? What on earth were you thinking?"

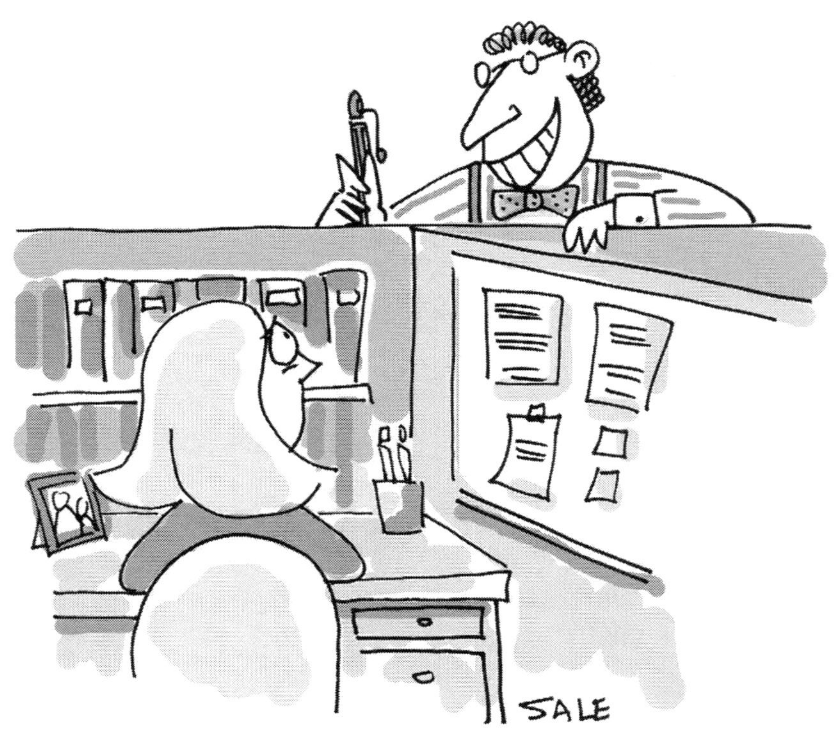

"Following his vasectomy surgery, Garrett totally creeped out his female co-workers by asking them to sign his cast."

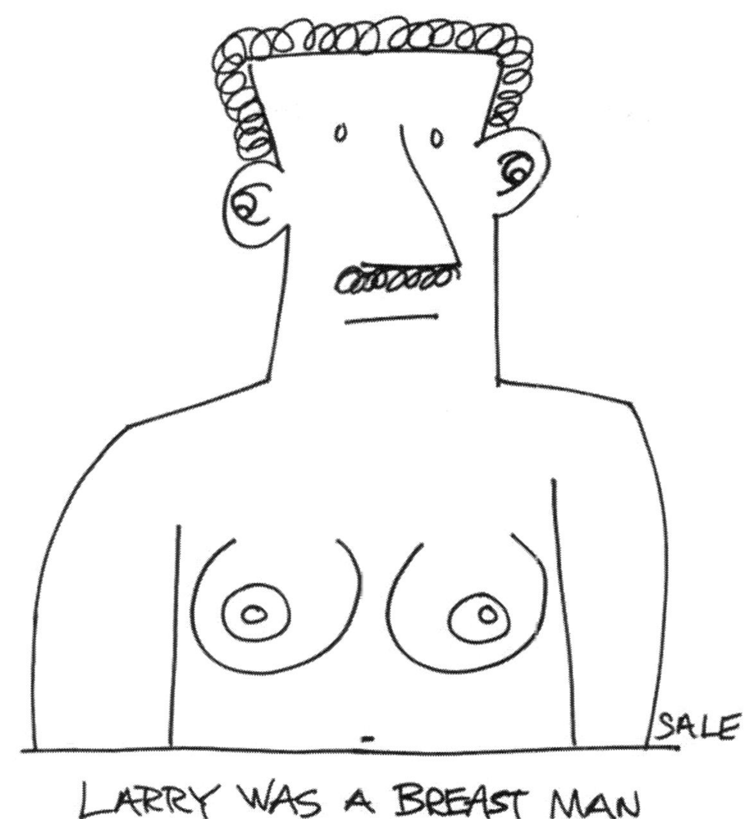

LARRY WAS A BREAST MAN

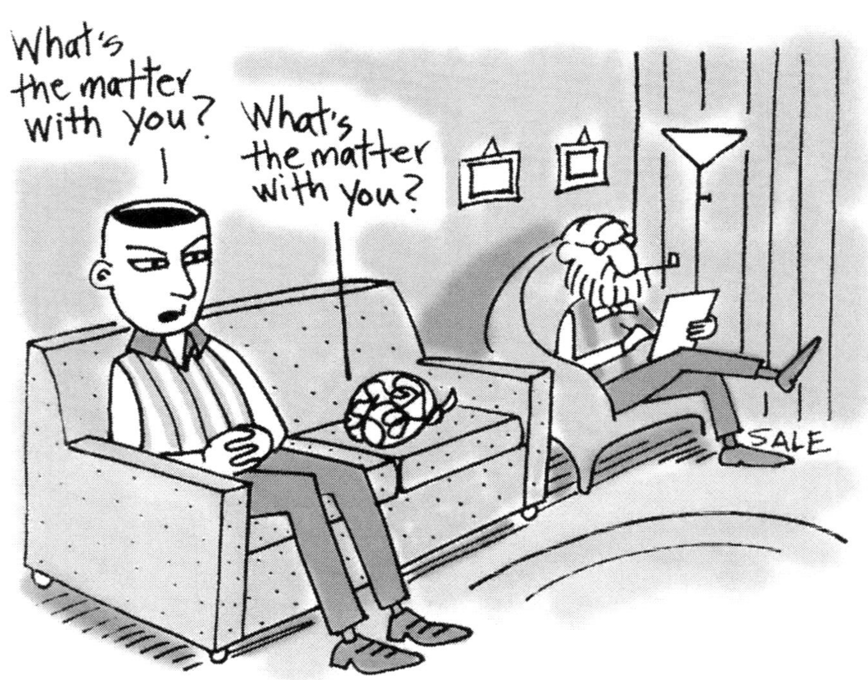

RELATIONSHIP COUNSELING.

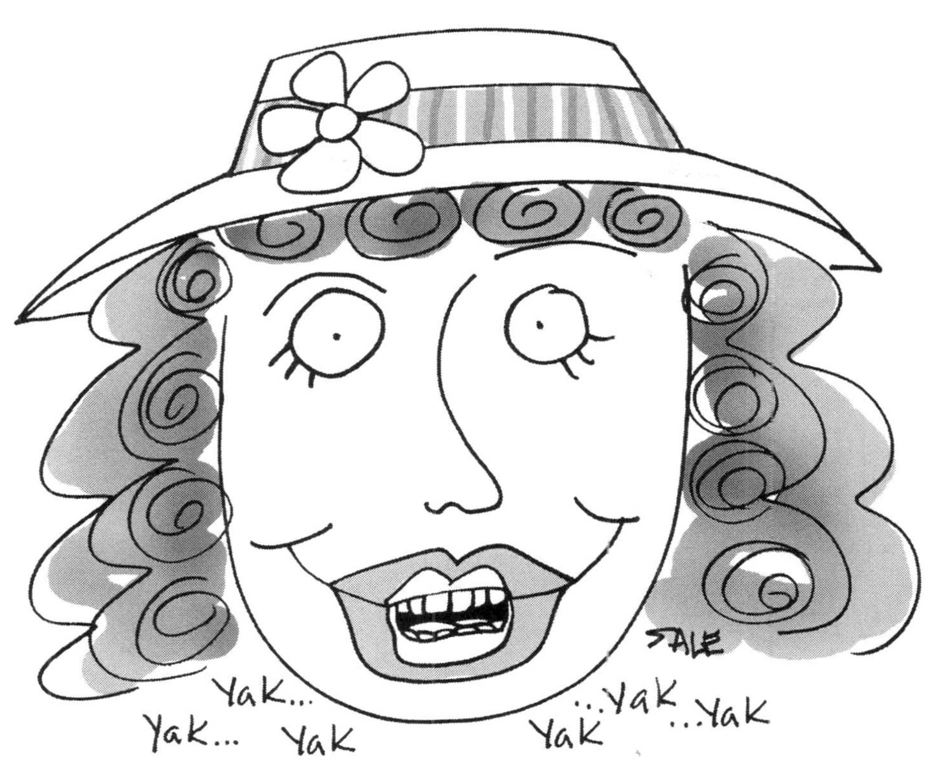

*"No one could shut Shelly up,
her mouth had a mouth of its own."*

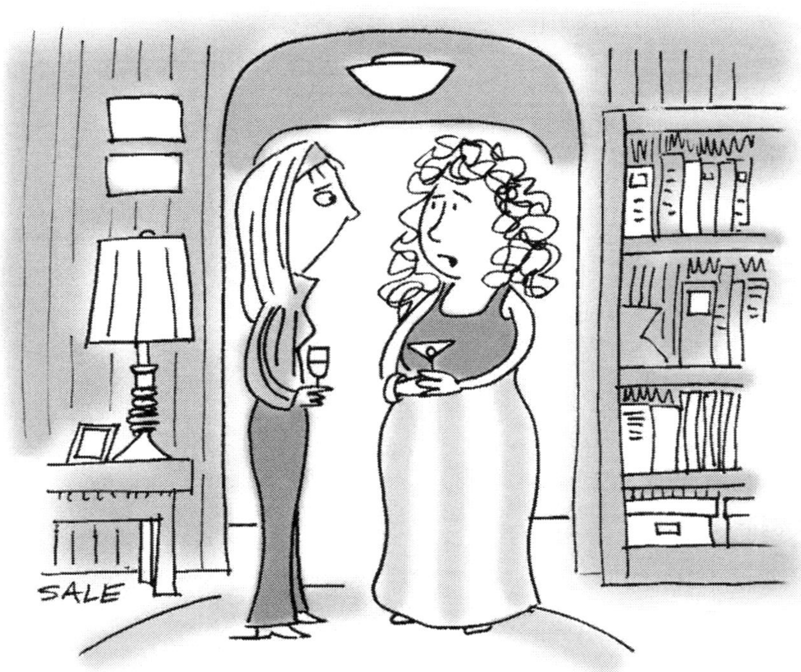

"I know Jeff was a great catch, but he made me look fat."

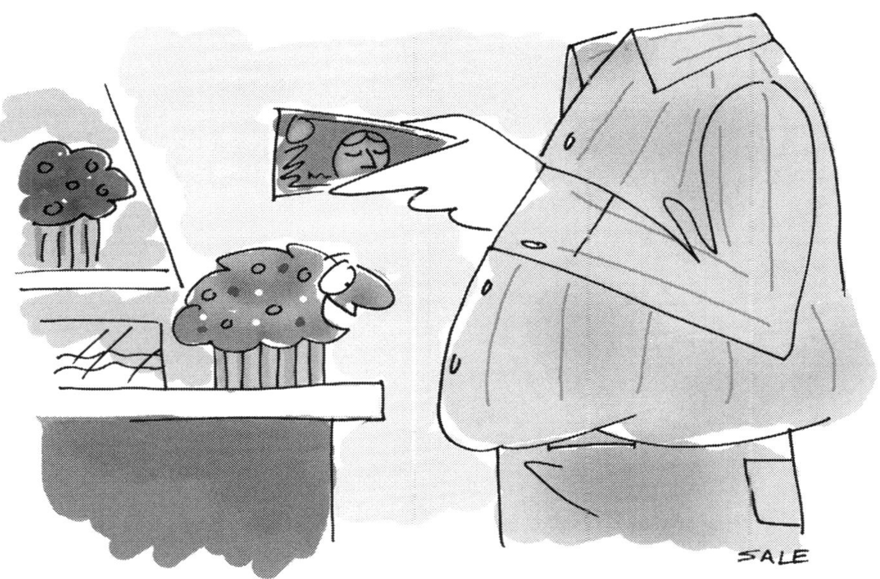

"See you soon."

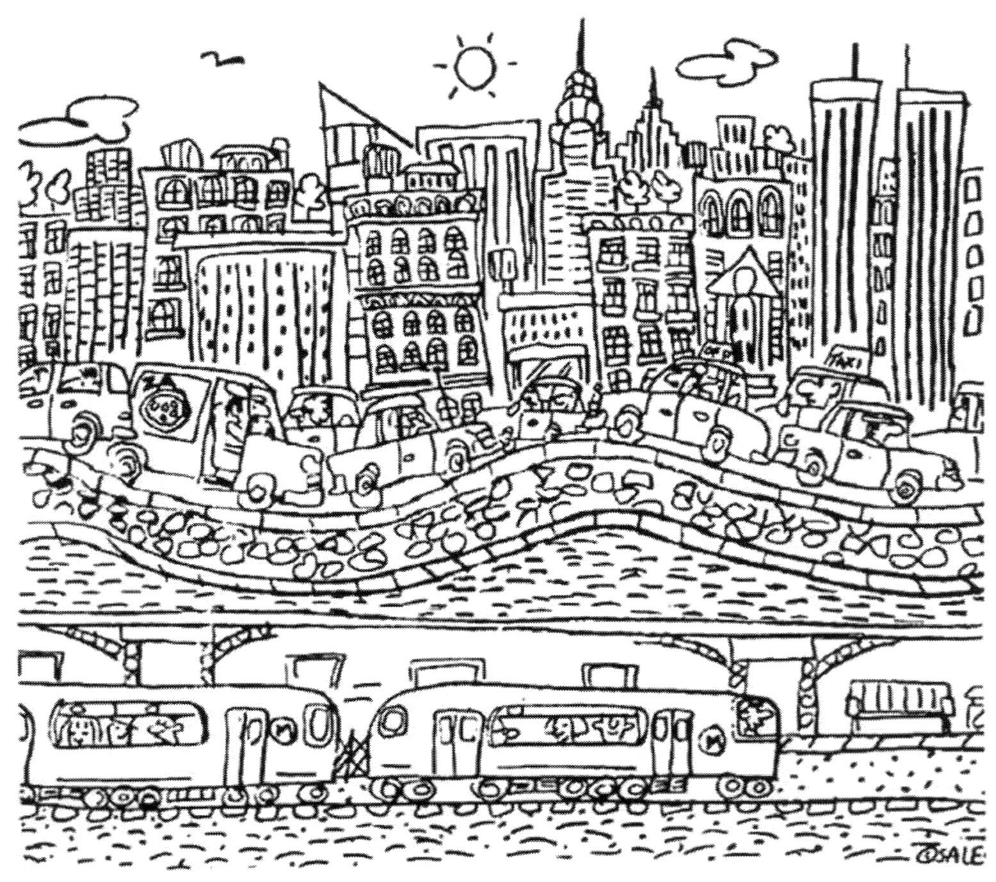

New York. A Busy Place.

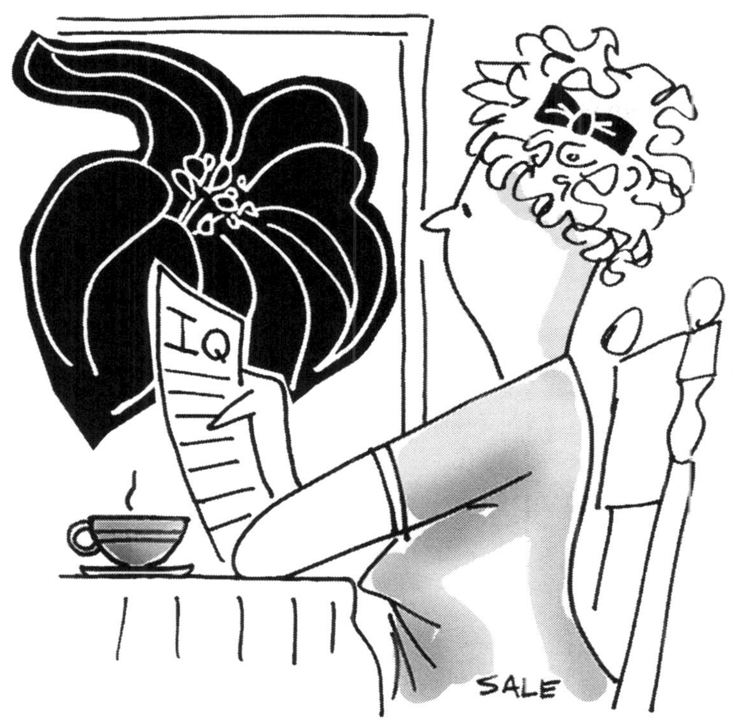

*The results were in. The good news was Marjorie
was far from stupid; the bad news was how far.*

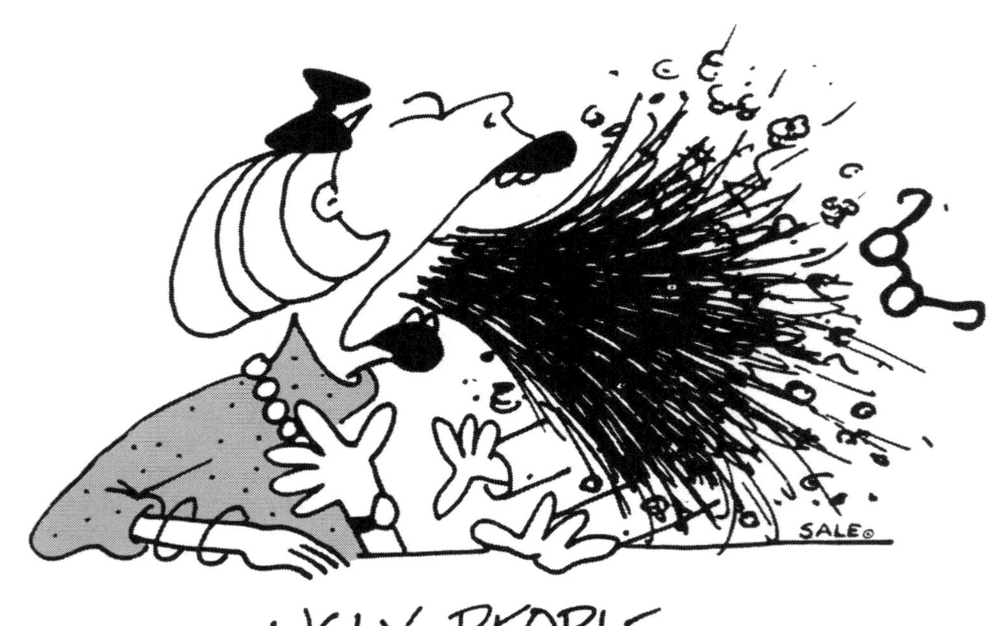
UGLY PEOPLE
MAKE MUFFY SICK.
SALE

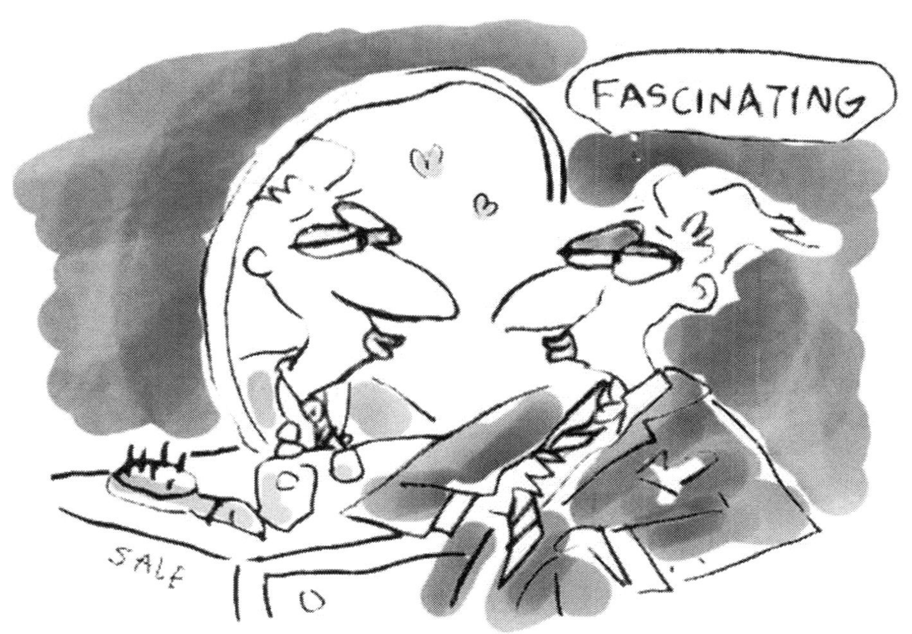

It began innocently as simple primping...a dab of product here, a maincure there, some discreet waxing...and before he knew it Ernesto was hopelessly irresistable to himself.

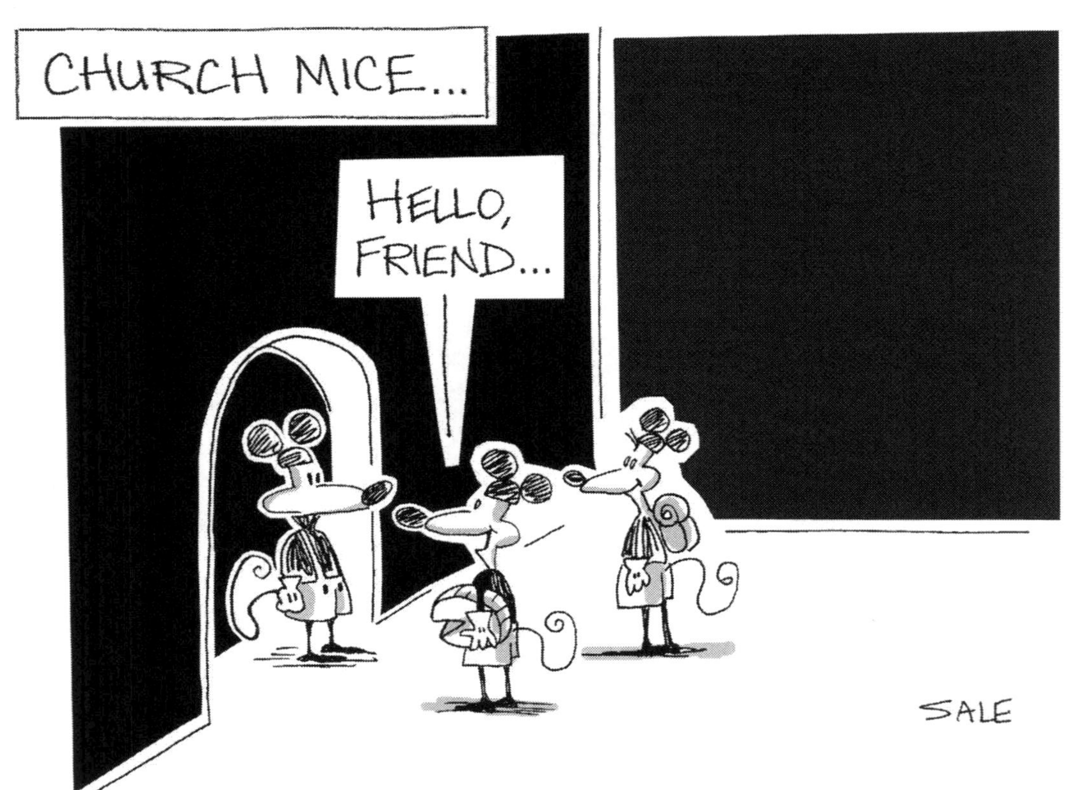

"We're Cheesitarians. Have you heard the good news
about the power of cheeses? Cheesus saves!"

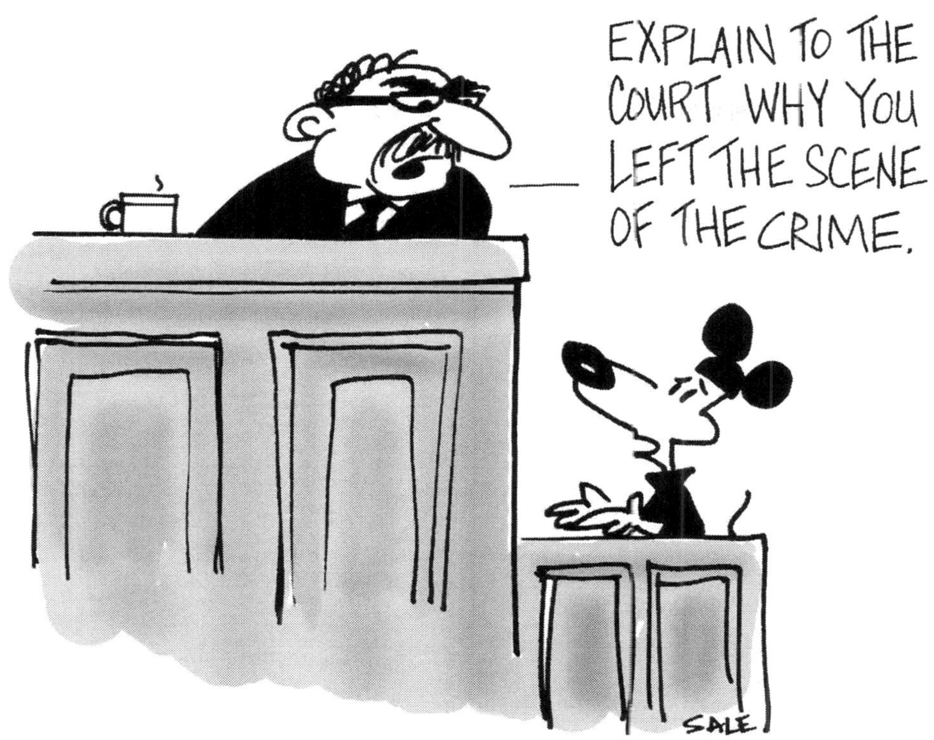

"Your Honor, I swear...I thought I saw a Puddy-Tat."

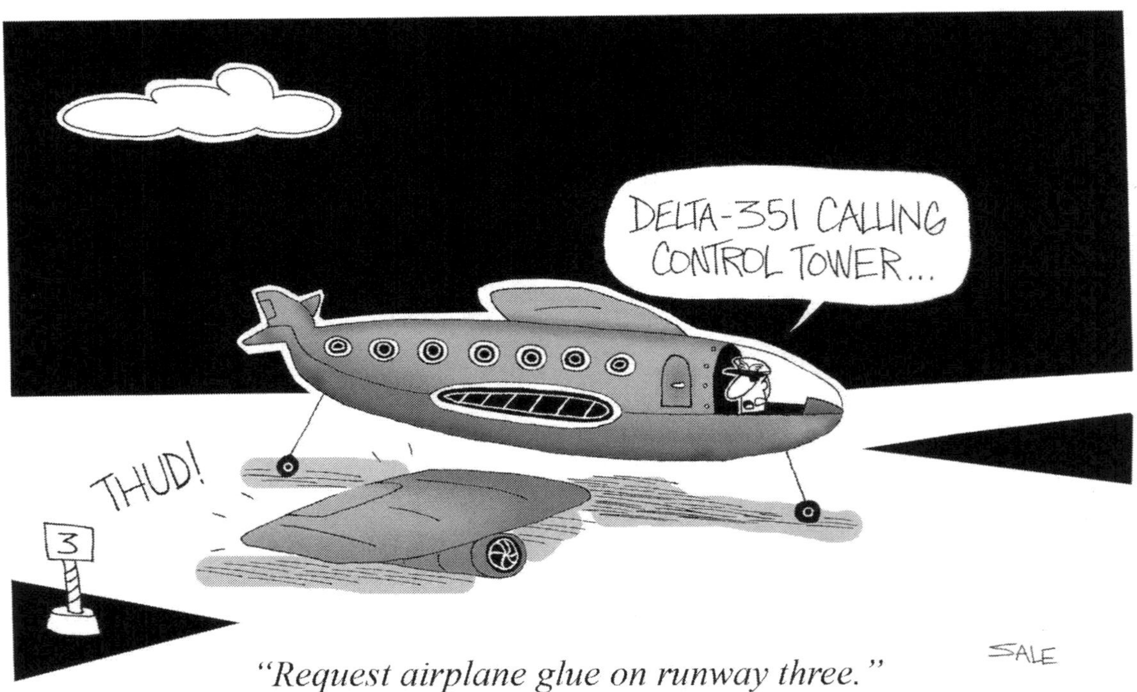

"*Request airplane glue on runway three.*"

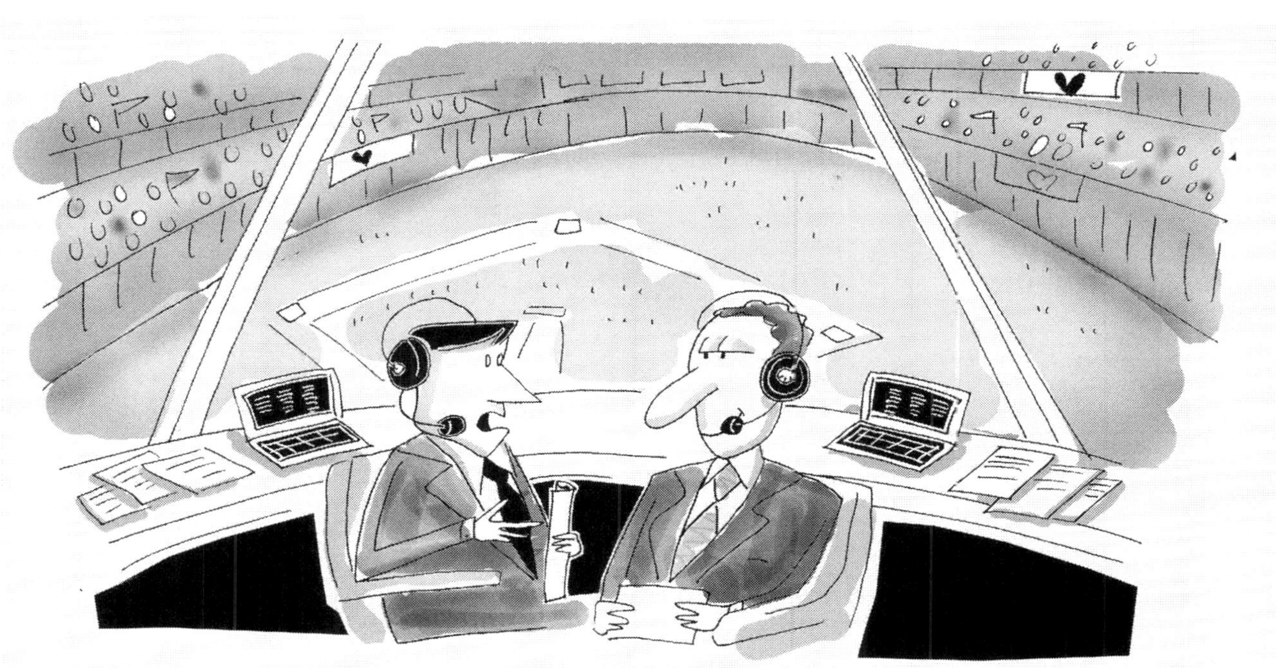

*"I know it's early in the season, Bob, but what's your prediction
that an American team will win the World Series?"*

Domestic Violence.

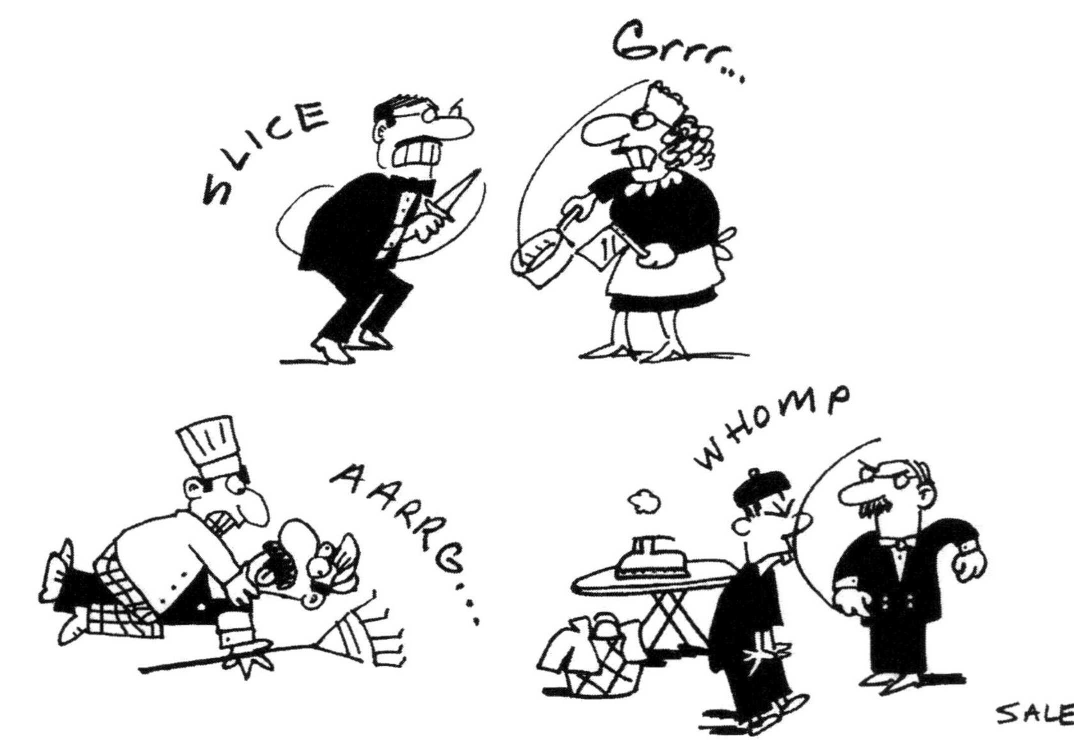

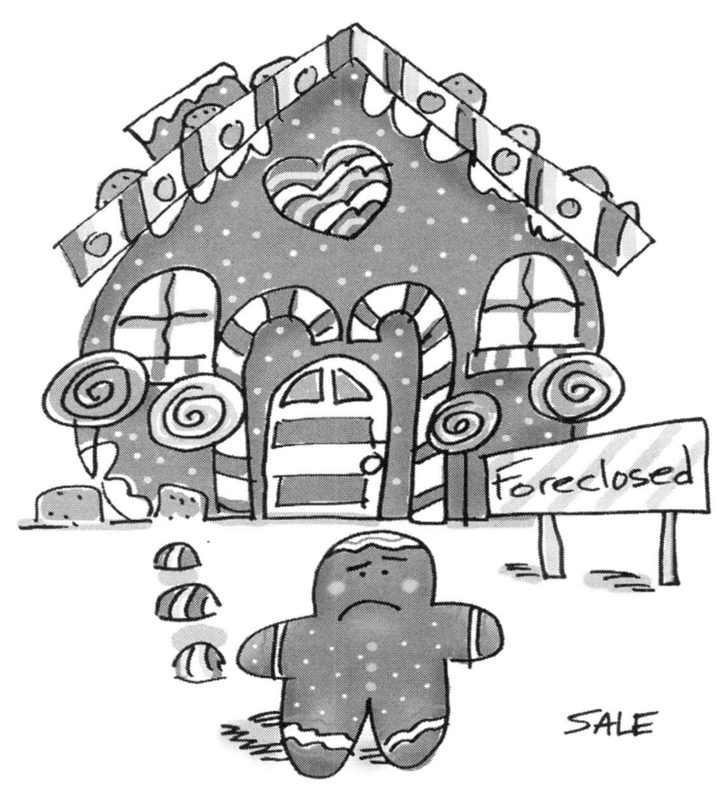

Christmas at the Gingerbread House.

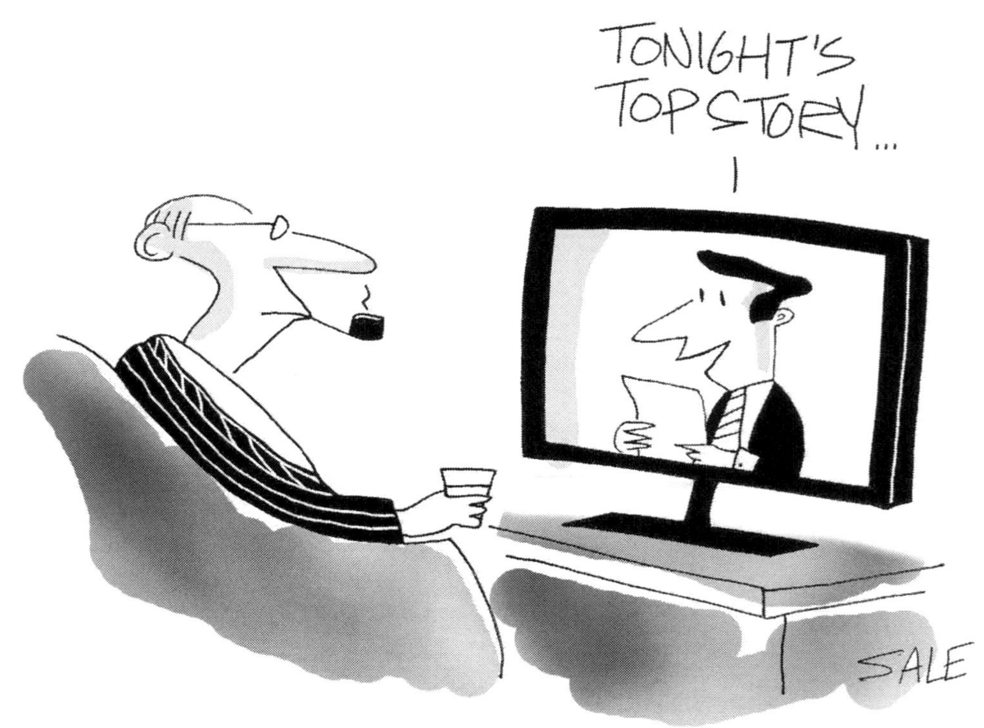

*"Lindsay Lohan fires her agents and hires the LAPD announcing...
She's quitting acting to focus on her life of crime."*

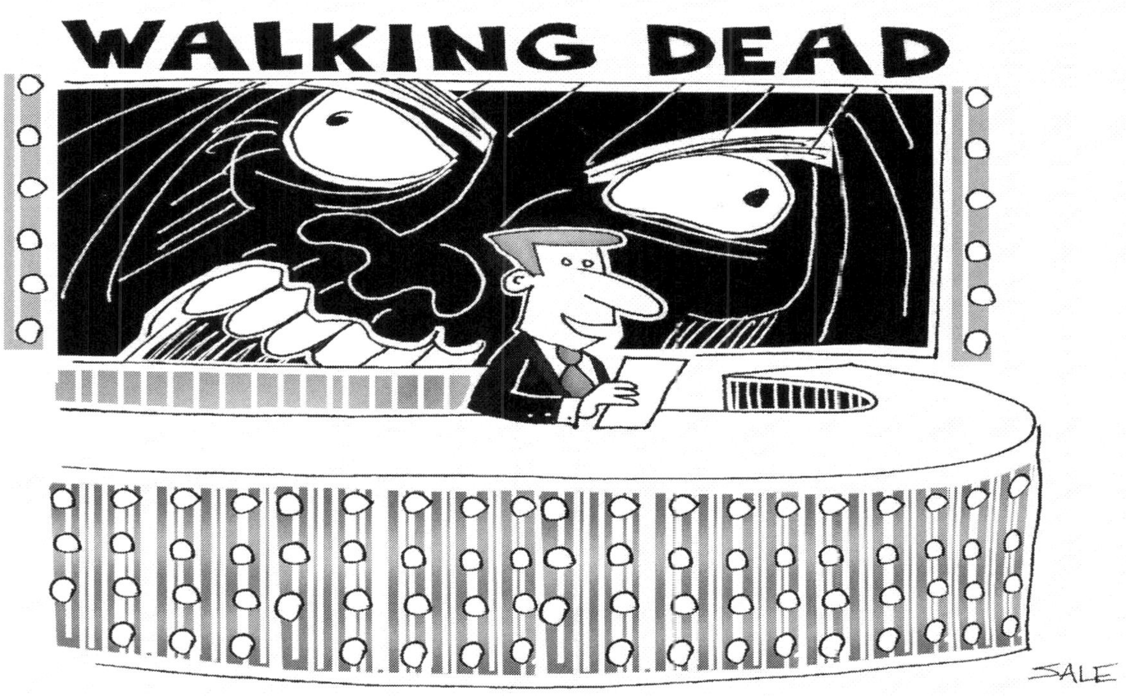

"Tonght's top story, Mark Burnett announces a new reality show,
The Real Zombies of Beverly Hills starring Joan Rivers, Mickey Rourke,
Donatella Versace, Carrot Top, Melanie Griffith and Gary Busey."

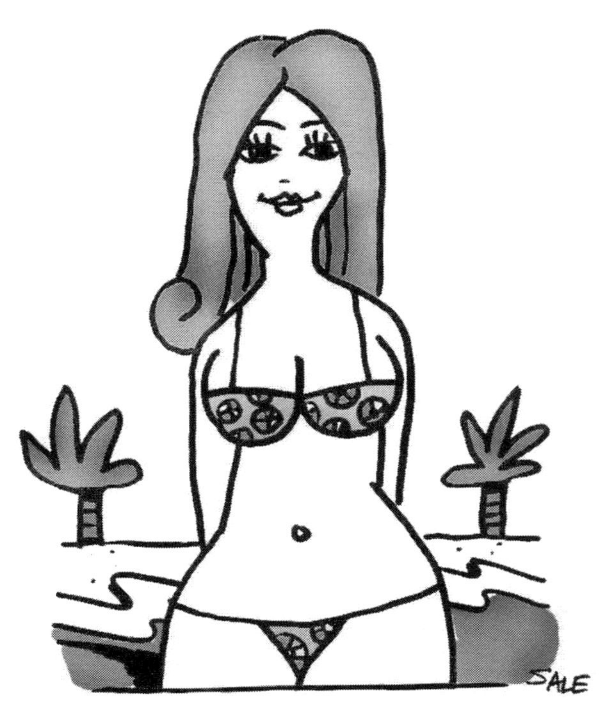

Thank You, Summer.

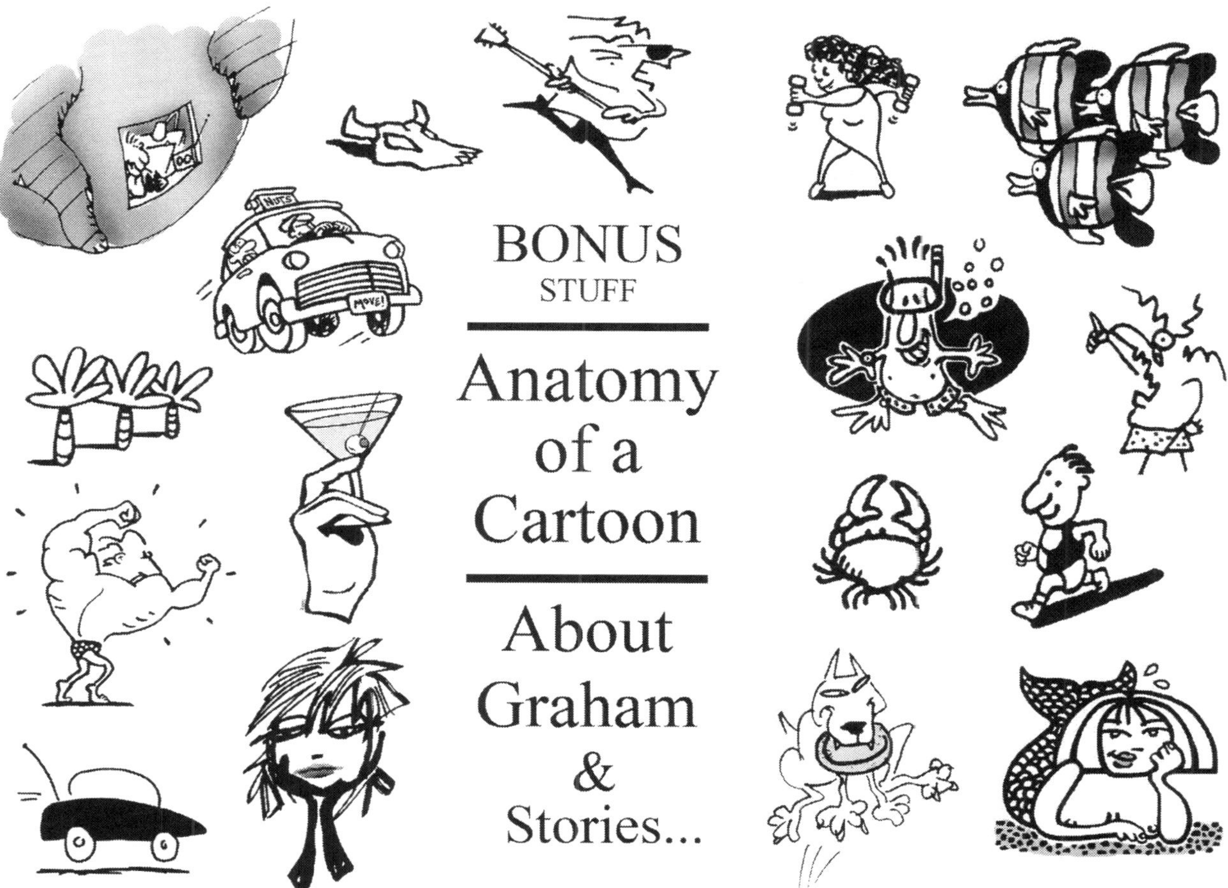

BONUS
STUFF

Anatomy
of a
Cartoon

About
Graham
&
Stories...

Anatomy of a Cartoon

Ever wonder how an idea turns into a cartoon?
Well, here's an example of how it works for me...

After the underwear bomber tried to ignite his short-and-curlies, the TSA and airports worldwide began installing devices to see through people's clothes to discover what nefarious goodies they might be concealing. This outrageous invasion of privacy was fertile ground for cartoonists and comedians.

The following are sketches and notes I made while coming up with a cartoon on this issue.

My first thoughts were:
1) Could this lunatic's actions have an upside?

2) Would the fear of being seen naked by strangers in a public place make people get healthy and fit?

3) Would the Nigerian Crotch Rocket do for health and fitness what Jerrod did for *Subway* and the submarine sandwich?

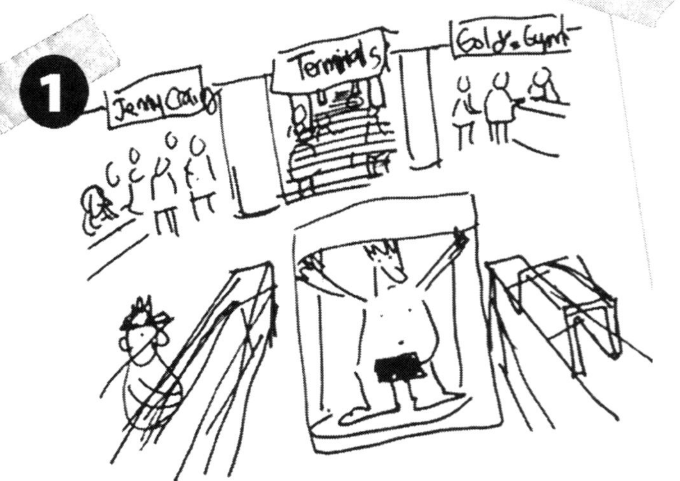

4) **What less invasive ways** could be used to see into the hearts and minds of passengers to discover their intentions?

Other possible consequences:

5) Would lingerie/underwear stores and tanning/waxing salons suddenly appear in airports to help travelers look their best?

6) Would women rejoice because their husbands finally replace their raggedy old drawers?

7) Would the sudden attention to personal fitness and grooming cause marital riffs, since they're often signs of an affair?

8) Will gyms start offering "Boot Camps for Travelers?"

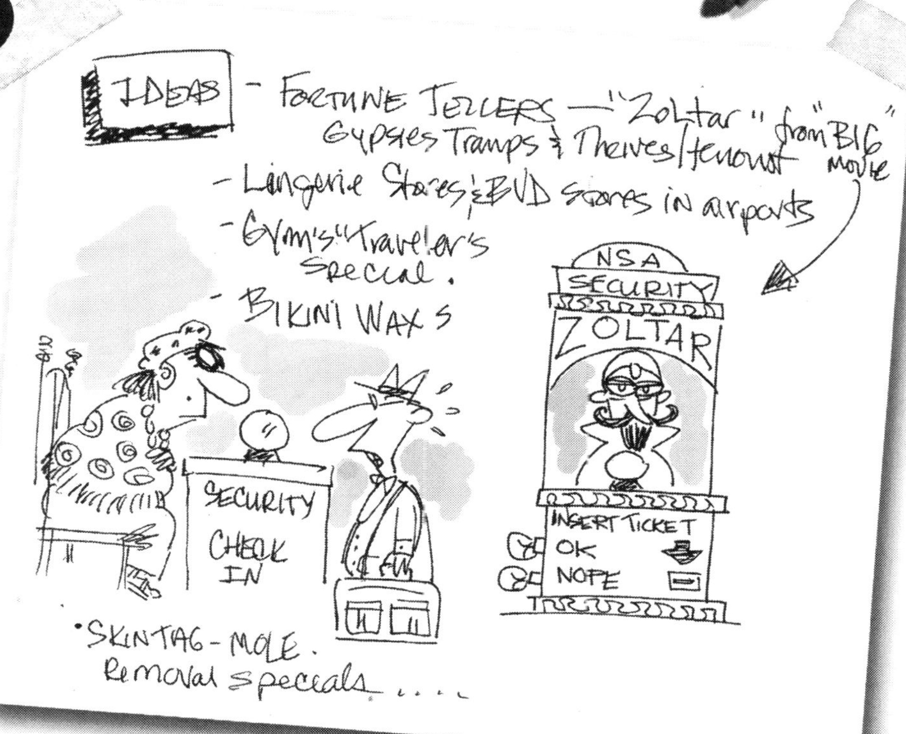

It was clear that several ideas had potential.

I decided to work on an image that would incorporate a few
of the ideas. I returned to my first sketch and changed
the perspective to read more quickly.

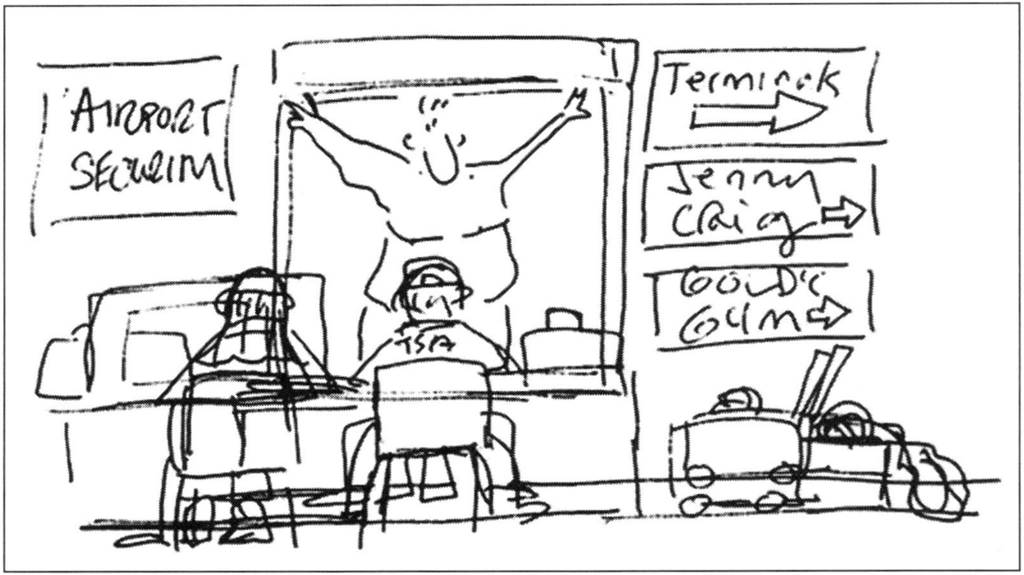

Then...
I redrew it over and over using a light box, and I scanned it
into photoshop to make final corrections and add shading
until it felt finished...

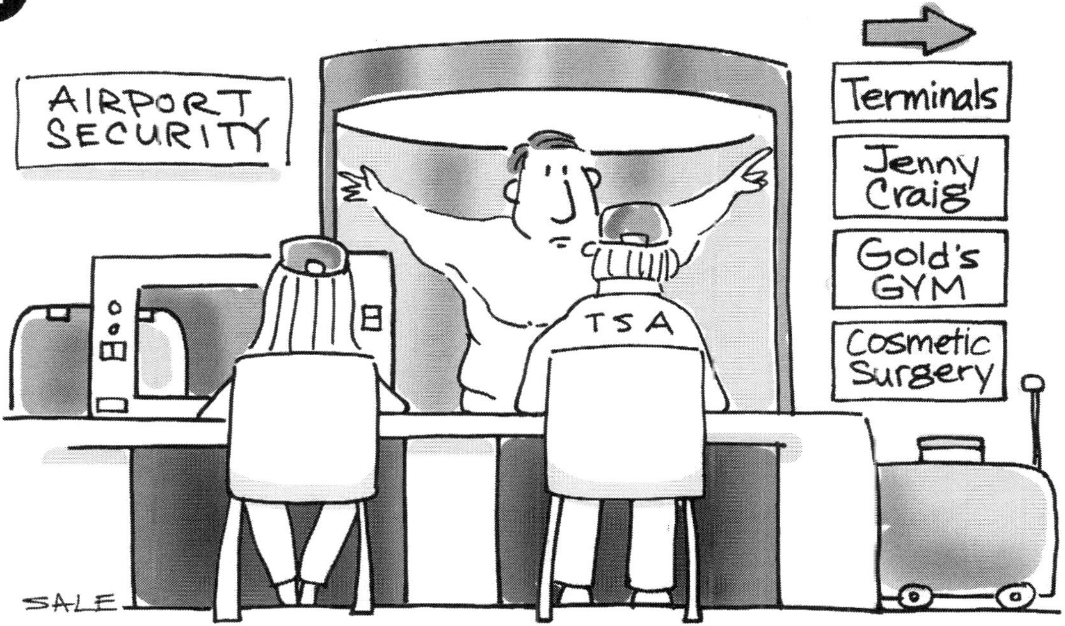

And I did a second cartoon from my notes...

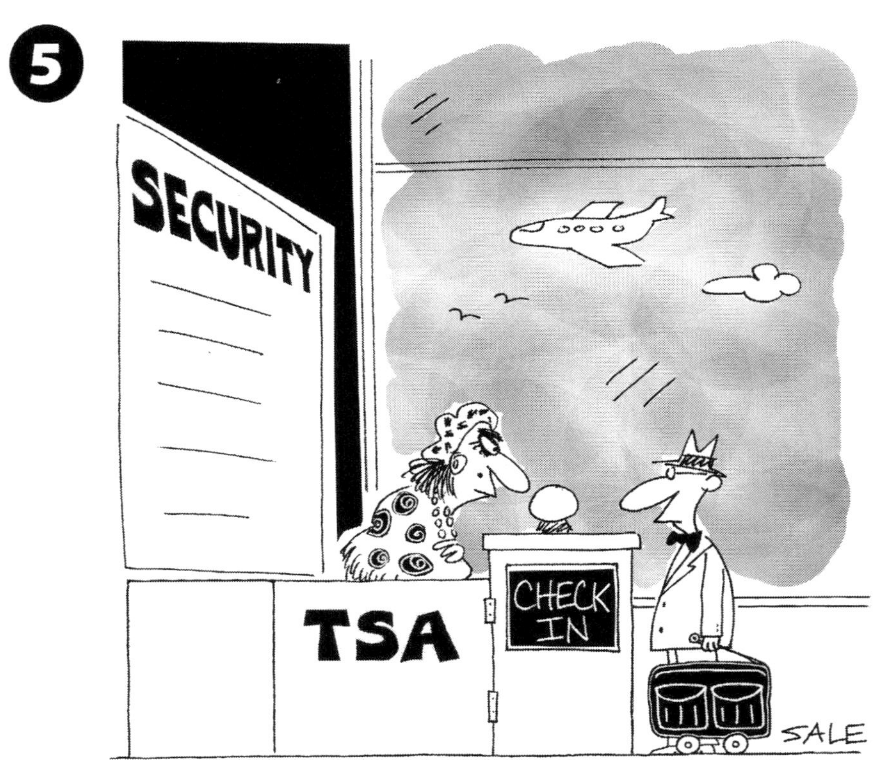

Airports tryout new less invasive screening procedures.

Mademoiselle

Banker, Broker, Lawyer, Crook was a reaction to the Wall Street banking scandals in the 1980's by Ivan Boesky, Michael Milken, Charles Keating and others. Sadly, it's worse and more prevalent today. Politicians have replaced lawyers as the sleaziest, lying, villianous, scumbags around. So, I made a **Banker, Broker, Politician, Crook** shirt.

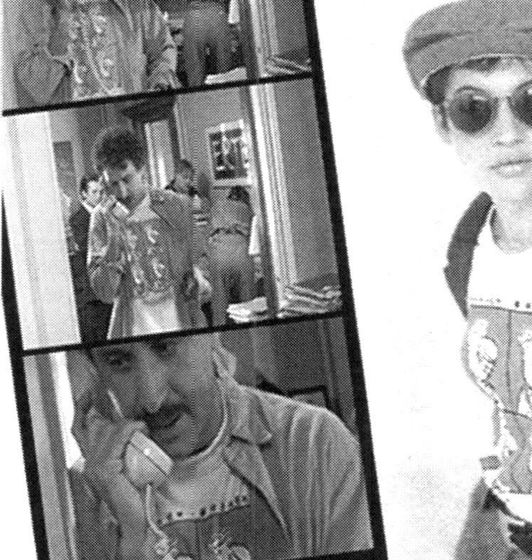

THE JOKE'S ON YOU.
Every girl needs a quirky conversation piece in her closet! Try this great shirt with a message, "Banker, Broker, Lawyer, Crook." Raise its level of sophistication with a blazer and khakis combo.

– Madamoiselle

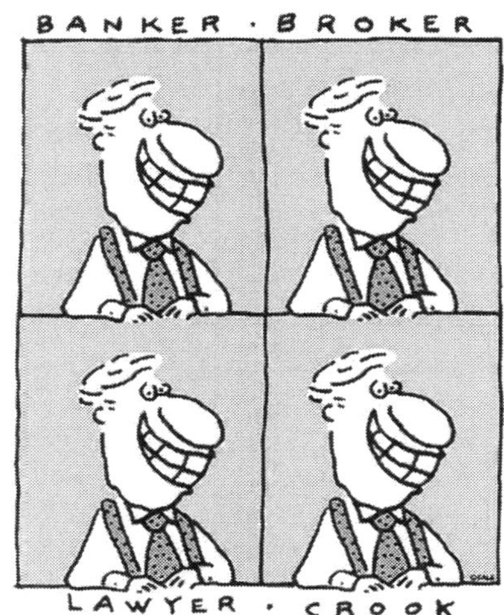

REVERSAL OF FORTUNE. Ron Silver wore my shirt when playing attorney Alan Dershowitz in the movie, *Reversal of Fortune,* starring Glenn Close and Jeremy Irons.

THE JOKE WAS ON ME. I was watching the movie when my shirt suddenly appeared on screen. I began shouting, "That's my shirt!" People looked at me like I was nuts. No one told me it was used in the film.

189

Who would want to take their phone with them everywhere?

You must be kidding.

In the early '80s, I did some cartoons for publications that made some pretty outrageous claims. For instance....

An article I worked on claimed that telephones would soon be so small that we would take them with us wherever we went---it'd be as normal as putting on your hat and coat when leaving the house. *You must be kidding.* Who would want their phone with them all the time and constantly be interrupted by calls? With answering machines, pagers and pay phones on every corner, this sounded crazy and totally unnecessary to me. *Good luck with that idea, guys.*

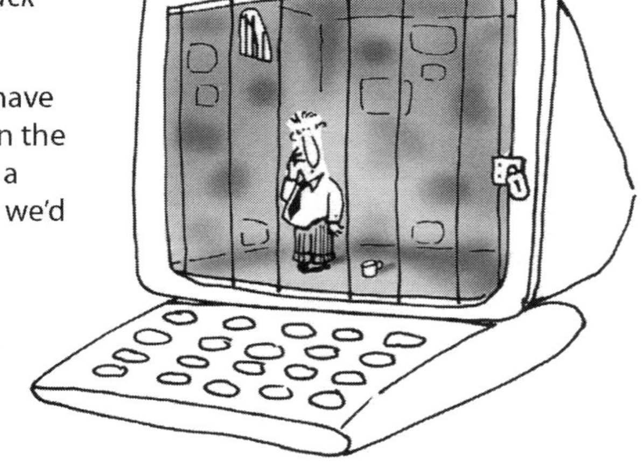

Another job I worked on predicted that everyone would have at least one or more computers at work, at home---even in the *kitchen*. And someday they'd be small enough to carry in a briefcase. Not only that, but instead of going to the store we'd shop on our computer. *Say, what?*

Computers were expensive. Almost no one except big companies, law enforcement, NASA and the government had computers.

Computers were gigantic and cost as much as a house. The operating system was DOS, a black screen with sci-fi computer type. So, it was impossible to imagine it looking like a store where you'd want to shop. Moreover, how would products get inside your computer in the first place? And how would you put money in it to pay for stuff?

Remember, the internet didn't exist. ATMs were just being tested and fax machines were like magic---how did images on paper travel through the telephone? Can you imagine how futuristic this sounded?

I'd only seen computers on TV — so, when the editor sent me a photo of what a "desk top" computer looked like, I didn't know what I was looking at. I thought the monitor was the actual computer.

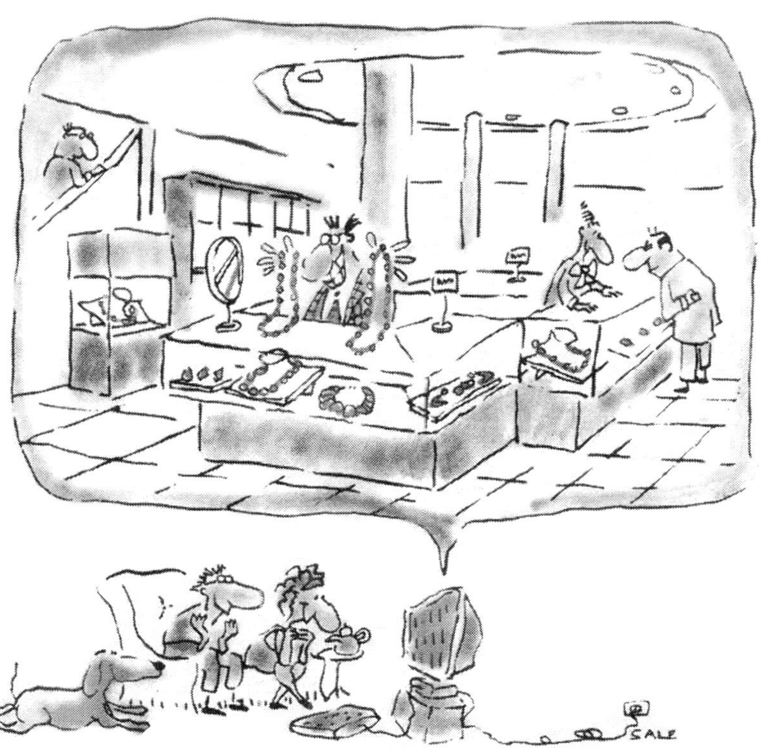

ONCE UPON A TIME IN NEW YORK CITY

There was a soggy frozen cartoonist...

NYC winters are just awful to get around in. Arriving at your destination looking as you did when you left home can be a challenge. If you don't need to be perfectly coiffed you can bundle up appropriately. Otherwise, you may find your-self incorrectly attired for the various climate changes your journey involves and feeling like Thor Heyerdahl outfitted by Hugo Boss.

Most New Yorkers pack them-selves into buses and subway cars like sardines. On days like these a heavy overcoat, scarf, gloves and hat quickly become claustrophobically hot and uncomfortable.

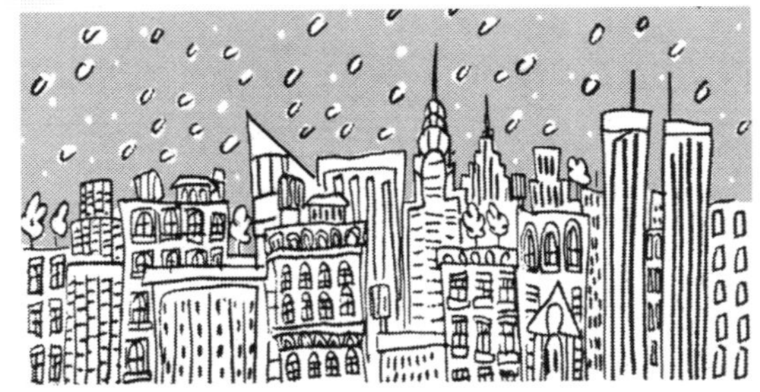

As you jostle along waiting for your stop, the snow and slush slowly begin to melt and saturate you. Then before you know it you're back on the street in freez-ing, 60 mph winds — a soggy, semi-frozen mess.

Luckily, an antidote exists for this misery — the hilarity of someone else in greater misery. Like the unlucky soul standing too close too the curb who gets wiped out by a tsunami of gutter slush from a passing bus. It's a perfect storm and comedy gold.

Thank God that wasn't me, you think, *I'll dry off but that poor shlub is going home and starting all over.* Eventually the shlub will also see the humor when retelling the story to friends. I know, I've been that shlub.

On this winter morning I was meeting a potential client, the French company, Club Med. Their offices were high atop fifty-seventh street featuring a spectacular view over the wintry expanse of Central Park.

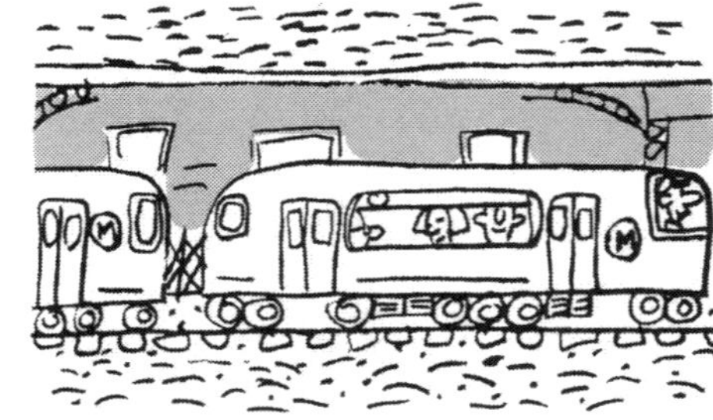

While the art director looked at my portfolio, I noticed how tan he was. *I bet he gets free trips to all their villages.* I hadn't had a vacation in years, and I'd never been to a tropical island.

As I dethawed and took inventory of my precious bits, I looked down at my fancy suede loafers. They were soaked and stretched hopelessly out of shape. Three of the four tassles were missing. My toes were numb, and my heels were red and bare because my flimsy dress socks had slipped down around my arches.

Several times I'd walked right out of my shoes and onto the icy sidewalk. To keep them on,

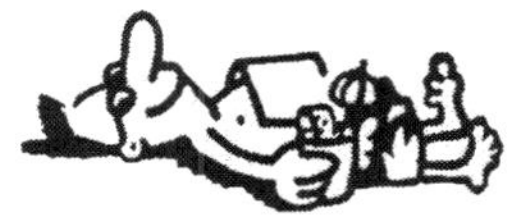

I'd adopted a herky-jerky shuffle-step, which elicited the ire of everyone around me. Freezing, harried New Yorkers have no patience for shufflers or fancy Arthur Murray dancers who impede their way.

Finally, Monsieur art director looked up, "I would love to use your work," he said, "But, I'm over budget. However, I can trade you all-expense-paid vacations in exchange for your artwork—if you don't object." Object? OBJECT?

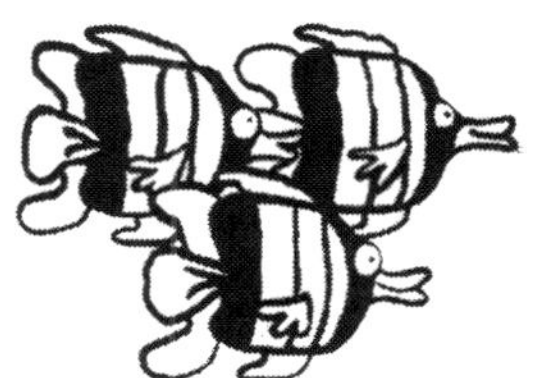

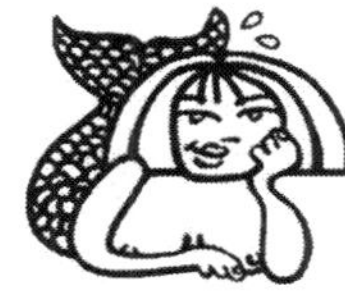

Stop yakking, Frenchie and start writing the contract---I've got to get home and start drawing! If Iwas a cartoon I'd have shot straight up in the air with my feet spinning and been gone in a cloud of dust.

I'll never forget that winter morning when I struck tropical gold.

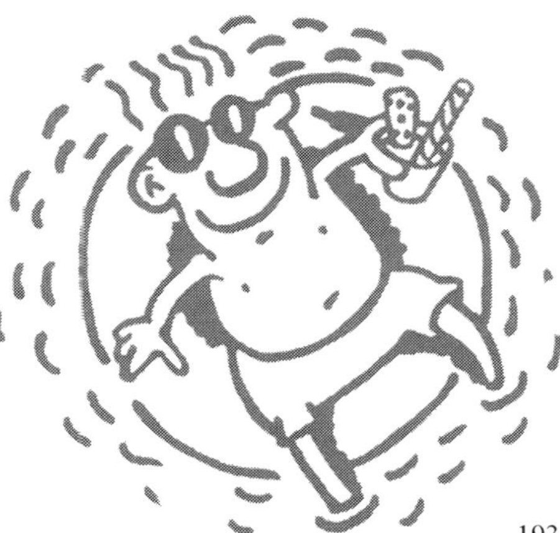

An Interview with Graham.

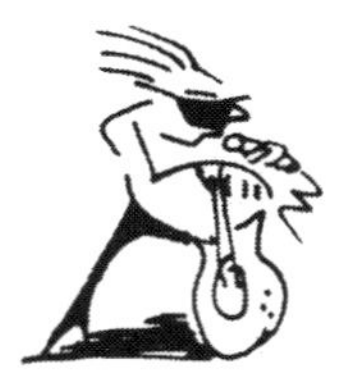

SB: It's really great to finally meet you after all these years.

GS: I know, and this is going to be fun.

SB: I think so too. Are you ready to spill all?

GS: I'll do my best. And thank you for bringing this delicious box of wine.

SB: Nothing but the best for a cartoonist of your stature.

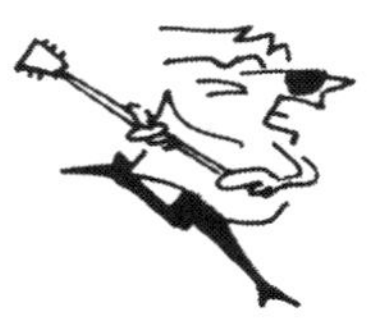

SB: So, where are you from?

GS: I was born in Detroit, MI where I was adopted by my wonderful parents, Ed and Virginia Sale. When I was three we moved to Elmira, NY where I grew up.

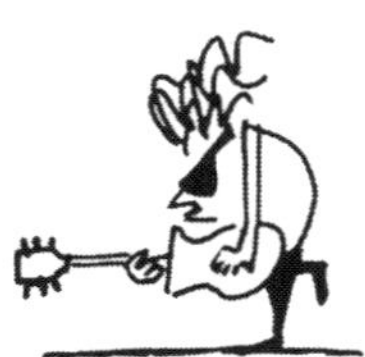

SB: Tell me about Elmira.

GS: It's a small town in western NY, near Corning and Ithaca. Some facinating people come from Elmira. Mark Twain lived, married, wrote and is buried there. Plus, Hal Roach, who produced *The Little Rascals* and *Laurel and Hardy*; Brian Williams, the anchorman; Ernie Davis, the first African-American to win a Heisman trophy; Eileen Collins, the first woman to command the Space Shuttle and Tommy Hilfiger was my neighbor.

...Continued.

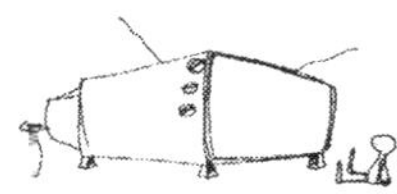

SB: Is anyone else in your family an artist?
GS: No, both my father and mother were Presbyterian ministers. But, my biological mother and her mother were artistic.

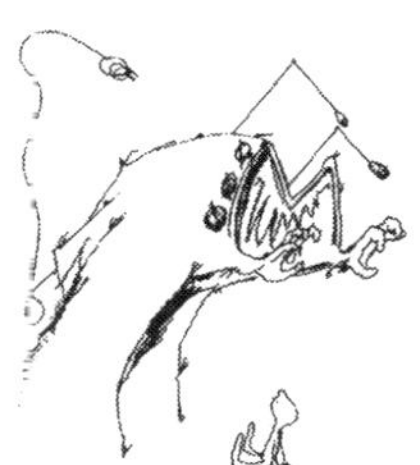

SB: Aha! You're a preacher's kid. That explains everything. So why cartooning?
GS: I ask myself that all the time. I've always drawn, but I've never "always wanted to be a cartoonist." As a kid I wanted to be either Jim Henson, Sid or Marty Krofft or play for the NY Giants. Then, when I discovered girls, there was no doubt in my mind that being a Playboy photographer was the life for me. My path to cartooning can be traced to an advertisement I read, "Draw your way to popularity, profit and girls! Be a cartoonist!" It's fair to say, I was spectacularly misinformed.

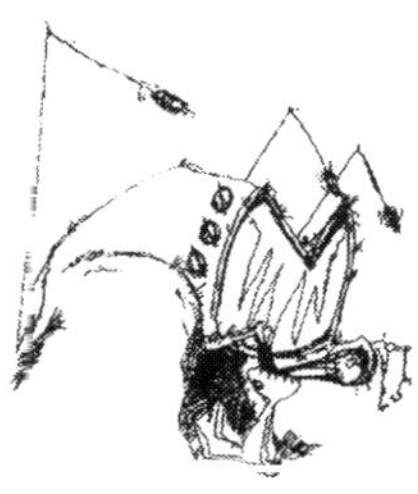

SB: When did you first sell your art?
GS: As a kid, I sold my drawings and various creations door-to-door in my neighborhood. In junior high, I sold drawings of naked women in the libray during lunch. But, after getting busted several times I went legit and started selling pen and ink watercolor drawings of people's homes (to buy a bike). Then I struck a deal with a real estate agency to buy my illustrations as gifts for home owners. My parents would drve around town and find me sitting on curbs sketching houses until the sun went down. I was the kid who put on plays, magic shows and neighborhood carnivals. I also contributed editorial cartoons to the local newspaper. So, I've always seen my art as commerce. The trick today, is finding a paying audience, which is a challenge since the internet has dramatically altered the publishing industry.

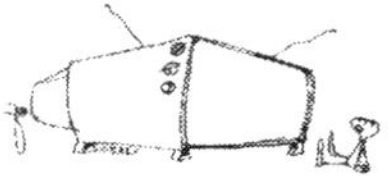

Rapid Fire...

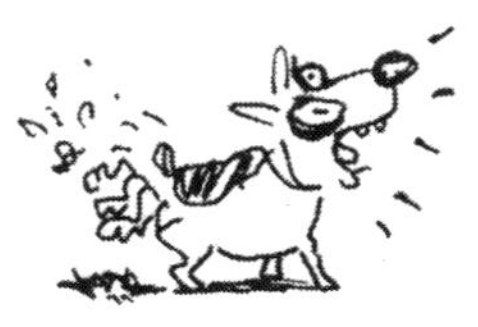

**SB: Let's try something different now. Finish the following sentences:
I draw in the style I do because...**
GS: All the other styles were taken.

SB: The hardest part of cartooning is...
GS: Spending all the money.

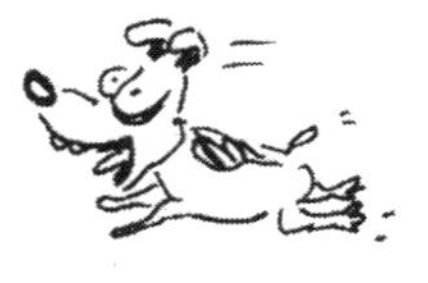

SB: I admire...
GS: The inventors of the potato peeler and salad spinner.

SB: When I'm having a hard time coming up with ideas...
GS: I'm sorry, I'm not familiar with that sensation.

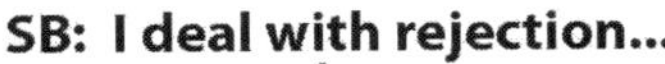

SB: I deal with rejection...
GS: Through righteous indignation, self-medication and phone calls to friends who support and enable my delusions of grandeur.

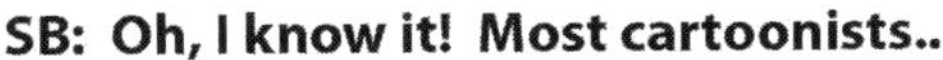

SB: Oh, I know it! Most cartoonists...
GS: Have IQs greater than their bank balance (also, they taste like chicken).

SB: When I'm not cartooning...
GS: I'm defending my choices and fighting with the person I could've been.

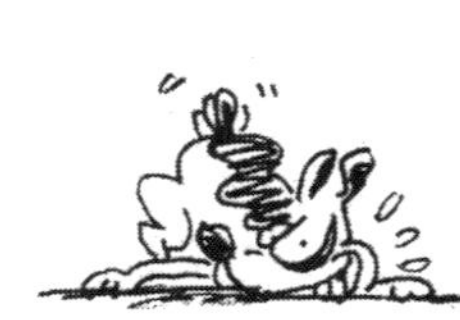

SB: My advice for aspiring cartoonists is.
GS: (1) Marry young while your youthful optimism is still sexy. (2) Learn to cook.

In Closing. 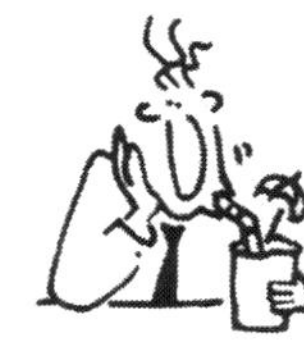

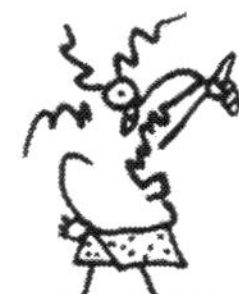

SB: I like cartooning because...

GS: I can say what I feel and communicate it with others fairly quickly - even without words, which can't be said of many art forms. In a flash, you can make a person laugh, touch their heart, or present them an alternative side to an issue. Cartoons can be like poetry or haiku in the sense that so much is captured and conveyed in a few seconds. All you need is a pen and paper. Anyone who uses their creativity knows the rush of excitement when you successfully work out an idea - it's a celebration of lightening striking; a magical, self-satisfied feeling. There's nothing like it.

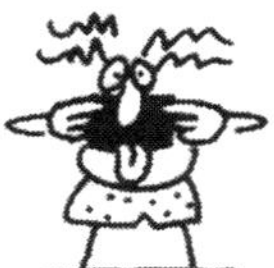

SB: What experiences have influenced you as a cartoonist?

GS: Selling seeds door-to-door, bartending for celebrities, being a life guard, swim instructor, dish washer, insurance salesman, moving man for dead peoples' stuff, singing telegrams (dressed as a penguin), actor, model, waiter, security guard, financial consultant, rubber band warehouse worker, Census taker, carpenter, party staffer, color copy engineer, an abundance of original sin, and living in New York City and Los Angeles have all served to twist my mind.

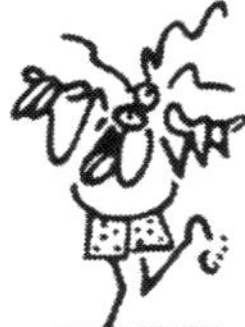

**SB: Thank you for your insights into cartooning, Graham. Now, one last question...
If you weren't a cartoonist, what could you see yourself doing?**

GS: Putting the red plastic strips on slices of baloney.

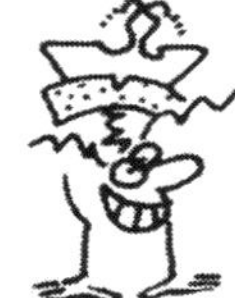

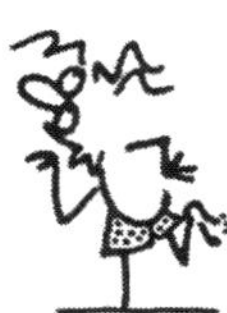

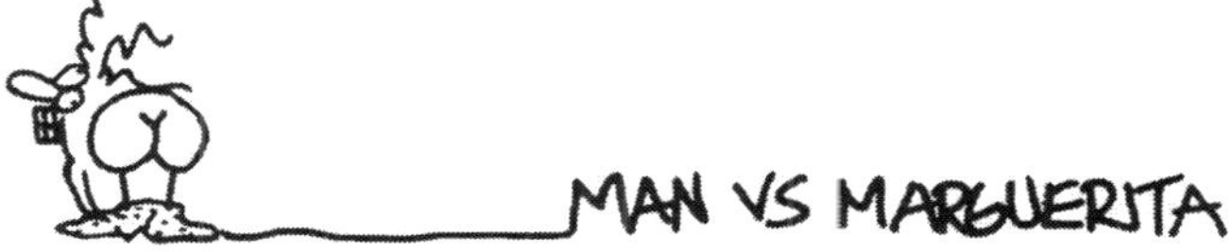

About Graham...

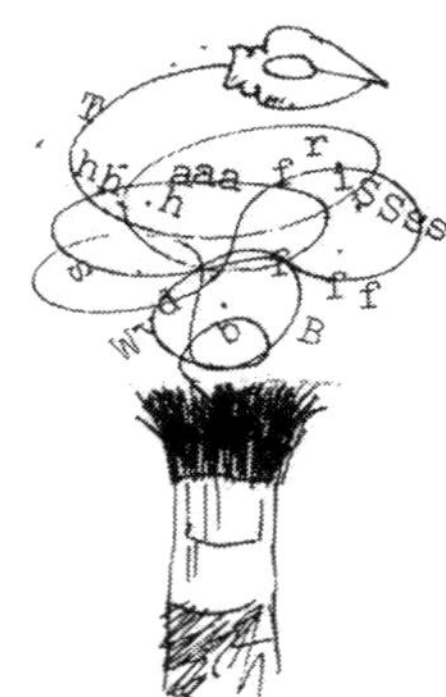

Graham Sale is a prolific artist, writer, and author best known for his cartoons and humorous illustrations that have appeared in advertisements, newspapers, books, on greeting cards, clothing and licensed products world-wide since the 1980's.

His clients have included, the NY Times, NY Newsday, Funny Times, AT&T, Prudential, Allstate, Adweek, NY Magazine, Club Med, Absolut, Citibank, Forbes, Money, Scholastic, various publishers, Forturne 500 companies and many others. His political cartoons and acclaimed series, MEN IN HATS appears in the Commercial Appeal of Memphis, TN, one of the nation's oldest newspapers.

Graham was born in Detroit and grew up in Elmira, NY. He attended the College of Wooster in Ohio and studied advertising at Parsons School of Design. He began selling his art on the street and soon built a successful freelance business. His t-shirt company, 90 Degree Angle, produced and sold his work world wide. His famous NY Gun shirt is still a New York City icon.

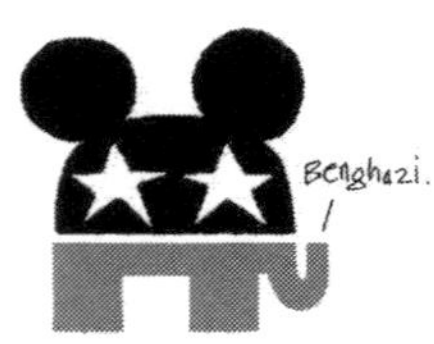

Graham is also the creator of Boneless Chuck the beloved character/toy loved around the world, Club Crib, the infant clothing line and he's the author of *What Women Want: A Gentleman's Guide to Romance,* and the soon-to-be-released, *Win at Work Without Losing* at Love.

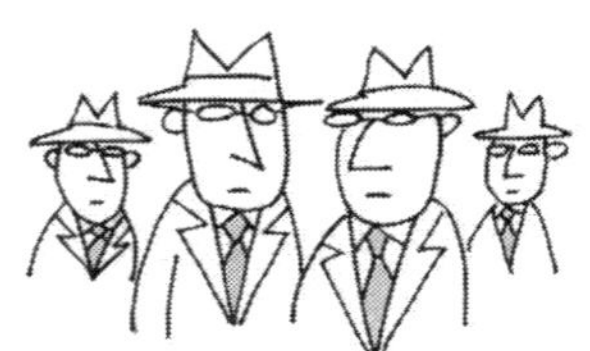

After decades in New York City, Los Angeles and Bucks County, Pa, Graham currently lives and creates in Memphis, TN.

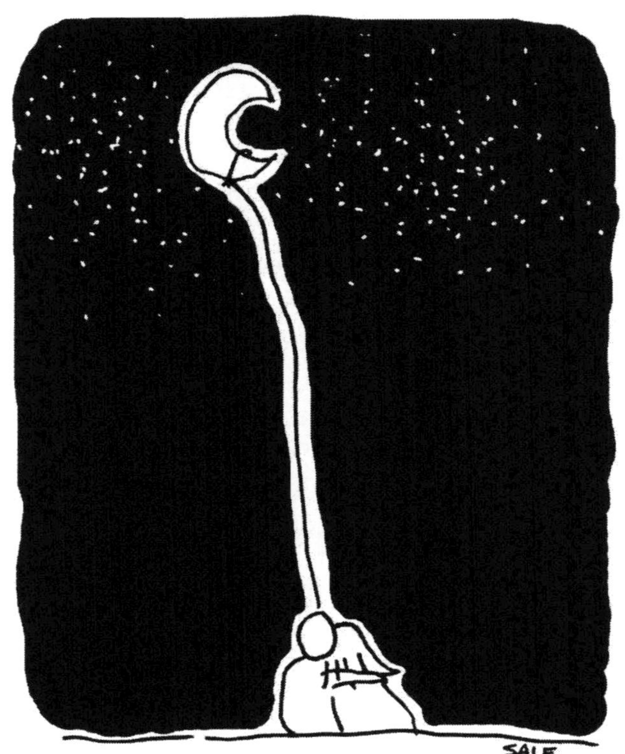

By the light of the silvery moon.

Acknowledgements

I wish to thank my wonderful parents,
Ed and Virginia for their love and support
and for allowing me to follow my bliss down
the meandering rabbit holes of my life.

I'd also like to thank my dear friend Lolly for
her ever present encouragement and belief
in me and for letting me try out my cartoons
on her even when she's tired or has better
things to do.

So, if after finishing this book you
feel the Spanish Inquisition had
more laughs - blame them - they
encouraged me.

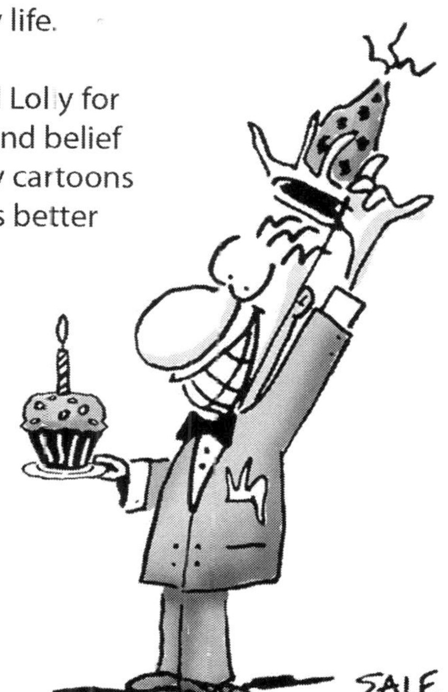

Made in the USA
Columbia, SC
19 May 2019